PRACTICAL LEAN ACCOUNTING

A PROVEN SYSTEM FOR MEASURING AND MANAGING THE LEAN ENTERPRISE

PRACTICAL LEAN ACCOUNTING

A PROVEN SYSTEM FOR MEASURING AND MANAGING THE LEAN ENTERPRISE

Brian Maskell and Bruce Baggaley

PRODUCTIVITY PRESS • NEW YORK, NY

Most Productivity Press books are available at quantity discounts when purchased in bulk. For more information contact our Customer Service Department (800-394-6868). Address all other inquiries to:

Productivity Press
444 Park Avenue South, Suite 604
New York, NY 10016
United States of America
Telephone: 212-686-5900
Telefax: 212-686-5411
E-mail: info@productivitypress.com

Composed by William H. Brunson Typography Services
Printed and bound by Malloy Lithographing in the United States of America

Library of Congress Cataloging-in-Publication Data

Maskell, Brian H.
    Practical lean accounting : a proven system for measuring and managing the lean enterprise / Brian Maskell and Bruce Baggaley.
        p. cm.
    Includes index.
        ISBN 1-56327-243-1 (alk. paper)
    1. Business enterprises—Finance. 2. Accounting. 3. Industrial management. I. Baggaley, Bruce. II. Title.

    HG4026.M3654   2003
    657—dc22

                                                        2003022870

07 06 05 04 03   5 4 3 2 1

DEDICATION

*This book is dedicated to our wives,
Barbara Maskell and Patty Baggaley.
Thank you for your love, help, and support—
especially over the last few years of travel, toil, and
tension as the Lean Accounting practice has taken shape.
This book is as much your work as ours.
With our love.*

Contents

Preface

The purpose of this book is to provide a roadmap for finance managers in companies seeking to transition their organizations into lean enterprises. The book came out of many years of working with companies introducing the powerful, culture-changing methods of lean manufacturing and lean thinking. We began to work on what is now known as *Lean Accounting* in the late 1980s and early 1990s. While helping forward-thinking manufacturers to implement lean methods (called *just-in-time manufacturing* in those days) we soon found that their accounting and measurement systems were an obstacle to success.

In those days, there was very little consideration given to changing accounting systems to support the new production methods. One of us worked with three companies that cancelled promising lean transformations because the improvements did not "hit the bottom line." Their financial executives made the assumption that if the lean improvements were good for the company then there would be marked, short-term financial benefits. When these benefits did not materialize, the efforts of the lean pioneers were summarily closed down.

In recent years there has been a lot more interest in and acceptance of Lean Accounting. Most companies introducing lean thinking realize that their finance and control systems are very wasteful and ineffective. They want to have practical methods to control the business, without the hugely wasteful, time-consuming, and misleading costing and measurement systems. We have found that once companies begin their lean transformation and have mapped their value streams, implemented cells and started getting their production to flow, they want to know how to sustain these efforts. Questions arise such as:

- What sorts of performance measures can be used in place of the current measures that seem to work against the lean improvements?

- Are there costing approaches that are lean themselves, that don't require us to track production that now speeds through the plant in a matter of hours or days?

- How do we understand the financial benefits of our lean efforts?

In many cases, they do not know how to answer these questions. Until now, there has been no *proven path* for Lean Accounting. In this book we are seeking to provide this proven path.

We have often been urged to change the title *Lean Accounting* and use another term. People say they are misled because they think Lean Accounting is just about applying lean principles to the accounting functions of an organization. Yet, when they learn more, they discover that Lean Accounting is a new method of managing a business that is built upon lean principles and lean methods. These principles, enunciated in the book *Lean Thinking* by Jim Womack and Dan Jones,[1] have been rigorously applied to the accounting, control, measurement, and management of the business. When these new methods take hold within the organization, the result is a very different—and very lean—way to manage, control, and measure the enterprise.

In one sense Lean Accounting is not new, because the finance, accounting, measurement, and management methods described in this book have been in use for many years; but this usage has been largely outside the realm of discrete manufacturing. These methods have been revamped and adapted to serve the needs of lean organizations. It is this melding of the principles of lean and the methods of lean, with the use of tried and tested accounting methods in a new context, that makes Lean Accounting what it is today. The result is a radically different way to run your lean business. Lean Accounting is a great deal more than just lean thinking applied to the accounting systems. It is the management framework of a lean organization.

In this book, we have tried to present, in very practical terms, the methods of modern Lean Accounting. We do not claim this to be the last word on the topic—there is so much innovation and change going on right now. But we offer in this book the lessons we have learned about how to manage and control the lean company. Our intent has been to include proven methods and enough detail so that finance people and lean advocates can implement them themselves.

It is our hope that those who use this book will extend the tools presented as they apply them in their organizations, and will share their experiences among a community of Lean Accounting practitioners. We are hoping that this book will foster and inspire this community of lean financial thinkers and doers. Our website *www.maskell.com* is already a popular resource for people interested in Lean Accounting. We plan to post onto the web-site more case studies and examples that will enhance the information contained within the book. We have also been running *Lean Accounting Roundtables* that are designed as *users-helping-users* conferences. These roundtables provide learning for newcomers and solutions for people already on the journey to Lean Accounting.

Through these initiatives, and those of others in the field, we hope to bring Lean Accounting up-to-speed with lean manufacturing, and to create a 21st century revolution in accounting, control, and business management.

---

1. James P. Womack and Daniel T. Jones, *Lean Thinking: Banish Waste and Create Wealth in Your Corporation* (New York: Simon & Schuster, 1996).

Acknowledgments

This book has come out of many years of work in lean manufacturing and lean accounting, and we owe an enormous debt to the many hundreds of people working in our customer companies. The Lean Accounting methods presented in this book have been forged on the anvil of their hard work, creativity, and willingness to innovate. There are too many people for us to mention them by name, but special appreciation must go to Mr. Fred Garbinski, Director of Cost Management at Parker Hannifin Corporation. Fred has been a thinker and doer in innovative financial management for a long time and working with him over the last three years has improved our "product," stretched our thinking, and he has helped us to develop the flexible and practical methods required to support a diverse, multi-national corporation like Parker.

We would also like to thank Maura May, Publisher for Productivity Press, for her patience over the last five years as we have worked to bring this book together, to our editor Emily Pillars, and the other production and editorial people at Productivity Press.

A special thank you goes to Susan Lilly, who is the lynch-pin of our consulting firm, BMA Inc. Susan's polymorphic capabilities, enthusiasm, hardwork, and good-humored willingness to go the extra mile has contributed greatly and pulled us out of many a scrape. Thank you Susan.

Brian Maskell and Bruce Baggaley
BMA Inc.
Cherry Hill, NJ
Tel: 609 239 1080
Email: *information@maskell.com*
Web: *www.maskell.com*

Introduction

Companies are at different stages with Lean Accounting, and with other aspects of lean thinking. The Lean Accounting methods that are appropriate for a company will vary according to the company's maturity with lean manufacturing, and the issues they are facing. There is a *Maturity Path* associated with Lean Accounting. As you mature with lean thinking, additional methods of Lean Accounting will become useful.

This book can be read from front to back, but that is not how it was written. The starting point for writing this book was the *Lean Accounting Diagnostic* that you will find in the Appendix. The diagnostic is designed to help you make an assessment of your company's progress with Lean Accounting and develop a plan for implementing these lean changes. Chapter 18 has instructions for using the Lean Accounting Diagnostic.

THE MATURITY PATH

As you examine the Lean Accounting Diagnostic, you will find three columns titled "Lean Pilots," "Managing by Value Stream," and "Lean Enterprise." In this book we call these "Maturity Path levels."

Most companies begin their journey into lean by creating pilot lean production cells, called "Lean Pilots" in the Diagnostic. They get enthusiastic about lean manufacturing and take some training classes. They learn how to create a value stream map and how to design production cells that flow much better than their current operations. They begin to implement lean cells in the factory. These cells use small batches, flow and pull methods, standardized work, and other lean methods. These cells prove to be remarkably successful and everyone is delighted with the operational improvements achieved.

There are four Lean Accounting methods that are required for a company in these early stages of lean thinking:

- Cell Performance Measurements (Chapter 3)
- Calculation of the Financial Benefits of Lean Improvements (Chapter 4)
- Elimination of Transactions (Chapter 5)
- Lean Financial Accounting (Chapter 6)

New cell measurements using a lean approach are needed to track and control the new production flow. If you continue to use traditional measurements in the cells, the measurements will actively work against the success of the lean cells and pull the people back to their old ways. If you are looking for the operational improvements in the cells to be reflected in financial or bottom-line benefits, you will most likely be disappointed. Many of the benefits of lean improvement do not provide short-term financial improvement. You need another way to assess the financial impact.

It is never too early to start dismantling the company's transaction-driven control systems. They represent huge amounts of waste and cost to the organization. There are not a lot of changes that can be made at the early stages of lean, but you can begin to remove a lot of the detailed reporting in the new lean cells and (perhaps) relieve inventories automatically based on units completed (or, in other, words backflush some of the information), instead of laboriously entering it manually. Also, you can apply the same thinking to the financial accounting processes and eliminate a good deal of waste in the accounting office. This will free-up some of the people's time to work on more important lean improvements—such as Lean Accounting.

Managing by Value Stream

Once the initial success of the lean cells has been achieved, most companies begin to realize that there is a lot more to lean thinking than just a few changes on the shopfloor. They realize that everything they do to create value and serve the customer is affected by lean methods. In fact, the improvements in the cells may not have had any real effect on service to the customers or the costs of the operation. The problems often just move from the newly improved cells to the next stage down the process. The next step in the maturity path is the realization that you need to change and improve the entire value stream, not just the shop floor cells.

Value stream management is a very different way of running the business. The departmental structure is significantly changed. The roles of people in the organization change. The culture of the business dictates such changes. Once the ideas of value stream management take hold within the company, there are several important changes required:

- Value stream performance measurements (Chapter 8)
- Value stream costing (Chapter 9)
- Box scores and value stream cost and capacity analysis (Chapter 10)
- Lean decision-making (Chapter 9)
- Radical elimination of transactions (Chapter 12)
- New methods for planning and budgeting (Chapter 13)

New measurements are needed for each of the company's value streams, and the value stream managers are accountable for the improvement of these measurements. The value stream manager's role is far wider than just production. That job description includes growing the value stream revenue, eliminating waste, creating more customer value, and making money for the company.

New financial reporting is required to support these value stream management endeavors. Value stream costing is simple to use, provides excellent and timely management information, and eliminates the need for the complex cost and management accounting systems that weigh down most companies. Value stream costing is also very easy to understand. Unlike traditional accounting systems (with their allocations, overhead absorptions, and variance reporting), value stream costing is the simple, direct accounting of the costs of the value stream. Everyone in the company can understand it.

Value stream costing leads to a number of different approaches. Standard product costs are eliminated because the costs are now collected and reported by value stream, not by product. Yet, most companies make a lot of their day-to-day decisions using standard costs. New methods are, therefore, required for lean decision-making for such things as profitability of customer orders, make/buy decisions, product rationalizations, inter-company transfers, etc.

If we are to manage the value streams, we need to plan and budget each value stream—not the departments. This leads to the introduction of *Sales, Operations, and Financial Planning,* where our plans and budgets are updated monthly and are always up-to-date and actionable. This kind of dynamic planning of the value streams is the powerful underpinning of lean strategy deployment.

The introduction of value stream costing, and the methods associated with it, enables us to radically eliminate transactions from the company's business processes. This brings huge savings of time, effort, and money, and it frees up the people to do useful, lean-continuous improvement, instead of spending their time feeding the computer systems with data resulting in late, often harmful, and misleading information.

THE LEAN ENTERPRISE

A characteristic of lean enterprises is their focus on the customers. The first principle of lean thinking focuses on creating value for the customers. Using target costing, described in Chapter 16, this principle becomes the primary driver of change and improvement throughout the organization. Target costing starts by understanding what creates value for the customer and creates integrated change programs to market, sell, design, manufacture, and support the products and services that create increasingly more value to the customer, while creating much higher revenue and profits for the company. There is no "magic wand" that brings instant business success, but target costing, correctly used, brings such focus on customer value, lean in everything, and profitability, that the organization becomes a radically lean enterprise.

A second characteristic of lean enterprises is their cooperative nature. They prefer to cooperate with customers, suppliers, and other third-party business partners as much as possible. This leads to the use of macro value stream maps, covering not only the company's operations, but those of their customers, suppliers, and third-party partners. This leads to a need for such powerful tools as costing and profitability analyses to help maximize the benefit of lean methods across the company and its trading partners. Instead of just negotiating prices with customers, the lean enterprise works with the customer openly to improve the flow, reduce the waste, and increase the value. Everyone is better off. Instead of bludgeoning suppliers for price reductions and better service, the lean enterprise works with the supplier to eliminate waste, improve the flow, and create more value. This way everyone is better off—especially the customers.

These more mature Lean Accounting methods are:

- Target Costing (Chapter 16)
- Expanding Value Streams Outside Our Four Walls (Chapter 17)

How to Use This Book

While some people will find it helpful to read the book from cover-to-cover, the book is designed to be read around the *Lean Accounting Diagnostic*. The best approach is to review your company's current status with Lean Accounting and then read the chapters relating to the topics you feel would be most useful to you at this time.

Included is a table that cross-references the sections of the Diagnostic to the chapters in the book. Certain of the recommendations included in the diagnostic are not included among the subjects covered by this book. These subjects were considered beyond the scope of a book on Lean Accounting and were therefore omitted. They are the subjects of many fine books that are readily available. We have noted these omissions in the footnotes to this chapter and included recommended reference books for those interested in pursuing these topics.

Have your lean teams use the Diagnostics and the related chapters actively as they implement the transformation to Lean Accounting. Post the diagnostic and related progress prominently so that it can be an active tool in this transformation.

In addition, this book includes a CD, which contains tools that support the methods of Lean Accounting. The files on the CD contain Excel templates and data that enhances the ECI Value Stream Cost Analysis case study detailed in the book. Each of the templates can be used with your own data.

Keep an eye on the BMA, Inc. website (*www.maskell.com*) for additional case studies and ideas for improving your Lean Accounting as you pursue the lean journey.

Diagnostic Section	Diagnostic Subsection (if applicable)	Lean Pilots in Place	Managing by Value Stream	Lean Enterprise
Financial Accounting		Chapter 6	Chapter 14	Chapter 14
Operational Accounting		Chapter 5 Chapter 20	Chapter 12 Chapter 20	Chapter 12
Management Accounting	Alignment of Lean Goals	Chapter 19	Chapter 19	Chapter 16[1]
	Performance Measures	Chapter 3	Chapter 8 Chapter 10	Chapter 16[2]
	Budgeting and Planning	Chapter 6	Chapter 13	Chapter 13
	Managing Product Profitability	Chapter 4	Chapter 9 Chapter 11	Chapter 16
Support for Lean Transformation	Role of Finance People	Chapter 6	Chapter 14	Chapter 14
	Continuous Improvement	Chapter 4 Chapter 21	Chapter 4 Chapter 8 Chapter 10 Chapter 21	Chapter 16 Chapter 17
	Empowerment and Learning	Chapter 3	Chapter 8	Chapter 13
	Financial Benefits of Lean Changes	Chapter 4 Chapter 21	Chapter 4 Chapter 21	Chapter 13
Lean Business Management	Value Stream Organization	Chapter 7	Chapter 7 Chapter 8 Chapter 9 Chapter 10	Chapter 7 Chapter 8 Chapter 9 Chapter 10
	Customer Value and Target Costing	Chapter 15	Chapter 15 Chapter 11 Chapter 16	Chapter 15 Chapter 16 Chapter 17
	Rewards and Recognition	Chapter 3	Chapter 8	Chapter 15

1. For a readable understanding of the use of "Design Of Experiments" methods, we recommend the excellent book by Mark J. Anderson and Patrick J. Whitcomb, *DOE Simplified, Practical Tools for Effective Experimentation*. Productivity, Inc., Portland, Oregon, 2000.

2. The subject of statistical variation is beyond the scope of this book. We encourage readers to refer to one the many excellent texts on the subject.

    One of the most readable that we have seen is written by Stephen R. Schmidt, Mark J. Kiemele and Ronald J. Berdine, *Knowledge Based Management, Unleashing the Power of Quality Improvement*. Air Academy Press & Associates, Colorado Springs, CO, 1998.

    Another very fine book, slightly more technical but very readable nonetheless, is by Donald J. Wheeler, *Understanding Variation, the Key to Managing Chaos*. SPC Press, Knoxville, Tennessee, 1993.

CHAPTER 1

Why Is Lean Accounting Important?

A great deal of mystique surrounds the subject of accounting, the third rail of management. It is governed by thick volumes of regulations presided over by auditors and regulators. One does not change the way accounting is done without a great deal of evidence that existing rules do not fairly present economic reality. And yet, increasing numbers of companies are questioning the validity of using existing cost accounting for their lean manufacturing operations. They are searching for methods of accounting that are consistent with the assumptions underlying the radical changes they have made in their manufacturing operations changes that have turned the traditional assumptions of manufacturing on their heads. So we begin our discussion of this subject by addressing the basic question, "Why is Lean Accounting important?" Our intent is to demonstrate that serious problems crop up when companies that adopt lean manufacturing use traditional cost accounting. Then we set the stage for succeeding chapters to explain the accounting methods that support the new manufacturing.

There are both positive and negative reasons why Lean Accounting is important. The positive reasons are that Lean Accounting

- Provides information for better lean decision making. These better decisions lead to improved revenue and profitability.
- Reduces time, cost, and waste by eliminating wasteful transactions and systems.
- Identifies the potential financial benefits of lean improvement initiatives and focuses on the strategies required to realize those benefits.
- Motivates long-term lean improvement by providing lean-focused information and statistics.
- Addresses customer value directly by linking performance measurements to the drivers of value creation and driving changes to maximize this value.

All the negative reasons relate to the shortcomings of traditional accounting, control, and measurement systems. Traditional systems do not work for companies pursuing lean thinking; indeed they are actively harmful. Traditional systems are not the wrong way to work, but they are designed to support mass production. Lean manufacturing and other lean methods violate the rules of mass production. When you try to use traditional accounting systems and lean manufacturing, you will find they conflict with each other.

Problems caused by traditional accounting, control, and measurement systems include the following:

- They motivate people to use non-lean procedures, such as running large batches and building inventory.

- Traditional systems are wasteful. They require huge amounts of unnecessary work, gathering and analyzing data, producing unhelpful reports, and generating additional non-value-adding tasks.

- Standard costs can harm lean companies because they are based on premises grounded in mass production methods. Lean manufacturing violates all the assumptions of mass production. Whereas mass production is based on achieving economies of scale through long production runs, lean focuses on making products one at a time. It is no wonder, then, that these accounting methods lead people to do the wrong things, such as out-source items that should be in-sourced. In addition, the methods are complex and confusing to generate, they provide a misleading understanding of cost, and they lead to wrong management decisions on important issues, such as make/buy, profitability of sales orders, rationalization of products or customers, and so forth.

Lean Accounting provides:

- Lean performance measurements, which replace traditional measurements.

- Methods to identify the financial impact of lean manufacturing improvements.

- A better way to understand costs, product costs and value stream costs.

- Methods to eliminate large amounts of waste from the accounting, control, and measurement systems.

- Time freed up for finance people to work on lean improvement.

- New ways to make management decisions relating to pricing, profitability, make/buy, product/customer rationalization, etc.

- A way to focus the business around the value created for customers.

How Standard Costing Can Drive Wrong Behavior

The manufacturing process shown in Figure 1.1 shows machine steel forgings creating industrial fittings. Prior to introducing any lean improvements, this company manufactured in batches of 2500 through a four-step production process that provides a six-week lead time, 25 days of inventory, and an 82 percent on-time delivery. The standard cost for the item is $21.50.

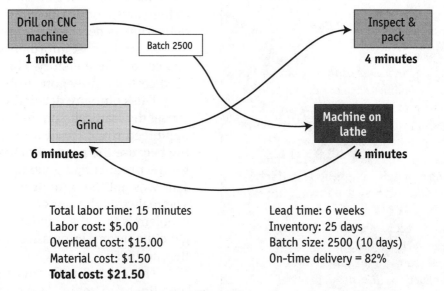

Total labor time: 15 minutes
Labor cost: $5.00
Overhead cost: $15.00
Material cost: $1.50
Total cost: $21.50

Lead time: 6 weeks
Inventory: 25 days
Batch size: 2500 (10 days)
On-time delivery = 82%

Figure 1.1

This company received training in value stream mapping and cell design. They decided to create a production cell and move to small batches and single piece flow. The obstacle to small batches was the long and complex changeover on the CNC machine. To overcome this, the team decided to use a straightforward drilling machine in the cell instead of the CNC machine. Changeover on the drilling machine was shorter than the CNC machine, and the production batch size was reduced to around 250. The new cell is shown in Figure 1.2.

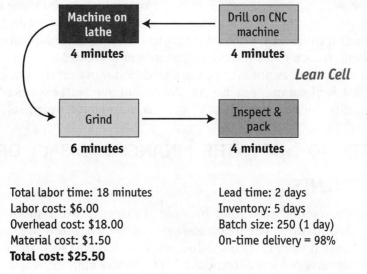

Total labor time: 18 minutes
Labor cost: $6.00
Overhead cost: $18.00
Material cost: $1.50
Total cost: $25.50

Lead time: 2 days
Inventory: 5 days
Batch size: 250 (1 day)
On-time delivery = 98%

Figure 1.2

IS STANDARD COSTING WRONG?

Standard costing is a perfectly good method of calculating product costs for companies that are committed to mass production methods. Standard costing is built on assumptions about the production process. These assumptions can be valid for traditional, batch and queue manufacturers because they will promote the creation of large production runs to create economies of scale. However, lean seeks to make items one at a time, so as to maximize the flow of production, and making an item only when demanded by a customer. Standard costing will tend to overproduce, creating excess inventories and reducing the flow of production—exactly opposite the intent of lean manufacturing.

Standard costing is not wrong, but it is inappropriate for lean manufacturing.

The results were impressive. The lead time came down to two days, inventory fell from 25 days to five days, and the on-time delivery was near perfect. But looking at the cost information you see a different story. The standard cost had now gone up!

This company decided to cancel the lean cell and go back to manufacturing the old way simply because the production costs for the product had gone up. This was not the right decision. The real costs did not go up. The problem is that the standard cost gave the wrong impression about the product's cost.

This kind of problem can be seen time and again. As a company introduces lean manufacturing methods, the traditional standard costing methods provide misleading information, causing managers to make the wrong decision.

Almost all companies introducing lean manufacturing methods bump up against these kinds of problems. They see great operational improvement, but little or no financial improvement. Often the financials show that bad things are happening when, in fact, good lean changes are being made.

Standard costing is not wrong for a traditional manufacturer, but it is inappropriate for lean manufacturing. We must have better ways of providing cost information for companies striving to create a lean enterprise.

WE NEED TO SHOW THE FINANCIAL IMPACT OF LEAN IMPROVEMENTS

A well-known manufacturer introduced lean manufacturing methods into one of its value streams. The income statement for the value stream is shown below. The current state is the monthly revenue and cost information before the lean improvements were introduced. The future state shows the results after the lean changes have been completed.

Income Statement			
	Current State before Lean	Lean Future State	Lean Improvement
Revenue	$216,200	$216,200	–
Production Costs	$121,043	$119,000	$(2,043)
Material Costs	$ 71,944	$ 71,944	–
Overhead Cost	$ 20,000	$ 20,000	–
Total Cost	$212,987	$210,944	$(2,043)
Gross Profit	$ 3,213	$ 5,256	$2,043

There has been some improvement; but it is modest. The reduction in production costs comes from a reduction in overtime worked by the people. The following questions were asked by the Chief Financial Officer (and others in the company):

"If this lean manufacturing is so great, why am I not seeing any bottom-line improvement. Sure, we are seeing improvement in the operational results, but that's probably caused by all the work and attention into that one production area. For all the work we put into making this lean manufacturing pilot, we should be seeing a substantial bottom-line impact."

When the future state was implemented, the company was able to make a significant reduction in inventory. This provided a welcome improvement in cash flow, which showed up on the Balance Sheet. However, this inventory reduction also had a negative impact on the Income Statement, caused by the

Income Statement			
	Current State before Lean	Lean Future State	Lean Improvement
Revenue	$216,200	$216,200	–
Production Costs	$121,043	$119,000	$ (2,043)
Material Costs	$ 71,944	$ 71,944	–
One-Time Inventory Reduction	–	$ 12,243	–
Overhead Cost	$ 20,000	$ 20,000	–
Total Cost	$212,987	$223,197	$ 10,200
Gross Profit	$ 3,213	$ (6,987)	$(10,200)

increased overhead burden on the reduced production volume associated with the inventory draw-down. This one-time inventory reduction pushed the gross profit negative.

These are common issues when adopting lean manufacturing methods. There is often little financial improvement in the short term, and the sudden reductions in inventory have a negative impact on profitability. Traditional accounting methods do not show the financial benefit of lean manufacturing. We need to have better ways to identify the financial impact of the lean improvements.[1]

WE NEED A BETTER WAY TO UNDERSTAND PRODUCT COSTS

A company creates a dedicated lean cell to manufacture product A. The cell is capable of making 10 items per hour and the total cost of the production process (including all the support and overhead costs) is $580 per hour. The raw material cost is $42 per item. What is the cost of Product A? It must be $100 per unit. The conversion cost is $580/10 units manufactured per hour.

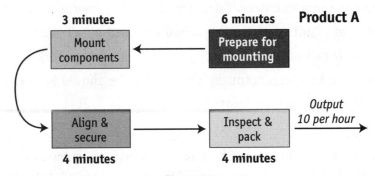

Figure 1.3

The company introduces a second product, Product B, into the cell. Product A and Product B are made interchangeably within the cell. The production rate is still 10 per hour, but the amount of labor and machine time required to manufacture B is much higher than that of Product A.

Despite the difference in labor and machine time, the cost of Product A and Product B will be the same. The company can make 10 As per hour and 10 Bs per hour. The cost of the value stream is $580 per hour and (let us assume) the material costs are the same also. The cost of Product B will be $42 materials and $58 conversion cost; total product cost $100.

This example is, of course, overly simplistic, but it does serve to show that as we move into lean thinking and our focus is on the flow of materials, products, and information through the value streams, the mass production

---

1. Chapter 4: "Financial Benefits of Lean Improvement."

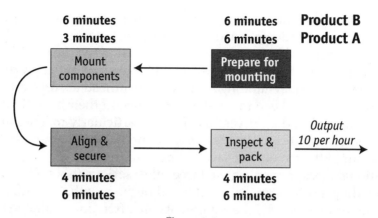

Figure 1.4

methods of standard costing become misleading and unhelpful. Here are the standard costs related to the Products A and B.

Product A	Product B
Standard Cost = $90.06 • Labor 17 mins @ $24.23 per Hr = $6.87 • Overhead @ 600% = $41.19 • Materials = $42	Standard Cost = $109.84 • Labor 24 mins @ $24.23 per Hr = $9.69 • Overhead @ 600% = $58.15 • Materials = $42
Real Cost = $100	Real Cost = $100
Standard Cost is too low	Standard Cost is too high

Lean organizations do not use standard costs for making day-by-day or week-by-week decisions. The cost information is related to the flow of products through the value streams. As lean manufacturing methods are implemented more fully, the organization ceases to be a job shop and the costing of production job and individual products are no longer relevant. The value streams become more like process manufacturing plants, and the methods of process costing are more useful than traditional job costing.[2]

WE NEED NEW KINDS OF LEAN PERFORMANCE MEASUREMENTS

Traditional accounting performance measurements lead to non-lean actions. Many manufacturers use measurements related to labor efficiencies and equipment utilization. These measurements lead people to make more products, build inventory, and increase their batch sizes. This problem is made

---

2. Chapter 9: "Value Stream Costing," Chapter 11: "Calculating Product Costs—Features and Characteristics."

worse when this same information is used to calculate financial variances that need to be discussed and explained at monthly cost meetings.

Many companies also focus on the absorption of overheads. This again leads production supervisors and operators to make too much product. They may not have a full understanding of how the overhead absorption works, but they know they can keep the cost accountants off their backs by making more products and building inventory. This is particularly marked at month-end and often contributes to the wasteful and non-lean month-end push of production out of the factory the last few days of the period.

Traditional measurements have three other serious flaws. First, they are too late; they mostly come out at the end of the month. Second, they are primarily financial. Financial measurements are often quite suitable for the finance people and the senior managers of the company, but are of very limited usefulness for improvement of the processes, creating customer value, and motivating the people towards lean goals. Third, they are too complicated. Most people do not understand them and this leads to lengthy and fruitless meetings, and to frustration and tension within the company.

Performance measurements within lean organizations are central to the control and improvement of the business. Lean organizations use simple and well-designed performance measurements to provide operational and financial control, to motivate people towards lean behaviors, to direct and initiate continuous improvement, and provide focus for decision-making and management direction.

Lean manufacturers need performance measurements at (at least) three different levels of the business:

- Production cell measurements,
- Value stream measurements,
- Company or plant level measurements.

There should be very few measurements, and these measurements must be focused on the lean issues we wish the people to address. The cell-level measurements[3] are primarily designed to assist the operations people to complete today the actions needed to be completed: to create quality products, on-time, in accordance with the customer's needs. These measurements are tracked visually (often manually) and frequently (often hourly); and they focus attention on the immediate needs of creating value for the customers.

Value stream measurements[4] are primarily designed to motivate continuous improvement of the value stream processes. It is the value stream continuous improvement team that works with these measurements, assuring they move in the right direction each week.

The plant or company measurements are more familiar measurements used by the managers of the company to monitor the achievement of the com-

---

3. Chapter 3: "Cell Performance Measurements."
4. Chapter 8: "Lean/Value Stream Performance Measurements."

pany's strategic objectives. The plant or company measurements are usually more financially focused than the cell-level or value stream-level measurements.

> BMA, Inc. recently conducted a detailed study with one manufacturer. The company has a single plant with 150 people. They make about 120 different products and their revenues are approximately $15M per year. They process approximately 4,000,000 transactions per year and this represents 38 people (equivalent heads) within the company. They spend 12.7 percent of their revenues processing wasteful transactions.

WE NEED TO ELIMINATE WASTE FROM ACCOUNTING PROCESSES AND SYSTEMS

Accounting and control systems are extremely wasteful. They are based around the premise that it is necessary to track and monitor every aspect of the business if we are to maintain financial and operational control of the business. These systems have been referred to as the hidden factory within a factory. The visible factory is the plant where the products are made. The hidden factory is the one where thousands and thousands of transactions are processed, reports produced, meetings convened, studies made, and projects initiated and completed. This hidden factory is hugely wasteful.

Although these transactions and processes are wasteful, they do serve a purpose. If the company's processes are essentially out of control, then detailed tracking can bring these feral processes to order. In reality, most traditional companies lack significant control within their processes, requiring detailed, transaction-based tracking. But as the methods of lean thinking are systematically and continuously applied to the company's processes, they gradually come under control, and it is no longer necessary to track all the steps in the process in great detail.

Companies using traditional systems try to create control from the chaos of forecasting, scheduling, rescheduling, expediting, material shortages, poor quality, machine breakdowns, etc. Lean companies address the root causes of these issues and, eliminate the chaos step-by-step. As we make progress with the introduction of control built into the processes, we can eliminate the wasteful tracking processes. We never jeopardize the financial or operational control of the business by removing transactions before their time. But we systematically and relentlessly eliminate the transactions by eliminating the need for them.

In Lean Accounting we define the maturity path for the elimination of transactions and wasteful systems. It would be wrong and irresponsible to eliminate transactions and systems that are currently providing financial and operational control of the business. However, we can define the changes needed to render those transactions unnecessary. As these changes are introduced and lean thinking takes hold within the organization, then we can eliminate the unnecessary transactions and systems. Using this maturity path, the wasteful processes are eliminated step-by-step.

We need to eliminate wasteful transactions and systems.[5] We need to free up the time of the finance (and other) people within the company, so they can engage in the more valuable activities of creating change and improvement.

WE NEED BETTER WAYS OF MAKING DECISIONS

The day-to-day decisions made by sales people, operations people, and others within the organization are (in most companies) based upon traditional accounting information. As we move further with lean manufacturing, this wasteful financial information becomes increasingly irrelevant and harmful. These decisions relate to such issues as pricing, make/buy, new product introduction, improvement priorities, product rationalization, and customer profitability.

As we progress with Lean Accounting and much of the traditional cost and management accounting system is dismantled, owing to its wastefulness, we largely eliminate the use of standard costing in favor of simpler and more relevant costing methods. But how do we make routine management decisions without this information?

Lean Accounting methods for decision-making revolve around an understanding of the flow of production through the value streams,[6] and the effect of these decisions on the value stream profitability and contribution. Value stream costs are clearly understood because they are calculated in simple, common-sense ways. Instead of relying on such things as profit margins based upon spurious standard costs, we focus on how the contemplated changes will affect the profitability and contribution of the value stream over the short and long term. These decision-making methods do not provide a simple, manufactured answer. All of these decisions require business judgment and a broader understanding of the company's strategy. Lean Accounting methods only provide the financial aspects of these decisions. But they are quick and easy to use, they focus our attention on the right things, and provide financial insight from a lean thinking perspective.[7]

---

5. Chapter 5: "Eliminating Wasteful Transactions," Chapter 6: Lean Financial Accounting 1," Chapter 12: "Eliminating More Wasteful Transactions," Chapter 14: "Lean Financial Accounting II."

6. Many organizations have additional value streams that are not production value streams. While in this book we are focusing on lean manufacturing, the principles of Lean Accounting apply equally well to value streams dealing with new product development, sales and marketing, service processes, and others.

7. Chapter 9: "Value Stream Costing."

WE NEED TO FOCUS OUR BUSINESS AROUND CUSTOMER VALUE

The first principle of lean thinking[8] is customer value, yet most companies have accounting systems that focus on internal costs. Lean Accounting focuses on customer value. The financial information is based around the value stream. We use methods like target costing[9] and performance measurements to address value rather than cost. As the organization matures with lean manufacturing and lean thinking, we move towards driving the business and the improvement processes from an understanding of how we create this value.

Does this mean that cost information is unimportant in Lean Accounting? No. Cost information is so important, in fact, that we need much better cost information than that provided by traditional cost and management accounting systems. However, we recognize that an important part of the cultural shift to a lean enterprise is the transition from thinking cost to thinking value.

Mass production companies have focused on cost reduction for years. An essential tenet of mass production is to "pile it high and make it cheap." The essential tenet of lean thinking is to maximize customer value and eliminate waste.[10] Lean Accounting is designed to address these issues.

SUMMARY

As an organization moves from mass production to lean manufacturing, the accounting, control and measurement systems need to change. Lean manufacturing and lean thinking cannot be sustained over the long term without significant changes in these systems. Traditional accounting systems are based on the rules and principles of mass production, and lean thinking violates these rules. Traditional accounting systems actively undermine a company's journey towards a lean enterprise because they motive non-lean behavior at all levels of the organization.

To overcome these problems we need to implement the methods known collectively as Lean Accounting. Based on proven and accepted accounting practice, Lean Accounting is simple and easily understood by everybody within the organization and provides business control systems rooted in lean thinking.

Lean Accounting addresses these needs:

- Replacing traditional measurements with few and focused lean performance measurements that motivate lean behavior at all levels of the

---

8. Womack, James & Jones, Daniel, *Lean Thinking*, Simon & Schuster, September 1996.

9. Chapter 16, "Target Costing."

10. Chapter 16: "Target Costing," Chapter 17: "Expanding Value Streams Outside the Four Walls," Chapter 21: "Value Stream Cost Analysis."

organization and engender continuous lean improvement. These measurements reflect the company's lean strategy and are the foundation of the company's operational and financial control.

- Identifying the financial impact of lean improvements and establishing a strategy to maximize these benefits.

- Implementing better ways to understand product costs and value stream costs, and using this cost information to drive improvement, make better business decisions, and enhance profitability.

- Saving money by eliminating large amounts of waste from the accounting, control, and measurement systems.

- Freeing up the time of finance people to work on strategic issues, lean improvement, and to become change agents within the organization.

- Focusing the business around the value created for customers.

CHAPTER 2

Maturity Path to Lean Accounting

Introducing Lean Accounting methods radically changes the accounting, control, and measurement processes of most companies. Lean Accounting creates a very different way to manage and control the organization as it evolves from traditional, mass production thinking to lean thinking. These changes must be made carefully. While the rapid introduction of lean manufacturing and lean thinking is desirable, the reality is that most organizations need considerable time to make the transition.

Lean Accounting does not stand alone. It is enabled by lean thinking and lean production methods. Lean Accounting only works when lean processes are stable and under control. This is a chicken-and-egg situation. Lean Accounting not only needs lean manufacturing, it also facilitates lean manufacturing. We need to introduce Lean Accounting in parallel with a transition to lean manufacturing and other lean changes.

The traditional control processes are there for a purpose. They are designed to maintain financial and operational control of the business. It would be wrong and irresponsible to remove those control processes too soon. We must maintain financial control.

Lean manufacturing (and other lean methodologies) eliminates the need for most of the traditional accounting processes because they bring the operation under control. For example, it is vitally important to maintain accurate and detailed inventory records if the company has high inventory and long production cycle times. The introduction of lean methods brings inventory levels down and creates short production cycle times. The kanbans, the pull system, the standardized work, and the performance measurements create operational control. It is not necessary to have separate financial control, because the operational control has been built into the process, and the detailed inventory records are no longer necessary. However, until this operational control has been established and stabilized, those traditional transactions still are needed.

THE MATURITY PATH

It is helpful to recognize that there is a maturity path toward the successful implementation of lean manufacturing. Most companies start off with a good deal of training, followed by the introduction of pilot lean cells or processes. Once the pilots are working well, these methods are rolled out across the plant and into other areas of the business. Over time, the company learns to apply lean thinking to every aspect of its business as it matures into a thoroughly lean enterprise.

There is, of course, no end to the lean journey and any simple model for the implementation of lean manufacturing and lean thinking will be inadequate. Also, all companies are different from one another, so they approach these fundamental changes in different ways. Having said that, we have found this simple model to be an effective way of addressing the changes needed to make Lean Accounting a reality within an organization.

The steps in the maturity path organize the five sections in this book.

Introduction to Lean Accounting	Chapters 1 and 2 set the scene for Lean Accounting.
Getting Started with Lean Accounting	Chapters 3 through 6 introduce the first steps in the maturity path.
Managing by Value Stream	Chapters 7 through 14 explain Step 2 in the maturity path.
The Lean Enterprise	Chapters 15 through 17 explain Step 3 in the maturity path.
Tools of Lean Accounting	These final chapters, Chapters 18 through 22, provide more depth on some of the key methods of Lean Accounting.

"Getting Started" is designed for companies that are in the early stages of lean thinking and have some pilots in place. The chapters on managing by value stream provide information on the more radical change and improvement your company needs to make as lean thinking is applied more widely. The chapters on lean enterprise focus on the more advanced aspects of Lean Accounting.

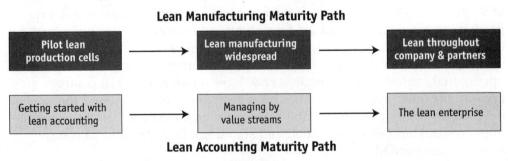

Lean Accounting Maturity Path

Figure 2.1

There is no clear-cut distinction between the three categories of maturity, but the table below shows the broad definitions we use in this book. It is common for a company to be at different levels of maturity in different parts of the organization. It is also common that there be varying levels of maturity within the same production plant or office. The purpose of the maturity path approach is to ensure that Lean Accounting is introduced in a sound and orderly manner, and that financial control is always maintained.

LEAN MANUFACTURING	LEAN MANUFACTURING ATTRIBUTES	LEAN ACCOUNTING
Pilot Lean Production Cells	• Successful lean cells in place • Extensive training in lean principles • Flow, pull, kanban • Quick changeover and SMED • Standardized work • Quality at source and self-inspection	Getting Started with Lean Accounting
Lean Manufacturing Widespread	• Wide-spread manufacturing in cells across the plant with standardized work and single-piece-flow • Extensive use of visual systems • Continuous improvement teams trained and established • Initial supplier certification program and kanban pull from some suppliers • Manufacturing managed by value stream • Processes under control; typically some use of SPC • Work-in-process and finished goods inventory relatively low and consistent	Managing by Value Streams
Lean Thinking Applied Throughout Organization and Partners	• Company organized by value streams • Extensive cooperation with customers, suppliers, and partners • Continuous improvement as way of life • Lean thinking applied throughout the entire organization	Lean Enterprise

Maturity Path—Stage 1

When an organization is in the early stages of lean manufacturing, it is not wise to make fundamental changes to the accounting, control, and measurement systems. However, important changes and waste elimination can be made to support the lean cells and the improvement teams.

New performance measurements are required in the production cells. New measurements are also required in the non-production departments that support the cells. These measurements are few and simple. They reflect the primary issues of lean thinking: making to takt time, standardized work, flow, and pull. The measurements are visual, timely, and action-oriented. The primary purpose of these cell-level measurements is to assist the production people to do today what needs to be done. Cell Performance Measurements are described in Chapter 3.

When lean pilots are introduced, it is unusual to see significant improvement to the company's financial reports. There can be some inventory reduction that leads to beneficial cash flow improvement, but this often takes some time to be realized. There is rarely any short-term improvement in cost or profitability, and, almost always, lean changes have a negative impact on the major financial variance reports. The classic dilemma is marked "operational improvements and no financial improvement," or worse. It is important in the early stages of the lean implementation to calculate the financial benefits of the changes being made. Most companies make the mistake of trying to identify the financial benefits of lean changes using the old mass production measurements. They are looking for head-count reductions and unit-cost reductions in the short term. This inevitably leads to conflict and wrong decisions. The discussion in Chapter 4 shows a better way to address the financial benefit of lean improvements. This method can be used in the early stage of lean manufacturing implementation, as well as in later stages.

LEAN ACCOUNTING CHANGES DURING THE GETTING-STARTED STAGE OF THE LEAN MATURITY PATH	
Lean Manufacturing	**Lean Accounting**
• Successful lean cells in place • Extensive training in lean principles • Flow, pull, kanban • Quick changeover and SMED • Standardized work • Quality at source and self-inspection	• Lean Performance Measurements in the Production Cells • Calculate the financial impact of the lean improvements • Eliminate many of the operational transactions • Eliminate variance reporting and other traditional performance measurements • Eliminate waste from the Financial Accounting processes • Identify the company's major value streams • Identify the primary drivers of cost and performance

During the first stage of the lean maturity path, it is necessary to continue most of the detailed reporting required by the traditional accounting, control, and measurement systems. These systems continue to be the primary financial control method. It is possible, however, to reduce the amount of waste associated with reporting this information. Most organizations use clear-cut methods like backflushing of materials and labor costs to eliminate a lot of the detailed manual transactions. It is important at this stage to eliminate the reports and measurements from the traditional system. The systems may well continue to be used, but it is not necessary to show the reports to anyone. We control the cells using the lean performance measurements, and ignore the old reporting methods. Chapter 5 addresses these initial steps to reduce wasteful transactions.

While improvements are being made to the production operations and the cost and management accounting associated with them, we can also begin to address the financial accounting processes. Typically, these processes contain a great deal of waste, much of which we can remove even in these early stages of the introduction of lean thinking. We also need to free up the time of the finance people within the company. There is a lot of important lean work to do and the finance people have a crucial role in the lean transformation of the company. Lean Financial Accounting is discussed in Chapter 6.

Finally, in the first stage of the lean maturity path there is some preparatory work to be done. This is a good time to start the process of defining the value streams. In the early stages of lean, most organizations focus their attention on the shop floor processes. The company's value streams are much bigger than just the production process; they include sales and marketing, procurement, engineering, customer service, production support services, and more. It is useful in the early stages to begin the process of defining the company's value streams. Chapter 7 addresses the definition of value streams.

Another useful action is to identify where (within the value streams) the costs occur and where the value is created. Later, we will spend a great deal of time on these issues. It is worthwhile to begin this process up front by identifying the extent of waste in the value stream. This is discussed in Chapters 4 and 10.

Maturity Path—Stage 2

Some of the more fundamental Lean Accounting changes can be made when the company's lean manufacturing has matured, and lean methods are widespread within the plant or an individual value stream. The widespread use of lean methods means that the processes are now coming under control operationally, inventory is low and consistent, visual methods are used to plan, initiate, and control production, and a culture of continuous improvement is developing.

Once the value streams are well defined, lean performance measurements are introduced to the value streams. These will be few and focused measurements designed to motivate continuous improvement and ensure the value stream is under control. Value stream performance measurements are discussed in Chapter 8.

The biggest change at this point is the introduction of Value Stream Costing (VSC), which is used to eliminate most of the wasteful transactions associated with production control, materials, and product costing. VSC eliminates the need for standard costing and overhead allocations, and creates a simple and effective cost accounting method. Value Stream Costing is dealt with in Chapter 9.

It goes without saying that the removal of standard costing must be done carefully. In most companies the use of standard costs is widespread for various kinds of decision-making from pricing, to make/buy, to inventory valuation. Value stream costing takes a different approach to these kinds of decisions. It is important that these changes are well thoughtout and the people well trained. The use of value stream costing requires people in the company to think differently—to think lean—about costs, profitability, and financial improvement. These issues also are dealt with in Chapter 9.

It is not necessary, most of the time, to know the cost of a product when using Value Stream Costing and lean decision making; but when it is required, we use features and characteristics to determine the product cost. The purpose is to identify the features and characteristics of the product and process that truly affect the costs within the value stream. It is usually possible to develop a simple matrix that relates the costs of products within a value stream to a small number of key features. Chapter 11, "Calculating Product Costs," describes the features and characteristics method of product costing.

LEAN ACCOUNTING CHANGES DURING STAGE OF THE LEAN MATURITY PATH, "MANAGE BY VALUE STREAM"	
Lean Manufacturing	Lean Accounting
<ul><li>Widespread manufacturing in cells across the plant with standardized work and single-piece-flow</li><li>Extensive use of visual systems</li><li>Continuous improvement teams trained and established</li><li>Initial supplier certification program and kanban pull from some suppliers</li><li>Manufacturing managed by value stream</li><li>Processes under control; typically with some use of SPC</li><li>Work-in-process and finished goods inventory relatively low and consistent.</li></ul>	<ul><li>Performance measurements at the value stream level and the plant or corporate level.</li><li>Integrated performance measurements reflect the company business strategy.</li><li>Value stream direct cost accounting replaces standard costing.</li><li>Value stream performance measurements and value stream cost information drive continuous improvement.</li><li>Expanded use of value stream cost analysis to understand where the costs are and where the value is.</li><li>Features and Characteristics used when product cost is required.</li><li>Financial planning integrated with the sales and operations planning.</li></ul>

Within stage two of the Lean Accounting maturity path, we also expand the value stream cost analysis, so the value stream team clearly understands where costs are generated and where value is created. We integrate the financial planning process with the sales and operational planning processes within the company so that we are no longer running the plant on spurious, out-of-date budgets, but have a single game plan, updated each month, for the achievement of the company's strategy. Also, we can eliminate a lot more waste from the transactions now that the value stream processes are coming under control. These issues are addressed in Chapter 12, "Eliminating More Wasteful Transactions."

Is Lean Accounting a Series of Methods and Tools?

While these Lean Accounting changes appear to be the introduction of new methods, in fact we are introducing a single lean management system. This lean management system applies the principles of lean thinking to the accounting, control, and measurement of the business.

- Lean Accounting uses visual measurement as the primary method of control. These measurements are few, primarily manual, focused on the creation of customer value, and require empowerment of people throughout the organization.

- Lean Accounting focuses business management around the value streams. All cost collection and financial decisions are made at the value stream level.

- Lean Accounting methods are designed to motivate ongoing, never-ending continuous improvement of the value stream.

- Lean Accounting eliminates most of the waste from the control systems through integrating control into the operational processes. The elimination of the need for wasteful transactions, reports, and meetings lead to the use of simple and understandable costing and reporting methods.

- Lean Accounting applies the principles of lean thinking (value, value streams, flow, pull, empowerment, perfection) to the accounting processes themselves.

A similar dynamic is evident in Lean Accounting and lean manufacturing. Some people regard lean manufacturing as a series of tools that can be learned and applied. While there is some truth in this, experienced practitioners recognize that the tools are less important than the underlying principles of lean. The tools were developed over time to support and apply lean principles.

The same is true of Lean Accounting. The methods and tools of Lean Accounting are not (for the most part) new. They have been used for many years in other kinds of businesses and under different circumstances. The power of Lean Accounting is that the use of these methods supports and applies lean principles.

The application of lean manufacturing and Lean Accounting methods varies from one organization to another. Companies really are different from each other. However, the lean principles are universal. Lean Accounting applies lean principles to the management of the business. When applied well, this becomes a quiet revolution.

Maturity Path—Stage 3

The first two stages of the maturity path deal with internal changes to the management of the business. Stage 3 addresses the outside world. Its two primary issues are the creation of customer value, and cooperation with third party partners.

A long-term objective of the lean enterprise is to drive the operation from the value we create for the customer. This is in stark contrast with traditional companies where the operation is driven with a firm focus on cost reduction. Simply put, mass production is a cost-down approach, whereas the lean approach is *value-up*. The lean method for bringing customer value into every aspect of our processes and improvement is called target costing.

Target costing starts with a profound understanding of the market, the needs of the customers, and how the company's products and services meet those needs. Once the value is clearly established from the customer's perspective, target costing moves on to calculating the costs required within the value streams to support the customer's need for value and the company's needs for profit and cash. We establish target costs for products, sub-assemblies, processes, and materials. The outcome of target costing is the development of action plans and continuous improvement initiatives designed to change the company's products and processes to meet or exceed the customer's requirements for additional value.

LEAN ACCOUNTING CHANGES DURING THE LEAN ENTERPRISE STAGE OF THE LEAN MATURITY PATH	
Lean Manufacturing	Lean Accounting
• Company organized by value streams • Extensive cooperation with customers, suppliers, and partners • Continuous improvement has become a way of life • Lean thinking applied throughout the entire organization	• Target costing used to understand customer value and drive continuous improvement processes. • Target costing used in product design to link the customer value to business operations, and product/process design. • Value stream mapping and value stream costing extended outside the company to suppliers, customers, and third party partners. • Most purchasing and inventory control processes eliminated as materials are pulled daily, expensed, and not tracked. • Most routine bookkeeping activities automated or out-sourced.

Target costing is a powerful method for bringing lean thinking into every aspect of the company's business. Target costing requires the integration of marketing, sales, product design, production, engineering, purchasing, and so forth. It focuses everybody within the value streams toward the creation of customer value. The value stream processes are changed to meet or exceed the value required and to generate exceptional profitability and cash flow. Target costing is described in Chapter 16.

The mature lean enterprise recognizes that its value streams extend beyond its own four walls. While there is still a great deal of continuous improvement to be completed, much of the internal waste has been eliminated. The external waste is now addressed. A touchstone of a lean enterprise is the profound level of cooperation with third-party organizations, including customers, suppliers, and other partners. Lean enterprises draw value stream maps that include external organizations. They work cooperatively with their customers and suppliers to improve their processes and eliminate waste.

The Lean Accounting methods required to support these extended value streams arise from the need to understand the costs of value streams that extend outside of the organizations, and the need to eliminate wasteful transactions and systems that are duplicated between the parties. This leads to new ways of pricing products, new approaches to selling and new ways of understanding the business control of the operation. These are discussed in Chapter 17.

In addition, there continues to be much waste that can be eliminated from the operational control processes, the financial control processes, and other administrative aspects of the business. These waste eliminations come about as a result of bringing our own processes, and those of our partners, under control. For example, is it necessary to provide an invoice to a customer receiving daily deliveries pulled from us by kanbans and delivered directly to their shop floor in standard containers? Is it necessary to maintain a perpetual inventory?

As these processes come under control within our own organization and the third parties we work with regularly, then we can eliminate the related transactions, processes, and bureaucracies. Chapter 14, "Lean Financial Accounting II," and Chapter 15, "The Lean Enterprise" addresses these issues.

GETTING STARTED WITH LEAN ACCOUNTING

So where do we start? The place to start is to understand where your company is on the lean manufacturing maturity path. You can use the simple definitions given in this chapter or you can refer to the more detailed breakdown given in Chapter 20.

Chapter 19 contains the BMA, Inc. *Lean Accounting Maturity Path Questionnaire*. The purpose of this questionnaire is to determine your company's status with Lean Accounting and to help you to map out a practical maturity path suitable for your needs.

Our experience with Lean Accounting has taught us that there is no cookie-cutter implementation method. Even within our own maturity path approach, we sometimes find that a company will easily be doing (what we would consider) advanced methods in the early stages of their lean transformation. Similarly, some of the changes we recommend for the early stages of maturity are, in fact, a complex challenge for other organizations. Every company, however, needs to go through a maturity path. The maturity path approach ensures that the introduction of Lean Accounting provides massive savings and improvements, while at the same time maintaining operational and financial control of the business.

SUMMARY

The introduction of Lean Accounting represents radical changes to an organization's accounting, control, and measurement systems. These changes need to be introduced carefully because the current systems are used to maintain financial control of the company's operations. It is essential to maintain sound financial control while, at the same time, eliminating most of the traditional cost management accounting and measurement processes. The successful implementation of lean manufacturing (and other lean methods) is the foundation for Lean Accounting. As the company's operational processes are brought under control through lean thinking, we can begin to dismantle unnecessary financial control and measurement processes.

When an organization is just beginning with their lean transformation, the early methods of Lean Accounting (as described in Chapters 3 through 6) are appropriate. Companies that are further ahead with lean thinking and have lean manufacturing methods widespread across their plants will be ready for the more fundamental Lean Accounting changes described in Managing the Value Stream (Chapters 7 through 14). Mature lean enterprises will want to take Lean Accounting further and use the methods discussed in the sections on Lean Enterprise of this book (Chapters 15 through 17).

Essential to Lean Accounting is an orderly, step-by-step transition of the company's accounting, control, and measurement systems as the organization matures with the lean transformation.

LEAN ACCOUNTING MATURITY PATH

Lean Pilots	• Successful lean cells in place • Extensive training in lean principles • Flow, pull, kanban • Quick change-over and SMED • Standardized work • Quality at source and self-inspection	• Lean Performance Measurements in the Production Cells • Financial Impact of lean Improvements calculated • Many operational transactions eliminated • Variance reporting and other traditional performance measurements eliminated • Waste from Financial Accounting processes eliminated • Identify the Company's major value streams identified • Primary drivers of cost and performance identified
Managing by Value Streams	• Widespread cellular manufacturing across the plant with standardized work and single-piece-flow • Extensive use of visual systems • Continuous improvement teams trained and established • Initial supplier certification program and kanban pull from some suppliers • Manufacturing managed by value stream • Processes under control; typically some use of SPC • Work-in-Process and Finished Goods inventory relatively low and consistent	• Performance measurements at the value stream level and the plant or corporate level • Integrated performance measurements reflecting the company business strategy • Value stream direct cost accounting replaces standard costing • Value stream performance measurements and value stream cost information drive continuous improvement • Expanded use of value stream cost analysis to understand where the costs are and where the value is • Features and Characteristics used when a product cost is required. • Financial planning integrated with the sales and operations planning
Lean Enterprise	• Company organized by value streams • Extensive cooperation with customers, suppliers, and partners • Continuous improvement has become a way of life • Lean thinking is being applied throughout the entire organization	• Target costing used to understand customer value and drives the continuous improvement processes. • Target costing used in product design to link the customer value, to the business operations, and the product/process design • Extend value stream mapping and value stream costing outside the company to suppliers, customers, and third party partners • Much of the purchasing and inventory control processes eliminated as materials are pulled daily, expensed, and not tracked • Automate or out-source much of the routine bookkeeping activities

CHAPTER 3

Cell Performance Measurements

Lean manufacturing and other lean processes need quite different performance measurements. Lean cells need to focus on customer takt time, flow rate, the effectiveness of standardized work, and the stability of the pull system and single-piece flow. Traditional measurements focus on efficiency, machine utilization, overhead absorption, etc. The measurements are different because we need to provide motivation towards different goals.

It is a mistake to mix lean manufacturing with traditional measurements. The operators and supervisors are pulled in two different directions; their lean training focuses on achieving takt time while their traditional measurements focus on earning hours and being efficient. When old measurements are mixed with lean operations the lean changes fail to achieve their objectives.

WHAT'S WRONG WITH TRADITIONAL MEASUREMENTS

- They motivate non-lean behavior, such as building large batches and increasing inventory, which ruin flow and lengthen cycle time.

- The measurements come too late to be useful and contain primarily financial information. Traditional reports usually address the efficiency of people, the utilization of machines, and such variances as labor (rate and usage), materials usage, and overhead absorption. In most companies these reports are available monthly and much time is spent explaining the variances. In some cases, additional reports provide daily information, but they do little to support the company's lean goals.

- The measurements waste a lot of time gathering data. Providing these reports requires the collection of detailed information about labor hours per production and machine time per job and job step, materials issued, scrap, and so on. These wasteful transactions do not provide helpful reports.

- As we move to lean manufacturing the burden of data collection becomes worse. If we make smaller batches we have more work orders, which leads to more tracking, more labor reporting, more machine time reporting, and more waste. Many organizations "perfume the pig" by automating these transactions, but they are merely automating waste.

WHAT'S RIGHT WITH LEAN CELL MEASUREMENTS

- Lean cell measurements are few and their focus is on the issues of lean manufacturing, providing motivation towards the company's lean goals.
- Information is gathered and used in the cell, and is presented visually. Operators and supervisors get the right information at the right time, in a form they can readily understand and use.
- Data gathering and reporting is quick, easy, and relevant. In most cases, complex data gathering or reporting is not required. The data is usually gathered manually by the people in the cell and reported on a white board or other visual board right in the cell.
- The measurements are developed directly from the company's business strategy and motivate people towards achieving that strategy.

In this chapter we will describe the performance measurements suitable for lean production cells. We will discuss these reports as if they are standalone measurements. In fact, the cell performance measurements are a part of the broader measurement set that supports the company's business strategy from the plant or division, through the value streams to the cells and nonproduction processes. We will address these broader issues in Chapter 8, "Lean Performance Measurements," and we will demonstrate how to link the business strategy to the performance measurement set in Chapter 19, "Lean Performance Measurement Linkage Chart."

BMA, INC. PERFORMANCE MEASUREMENT STARTER SET

There is no right set of measurements for a lean cell, but over the past 10 years we have worked with many companies implementing lean manufacturing cells and have developed our own starter set. These measurements are not perfect and they do not fit every situation, but they are tried and tested in many organizations and are a good starting point for most lean pilots.

The complete starter set is shown in Table 3.1. In this chapter, we will address the cell measurements only. The other starter set measurements are described in Chapter 8.

DAY-BY-THE-HOUR REPORT

The most fundamental measurement of lean performance is the Day-by-the-Hour report (Figure 3.1). It tracks the cell's success at the achievement of takt time. Lean cells are designed to achieve a predetermined cycle time for the

Table 3.1: Performance Measurement Starter Set

Strategic Issues	Strategic Measures	Value Stream Measures	Cell/Process Measures
Increase cash flow Increase sales and market share Continuous improvement culture	Sales growth EBITDA Inventory days On-time delivery Customer satisfaction Sales per employee	Sales per person On-time delivery Dock-to-dock time First time through Average cost per unit AR days outstanding	Day-by-the-hour production WIP-to-SWIP First time through Operation equipment effectiveness

products manufactured. The cycle time of the cell is determined by the takt time required by customer demand. The takt time is the rate at which customers demand product. If customers need a product every five minutes, for example, then the cycle times at each of the cells involved in manufacturing the product must match the five-minute requirement.

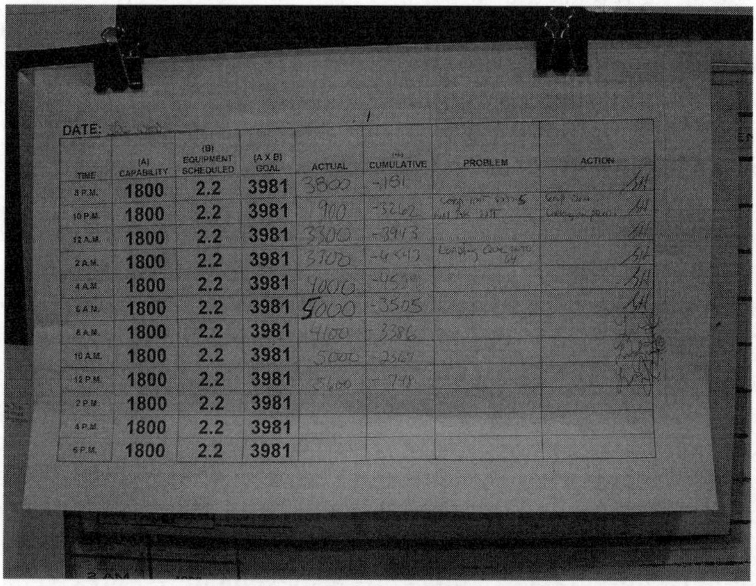

Figure 3.1: The Day-by-the-Hour Report

The Day-by-the-Hour report tracks the cell's ability to achieve the takt time and provides fast feedback when problems arise. The Day-by-the-Hour information is usually reported on a white board within the cell and shows the production quantity needed each hour to support the customer takt time. At the end of each hour one of the cell people writes up the actual quantity achieved that hour, and the cumulative quantity achieved this shift or this day.

There are three purposes for this measurement. The first is to keep the operating people in the cell focused on maintaining a consistent output of products in line with customer demand. The second is to provide fast feedback when problems in the cell need to be fixed quickly. The third is to gather data about the problems so they can be studied and permanently corrected.

For a cell to maximize flow and minimize waste, the cell must manufacture the product at the same rate as customer demand for the product. This is why cells are designed to run at the same rate as the takt time. To maintain this constant rhythm of production, the cell people need to be well trained in the standardized work methods, effectively supplied with parts and materials, and have a method to track their production rate. The Day-by-the-Hour report helps them track their rate of production and keep it in line with the customer's takt time.

When the production rate of the cell falls back and the hourly quantity is not achieved, it is imperative the issues causing the problem are quickly resolved. The cell people are trained to raise the alarm when the hourly production quantity (or cumulative quantity) falls below a certain level. Andon lights (Figure 3.2) are often used to provide a visual method of raising the alarm. When the light goes on, an alarm is raised, which alerts managers, engineers, and production specialists to go to the cell and help resolve the problem quickly.

The achievement of takt time is so vital to the success of lean flow within the plant that it is important to have an effective mechanism in place for people to raise the alarm, resolve the problem, and have the cell catch up on the shortfall over the next few hours. This instant problem resolution and emphasis on the importance of takt-time achievement requires a change in management style for companies moving from traditional manufacturing. However, because there is so little inventory and the focus is on production flow and takt time, one cell cannot be allowed to fall behind. Production managers, supervisors, engineers, maintenance, materials, planning specialists, and others must be readily available to attend to problems immediately and resolve them quickly.

To avoid constant production fire drills it is necessary for the cell people to stop the line and call for help only when the production slow-down is significant. Usually a percentage or quantity below the hourly requirement is

---

TAKT TIME

A company that manufactures high-quality radios has an average customer demand of 635 units per day. The factory works two shifts of 7½ hours each. The takt time is 85 seconds. To fulfill the customer demand the factory must make one radio every 85 seconds.

The cycle time of the final assembly cell must be no less than 85 seconds. Every step in the final assembly cell processes must take 85 seconds or less.

The takt time for the cell assembling the speaker unit sub-assemblies is 42.5 seconds. The cell must make two speakers for every radio manufactured.

Figure 3.2: Andon lights in action.

established. If production falls below this amount, raise the alarm. When good data is available, this shortfall quantity is calculated statistically to ensure that the people are reacting to a real problem and not to the production noise or expected variability of the process.

Thirdly, the Day-by-the-Hour report is used to gather information and data about the problems the cell experiences over time. Every hour, when the production quantity is reported, the cell people write down the problems they encountered during the hour. If there has been a shortfall that hour, they write up the reason for it. This information is used by the cell people themselves, the value stream continuous improvement team, and managers or engineers within the value stream to introduce changes that permanently resolve the problems. This is part of the work of perfecting the process that leads to continuously improving process quality.

All cell performance measurements must report the result of the work, and also have a method for collecting data that relates to problems. These performance measurements are not used to measure people's efficiency or capability. The measurements are used to enable the cell team to complete today what needs to be done to serve the customer's needs and create value. The measurements are also used to gather the first-level data required in the cell's pursuit of perfection.

The Primary Reason the Cell Team Neglects the Day-by-the-Hour Report

If managers, supervisors, and others in authority do not look at the results or use the information, the cell team members soon know whether their managers and supervisors are paying attention to the information they report on the Day-by-the-Hour report. If they find that the managers and supervisors do not walk the production floor regularly and monitor the cells' progress throughout the day, they (rightly) conclude that the managers and supervisors are not serious about the importance of takt time.

If you (as a manager or supervisor) want your cell people to use the Day-by-the-Hour report effectively, you must make sure you are constantly out on the shop floor working with the people, reviewing the issues, understanding the problems, resolving problems, and managing the processes visually. If you spend much of your time in your office looking at computer screens and reading reports, they will conclude (again, correctly) that visual management is a buzzword they should not take seriously.

This different way of managing the production process is a major change for many companies moving into lean methods for the first time. However, it is an essential part of lean management that cannot be neglected if you are looking for successful lean cells and value streams.

Why By the Hour?

Measuring by the hour is not a requirement. You need to select a time frame that matches the production rhythm of the process and is convenient for the people to use. It is important, however, that the measurement is frequent because one purpose of the reporting is to enable the cell team to resolve problems quickly and get back on track to achieve takt time. If you only measure daily or by shift, for example, this important purpose cannot be achieved.

Some companies set the measurement time to be the same as the pitch[1] of the process. This means that it will measure at the same frequency as the value stream releases work at its pacemaker cell. The pacemaker cell sets the pace of work for the whole value stream, so that the work will flow at a constant rate—so-called levelized scheduling. This can be convenient because it links scheduling, materials handling, and production reporting into a single process. One of our clients sets this report every 20 minutes. This is the pitch they use for the flow of materials through the value stream. This 20 minute pitch was set because the materials required for 20 minutes of production fitted well onto the carts used to move the material from one cell to another within the value stream.

Our Cells Only Make a Few Products Each Hour and the Cycle Times Vary Considerably.

The Day-by-the-Hour report works most simply when the cell makes a large number of products each hour and these products have roughly the same pro-

---

1. See Shook, John and Rother, Mike, *Learning to See*: page 76, LEI, 1999.

duction cycle time (Figure 3.3). However, when this is not the case, it is even more important to maintain and monitor the rhythm of production.

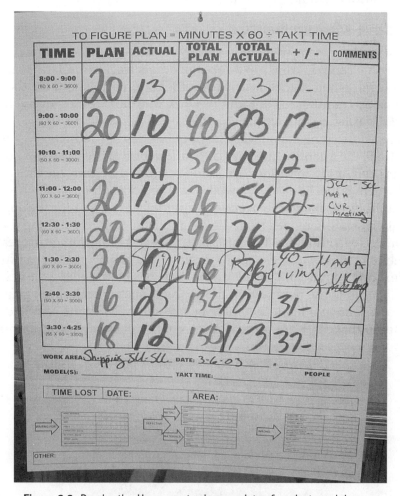

Figure 3.3: Day-by-the-Hour report using a variety of products each hour

Some companies use the Day-by-the-Hour report to provide the production schedule to the cell. The specific products to be manufactured each hour are written on the board. These products are, of course, scheduled from the kanbans or customer orders pulling the need for the item. The quantity per hour may be different each hour according to the production cycle time of the products. The cell team reports the quantity produced each hour and this is compared to the scheduled quantity and the cumulative quantities.

When the products need to be manufactured in a specific sequence, this can also be provided on the Day-by-the-Hour board. The cell team can then report the quantity manufactured that hour, and whether they were completed in the appropriate sequence.

Companies using heijunka methods to levelize production will often match the reporting interval to the time within which a full cycle of levelized production is completed. This usually means that the quantity per cycle (or pitch) is always consistent despite the fact that the products are widely different and their individual cycle times vary considerably.

Alternative Measurements

Day-by-the-Hour measurement is used by almost all lean manufacturing companies. Some companies use exit reports, others track cumulative output over time, and still others track linearity. Another approach is to track the cell's cycle time by counting the amount of work-in-process inventory within the cell and dividing by the output quantity.

When a machine makes very large quantities of products, it is usually best to track the quantity automatically and report it on an andon board above the cell or the machine. An andon board is an electronic message board, placed where it can be easily viewed. It automatically posts in lights the planned production and the production actually achieved for the shift. This automatic posting removes from the operator the task of counting the actual units produced and makes the information very visible. Other processes lend themselves to an electronic counter (Figure 3.4). The operator can flip a switch each time one item is completed, or the item can be counted as it passes out of the cell and on to the next step in the process. These results are again presented on prominent lighted display boards (along with the required production rate) so that cell-team members can continuously monitor their progress.

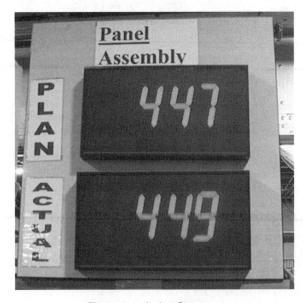

Figure 3.4: Andon Counter

FIRST TIME THROUGH REPORT

The purpose of the First Time Through (FTT) measurement is to monitor whether the cell is making the products right the first time. Some would see this as a quality measure because it tracks scrap, rework, and repair. A better way to look at the FTT, however, is as a measurement of the effectiveness of the cell's standardized work.

Standardized work is an essential feature of lean manufacturing. When a cell is designed the precise method of manufacture is specified. The physical flow of the product through the cell is defined and diagrammed. The steps in the production process and how to perform them is defined and diagrammed. The combination diagram shows the exact sequence and timing of the production process.

The two primary purposes for standardizing work are to ensure the product is made correctly and to the cell's production cycle time. Cell operators are trained to complete the production processes exactly in accordance with the standardized work. This way the product is made perfect the first time and at the right rate.[2]

The cell FTT report shows the percentage of product made in the cell without any need for rework, repair, or scrap. If the standardized work is adhered to, the product will be made right first time; and FTT will be 100 percent.

There are other reasons, however, for scrap and rework. The materials and components may be faulty, for example, but most scrap, rework, and repairs owe to the operator not completing or not adhering to the standardized work.

How Do I Measure First Time Through?

$$FTT = \frac{\text{Total Units Processed} - \text{Rejects or Reworks}}{\text{Total Units Processed}}$$

If the production quantity for a time period an hour, for example, 40 units and three of these units required rework; then the FTT is 92.5 percent. This is calculated as 37/40 because 37 units were competed right the first time.

The FTT percentage may be calculated at more than one workstation within the cell. For example, a cell may have three workstations, each of which is tracking the FTT. If the FTT for workstation 1 is 90 percent, for workstation 2, 95 percent, and for workstation 3 85 percent, the FTT for the whole cell is the product of the three individual FTT's.

$$\text{Cell FTT} = FTT_1 * FTT_2 * FTT_3 = 90\% * 95\% * 85\% = 72.7\%$$

How is the Data Collected?

The data required for the FTT calculation is collected by the cell people themselves monitoring their own production processes. Each person included in the FTT monitoring is given a check sheet (or similar data gathering method)

---

2. For more information about standardized work, see Rick Harris and Mike Rother, *Creating Continuous Flow*, LEI, 2001, or Larry Rubich and Madelyn Watson, *Implementing World Class Manufacturing*, WCM Associates, 1998.

and they keep track of the products that require rework, repair, or scrap; and the reasons for the problem. Typically the check sheet has columns for the most common problems and extra space for noting other issues and problems.

It is not necessary to track and monitor every step in the process and every person involved. You need to decide which steps in the production process are most critical or problematic. Do not monitor for the sake of monitoring. Only gather information that is required and meaningful.

How Do I Report FTT?

First Time Through can be reported a number of ways. Some people combine it with the Day-by-the-Hour report and have their cell people track the FTT information on the same white-board or flip chart they use for Day-by-the-Hour. Alongside the completed quantity, the cell team reports the FTT for that hour's output.

FTT can be reported on a graph or bar chart on the cell performance measurement board. It can be reported throughout the day at regular intervals, or at the end of the shift or the day. Alternatively, it can be reported on a diagram of the cell. The individual FTTs are shown for each workstation and the summary for the cell shown at the end of the cell.

What is the Number One Reason for the FTT to Fail?

The most common reason FTT reporting fails is that the information is used to blame or criticize the operators. The people gather their own data within the process. If they feel that accurate reporting will put them in danger of discipline or criticism, they will falsify the numbers.

It is essential to develop a no blame environment on the shop floor (and other places within the value stream) because information must be correct and up-to-date. The purpose of the information is never to judge people, but to discover problems and issues that need resolution. Even if a person is at fault, this is mostly likely the result of a problem within the process for example, lack of training, lack of fail-safe or mistake-proofing methods, or inadequate documentation. Again, lean thinking requires a thoroughly different style of management in which we monitor the process and not the people, and where problems are seen as opportunities for improvement.

Alternative Measurements to FTT

There are several methods of measuring quality. Some organizations track rejects in terms of parts per million. Others keep careful track of the quantity or value of scrap material. Yield is also a common way for measuring product quality, particularly when manufacturing less discrete products.

While quality measurements are often successful, they typically address the outcome of cell process. First Time Through is designed to measure not only the success of the process at making good parts or products, but also to indicate the capability of the standardized work. The most important issue is not only how many were made perfectly, but how many were made right the first time, without additional wasteful work.

WIP-TO-SWIP REPORT

The WIP-to-SWIP report shows the inventory levels in the cells. WIP is work in progress. SWIP is standard work in progress. Cells are designed to contain a certain amount of inventory. This inventory is often determined by the number of kanbans between the cell's work centers. The purpose of these kanbans is to buffer the production processes within the cell against delays or problems, as well as to trigger production and maintain the one-piece flow (Figure 3.5).

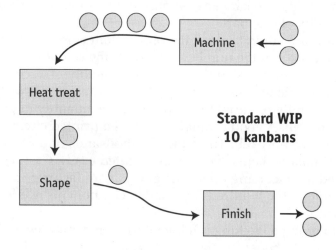

Figure 3.5: Diagram of Production Cell Standard Inventory

The kanban method in its various forms is the backbone of a lean pull system. If the kanbans go awry, the pull system within the value stream fails: production cycle times extend, production rates fall, and the processes become unstable. It is essential to maintain the pull system effectively.

We measure WIP-to-SWIP because it tracks the success of the pull system. If the actual inventory within the cell is always the same as the standard WIP designed for the cell, then the pull system is working correctly. If the inventory goes much higher or much lower than designed, then the pull system is failing. WIP-to-SWIP is a measure of the pull system.

How is the Report Calculated?

The WIP-to-SWIP is calculated by dividing the inventory quantity within the cell by the standard WIP inventory quantity.

Total Inventory on the Cell / Standard Cell Inventory

The ideal result is 1. The WIP is equal to the SWIP. If the result is higher than 1, there is too much inventory in the cell. If the result is less than 1, there is too little inventory and the cell is in danger of running short.

How is the Data Gathered?

The information is most commonly gathered by simply counting the number of kanbans in the cell. A kanban contains the number of items that are to be manufactured at any one time. Kanbans may be in the form of containers or totes, squares painted either on the benches or on the floor or physical cards denoting the items.

A kanban always has a fixed quantity associated with it. It may have 10 pieces in a standard container, a single piece in a kanban square, or a certain amount contained on a shelf or rack. It is not necessary to count all of the individual parts, just the kanbans, because they represent the part and the standard quantity of that part.

If kanbans are not in use and the pull system is maintained another way, then you can just count the number of units in the cell. If the cell contains a very large number of items, perhaps for the assembly of a complex product, it may be impossible to count all the parts. In this case, you will select a major part (or family of parts) that represents the quantity of products flowing through the cell. A good example of this is a printed circuit board within an electronics assembly cell. There may be thousands of parts and components, but the boards themselves can be counted easily. Castings or forging are often used in machining cells. One guitar manufacturer counts guitar necks from among the hundreds of wooden components needed to manufacture the instrument.

If possible, avoid tracking cell inventories on computer systems. Visual management works better.

How Do I Report WIP-to-SWIP?

WIP-to-SWIP may be reported by the hour, but it is more common to report by the shift or day. The inventory is counted and the ratio is calculated. The results can be plotted on a run chart or bar graph. A better way is to use a color-coded visual report like the one shown on the next page.

The gray blocks mean the inventory is in line with standard WIP. The black blocks mean the inventory is significantly too high. The checked block means the inventory is significantly too low. Again, it is important to have a method of tracking the reasons for the problems so these can be addressed and resolved quickly.

Train the people using the report so that they know how much over or under inventory is acceptable. This avoids reporting a problem when it is merely the noise within the kanban pull process.

Alternative Measurements to WIP-to-SWIP

Some companies simply track the amount of inventory within the cell and report it. This may be as a quantity, a number of kanbans, or the value of the inventory. Often the chart that reports inventory will also show the planned inventory. Others use dock-to-dock tracking, where the inventory throughout

Monday Aug 6			
Tuesday Aug 7			
Wednesday Aug 8		14	Shortage of clips
Thursday Aug 9		16	Shortage of clips and holders
Friday Aug 10			
Monday Aug 13		8	
Tuesday Aug 14			
Wednesday Aug 15			
Thursday Aug 16			
Friday Aug 17			
Monday Aug 20			
Tuesday Aug 21		13	Product mix not level
Wednesday Aug 22			
Thursday Aug 23			
Friday Aug 24			

Visual Report Chart

the cell is counted and divided by the output rate. This gives the number of days or hours of inventory within the cell.[3]

OPERATIONAL EQUIPMENT EFFECTIVENESS

The three measurements we have discussed so far address the manual operation of the cell. Operational Equipment Effectiveness (OEE) addresses the machines within a cell. OEE is a combination measurement that tracks the ability of a machine to make product on time and to the right quality. In many processes the cell cycle time is determined by the ability of the machine to make to cycle time. OEE tracks this and the reasons for problems.

OEE is a little complicated. It requires the tracking of three attributes of the machine: downtime, production rate, and first time through. These three measurements are then combined into the single measurement of OEE.

We do not recommend applying OEE to all the machines in the cell or the value stream. OEE takes time to track and measure. The most important place to use OEE is with the machine that creates a bottleneck in the cell. This machine determines the flow rate and cycle time of the entire cell. If this machine fails to operate effectively, the whole cell fails. When you first start with these measurements, use OEE at the bottleneck (or constraint) machine.

---

3. There is a further discussion of dock-to-dock tracking in Chapter 8, because we include this measurement in our starter set for value stream measurements.

Once your measurement system has matured and the people are using the measurement as a regular part of their daily work, you can extend the use of OEE to other machines within the cell.

OEE is often used to support a total productive maintenance (TPM) program. TPM is a formal method for ensuring the correct maintenance on production machines. TPM puts the responsibility for maintenance with the machine operators, rather than the company's maintenance department. The machine operators use OEE to monitor the production capability of their machines and initiate preventive maintenance to ensure their machines are always capable of making product on time and to quality.

How Do I Measure OEE?

The OEE calculation requires three pieces of data; machine availability, machine performance, and the quality of products.

OEE is the product of these three factors.

OEE = Availability * Performance Efficiency * Quality

To track availability we need to track the amount of time the machine was not working when it should have been available. If the machine is not working at a time it is needed, then it is down. The machine operators track the downtime and the reasons for the problem. The availability of the machine is the percentage of time the machine was up and running when it was needed.

Availability = (Total Time – Downtime) / Total Time

If the production shift is eight hours (480 minutes) and the machine is down four times during the shift, for a total of 40 minutes, then.

Availability = (480 – 40)/480 = 440/480 = 91.67%

AVAILABILITY

- Operating Time / Net Available Time
- Net Available Time = Total Scheduled Time less Contractually Required Downtime
- Operating Time – Net Available Time less Downtime
- Contractually required downtime is usually set by union contracts, local regulations, or management policy.
- Downtime is caused by equipment breakdowns, setup and adjustments, tooling losses, changeovers and other documented minor stops.

Performance efficiency is concerned with the rate of production from the machine. A machine may be designed to run at a rate of 100 per hour, but if it is running at only 90 per hour then its performance efficiency is 90 percent. The ideal production rate is not necessarily the maximum run rate for the machine. The ideal rate is the run rate we have designed it to run at within this cell. This will often be slower than the maximum run rate because we need to run the machine in line with the cycle time needed to achieve customer takt time.

Performance Efficiency = (Ideal Run Rate – Actual Run Rate) / Ideal Run Rate

Such issues as speed losses, losses associated with undocumented idling or minor stoppages, or resulting from blocked or starving upstream and downstream equipment, can affect performance efficiency.

Quality is measured using the first-time-through method. FTT is the percentage of parts manufactured without rework, rejects, or scrap. The machine operator keeps track of how many items are reworked, rejected, or scrapped. This is contrasted to the total number of items manufactured.

Quality = (Total Quantity Manufactured – Number Rejected) / Total Quantity Manufactured

If we manufacture 126 items and need to rework seven, then the quality measure is:

Quality = (126 – 7) / 126 = 119 / 126 = 94.44%

The overall equipment effectiveness is calculated by multiplying these three factors.

OEE = Availability * Performance Efficiency * Quality

OEE = 91.67 * 90.00 * 94.44 = 77.92%

How Do We Gather the Data?

The data for OEE has to be gathered by tracking the machine carefully throughout the day. The downtime must be documented as it occurs and the reasons for the downtime tracked. The run rate is tracked by comparing the hourly production quantities to the designed run rate. The operator tracks the FTT by recording the rejects and the reasons for the rejects. This information is brought together at the end of the day or shift and the OEE is calculated.

How Do We Report OEE?

OEE should be reported at the machine on a graph or chart showing the OEE result and the breakdown between the three elements of the measurement. The chart also highlights the level below which the operator should notify a supervisor or engineer that the machine is malfunctioning. This level may be calculated statistically as a lower limit outside of which the machine no longer displays normal variability, but needs repair.

As well as reporting the results of the OEE (and the three elements of OEE), the reasons for problems should be recorded: the number of occurrences and duration of downtime, the reasons for quality problems, or machine slow-downs. This information is used to build up a history of the machine's operation that the continuous improvement team, the operator, or engineers use to resolve machine problems permanently.

Is OEE Used for Other Things?

OEE is often used as the primary measurement when a company introduces Total Productive Maintenance (TPM). TPM is a systematic method that allows machine operators to use preventive maintenance methods to ensure the availability and productivity of the machines they use. Maintenance people assigned to the value stream perform major maintenance activities on the machines, but the operators themselves are responsible for the effectiveness of their machines, and perform much of the routine maintenance tasks themselves. This is similar to our private cars. We are responsible for our cars being in good working order. We perform simple routine maintenance such as cleaning, filling up with gas, checking the oil level, etc., but we delegate major maintenance and repairs to specialist service garages.

The operators use OEE to measure the success of the TPM efforts. If TPM is applied correctly, even old and troublesome machines can be brought up to good working order. OEE and, sometimes, statistical process control are used to notify the operator whenever the machine's performance begins to deviate.

Another use of OEE is in the design of the cell, or when the value stream takt time is recalculated. For example, a value stream takt time is 120 seconds and a cell within the value stream has a required cycle time of 100 seconds. However, the bottleneck machine within the cell has a regular OEE of 85 percent. Then the cell needs to be set up to run at a rate of 85 seconds (100 secs * 85 percent OEE) because the effectiveness of the machine will, over time, slow down the cell run rate to an average of 100 seconds.

It is essential to know the normal OEE of a machine when designing a production cell. To design a cell assuming the machines will be 100 percent available, 100 percent productive, and provide 100 percent perfect quality is usually a mistake. The OEE of the bottleneck machine needs to be applied to the required cycle time to obtain the design cycle time.

Alternative Measurements to OEE

Some organizations find that OEE is overkill. Their machines do not have problems with their speed of performance, for example. They just use measurements of downtime and FTT to keep track of the machine's effectiveness. These are either reported individually or combined into a simpler version of OEE.

Other companies find that downtime is the big issue, and they just keep track of the downtime of the bottleneck machines. A bottleneck machine produces at the slowest rate of any in the cell. It determines the maximum rate of production of the cell—hence its designation as a bottleneck. Many companies use full OEE on bottleneck machines, and also track the downtime of non-bottleneck machines. This provides the data required to understand why cycle times are sometimes missed and to resolve production problems in the cell that are caused by machines other than the bottleneck.

OTHER SUPPORT MEASUREMENTS IN THE CELL

The four measurements given above are the primary cell measurements. It is not always necessary to use all four in a cell, but these measurements motivate the cell operators toward lean manufacturing goals. They are designed to measure the lean goals, and they assist the operators in achieving the planned rate of production as they maintain the focus on producing at the desired rate of production.

It is usual for cell operators to maintain other support measurements. While not primary measurements, these can be important to the success of the cell.

Cross-Training Chart

This chart shows how much cross-training has been achieved among the cell team members. The chart lists the name of all the cell team members on the horizontal axis. Across the top of the chart are listed all the topics the people need to be trained in over time. Typically, the first set of topics are tasks required within the cell to make the products. The second set of topics includes the skills required to do preventive maintenance, problem solving, and lean improvement. The third set of topics are tasks required to support other cells. And the fourth set includes skills in facilitating continuous improvement teams and kaizen events.

When a person receives training, this is marked on the chart. Many organizations designate skill levels. For example, a red circle on the chart may denote that the person has received training, an orange circle may denote the person is trained and certified, a green circle may denote the person is a trainer of that task.

It is possible to assign a numeric score to each level of skill (1 for training, 3 for certification, and 10 for trainer status, for example) and then calculate the average amount of cross training per person within the cell.

Five S

Most lean companies have a formal 5S program, which is used to create an orderly cell work area. It is important for the cell operators to maintain their own 5S. The results from 5S audits should be posted in the cell. Self-audits are the best kind. Provide people with a photograph of the cell in perfect condition, and have them assess themselves currently, using a 5S check-sheet. 5S is usually reported on a bar chart or radar chart showing the level of achievement in the 5 of the S's (Figure 3.6).

Safety

While not a performance measurement as such, tracking safety within the cell is of the highest importance Figure 3.7 shows a Safety Cross Calendar chart that can be used in a cell or for an entire value stream.

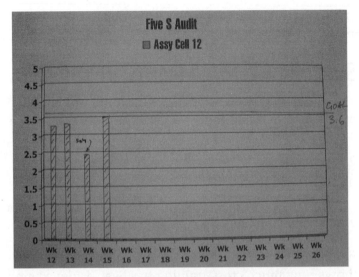

Figure 3.6: Five S Audit Chart

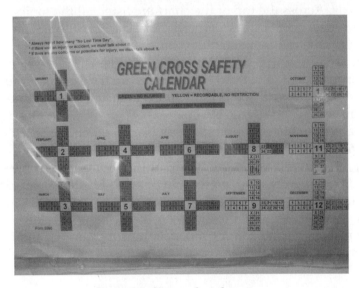

Figure 3.7: Picture of a safety cross

Absenteeism

Some organizations track the attendance of people within the cell. This may be used for payroll reporting as well for keeping track of problems.

Set-Up Times

It is common to track machine set-up times in production cells where the set-up or changeover of machines is an important driver of success with the achievement of takt. Figure 3.8 shows press changeovers tracked on a simple graph. This photograph comes from a company that achieved significant improvement in changeover time just from the focus created by the requirement to measure it.

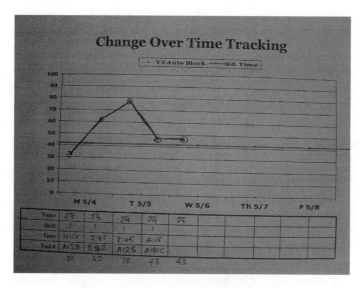

Figure 3.8: Changeover Time Tracking Chart

PRESENTING THE INFORMATION

Cell performance measurements should be presented visually in the cell and maintained by the cell operators. A performance measurement board (Figure 3.9) is a standard part of all lean cells. The board has a place for showing the current performance measurements like the Day-by-the-Hour report, First-Time-Through, and so on. It also has a place for reporting the problems and issues the cell people are having. These problems are written on a flip chart or white board, and the problems can be divided into two types; those problems

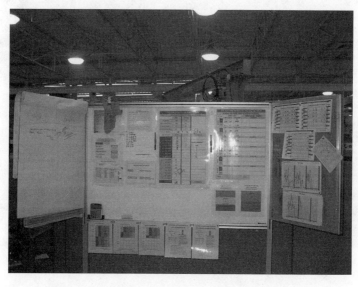

Figure 3.9: Typical Cell Performance Measurement Board

that can be solved by the cell team (Can Do problems) and those requiring help from other people (Need Help problems).

The performance measurement board may also contain other information, such as standard work charts, the cell's continuous improvement project information, process maps, and other information about the cell process.

It is useful that performance measurement boards be on wheels so they can be easily moved when cell layout is changed. It is also helpful to be able to move them into a meeting room or the continuous improvement room when the people need to discuss the information.

These boards become the focal point of the cell because they provide the information required by the cell team to monitor their progress and record the issues and problems that need to be resolved. The boards are also important to the supervisors and managers because they can see at a glance the status of the cell and what issues need urgent attention.

It is typical for lean cells to have a 10-minute team meeting before each shift. This is used to review the performance from the previous day, discuss the problems noted on the board, assign people to resolve the problems, and decide on any changes needed. This meeting also may be a forum for discussing the production schedule and the progress of improvement projects.

Some companies find it helpful to keep track of the issues and problems raised on the cell performance boards. Figure 3.10 shows how one company reports the progress of these problem resolution processes.

Figure 3.10: Visual board showing how many problems have been resolved

Making the Cell Performance Measurements Work

Performance measurements are used differently in lean manufacturing than in traditional manufacturing. In lean, the purpose of the cell measurements is to help the cell team manufacture its products to meet the takt time of the customer. The focus is on flow, standardized work, pull, and timeliness. To make these measurements work they must be managed from a lean perspective:

1. The supervisors and managers must use the measurements to monitor the progress of the shop floor. The managers and supervisors with direct responsibility for the shop floor must get their information from the performance measurement boards. The engineers, maintenance people, inventory and production planning people, accountants, and others must also get the information from the performance measurement boards.

   This represents a different way of managing the business. Those people with direct production or production support responsibilities must walk the floor regularly and often throughout the day. This is visual management at work. To use visual management you must observe the information regularly and systematically.

   The operations people will soon know if their information is being used or not. If they find that their issues are not being resolved and their data is not used, they will stop posting it and go back to running the cell the old way. They will know that their managers did not mean what they said about lean manufacturing and visual management.

2. Eliminate any other measurements. The visual measurements in the cell must be the only cell measurements. If there is another set of management reports on the cell, perhaps coming from the cost accounting system, then the tendency will be to use the old and familiar measurements rather than the lean measurements.

   It is vital to eliminate the other measurements from the cell. It may be, in the early stages of lean manufacturing, that your company is still running a traditional cost accounting system with variance reports, etc. The finance people may still need to run these reports, but they should not show them to anyone. The cell must be run using the new, visual measurements.

3. The measurements must be easy for people to do. It is essential that the information is easy to gather and the reporting quick and simple. Select measurements that are relevant and for which the data are readily available to the relevant people. Provide them with simple methods of gathering and reporting the numbers.

   If necessary, provide automatic data gathering. If the cell contains fast running machines, introduce automatic counters. If the machines automatically reject faulty parts, have the machines count the quantities and report them visually on an andon board, or something similar.

We have one customer with a cell that is noisy and dirty. The operators wear heavy protective clothes and thick gloves. The operators cannot easily count parts and write down numbers. The company introduced a simple counting system whereby the operator hits a large plastic button every time a product is completed. This simple method adds up the numbers manufactured every 15 minutes; which is the pitch of production in the cell.

4. Listen to the users. The cell-team members are the primary users of these performance measurements. Listen to their ideas and suggestions. Lean performance measurements should change over time. There is no reason why we need to keep exactly the same measurements forever. Indeed, measurements can vary from one cell to another. Allow the people to change and fine-tune their measurement systems until they have useful and relevant information to help them achieve the planned rate of production.

5. Provide a no-blame workplace. The information reported on the performance measurement boards is gathered and presented by the cell-team members. It is important that the cell-team members are confident they can report the true information without risking discipline or censure from their supervisors or managers. If the people are to provide the true information there must be a practical no-blame atmosphere within the plant. There must be a general principle agreeing that problems and errors are regarded as opportunities for improving the process and getting a step nearer to perfection.

6. Summarize the data. The data being collected in the cell by the hour and the shift, is the basic raw information used by the value stream continuous improvement team(s). It is useful to collect the data and summarize it into a spreadsheet or database. The cell operators can do this, but it is more common for the manufacturing engineers or an accountant within the value stream to do this.

NON-PRODUCTION CELLS AND DEPARTMENTS

In this chapter, we have been discussing performance measurements for manufacturing cells. However, there are many other cells within the value stream. These are the support areas the non-production cells and departments so essential to the success of the value stream. These also need performance measurements.

The same methods used for production cells work for non-production cells. The measurements themselves, and also gathering data, may differ, but the lean approaches are the same. Take an order entry cell, for example. Does an order entry process have a cycle time? Does an order entry process have standardized work? Does an order entry process have inventory flowing through it?

The answer to all of these questions is yes. There is takt time for the order entry process. If customers order 800 items per day and there is an eight-hour shift, then the product takt time is (8 * 3600)/800 = 36 seconds. If the average order quantity is 25, then the order entry takt time is (8 * 3600) / (800/25) = 900 seconds or 15 minutes. We need to enter one order every quarter of an hour. We can use a method similar to the Day-by-the-Hour report to track the achievement of the cell cycle time to match the customer takt time. We may not track by the hour; the half-day may be appropriate, but the method is the same.

We can and should establish standardized work for the order entry process, and we should use first time through (or something similar to it) to track the effectiveness of the processes and the standardized work. It may be that the problems with orders may not be found until later in the process, but we can assess the number of orders being entered right-first-time without rejects or rework.

The inventory in the order entry process is the number of order documents in the flow through the order entry process. We can flow this material using kanban squares in a similar way to a shop-floor process, and we can measure the flow of these orders using something similar to WIP-to-SWIP.

This kind of measurement may be overkill for a simple order entry process, especially as simple order entry processes will be gradually replaced by visual pull systems. However, an order entry process requiring quotations, configuration, validation, and the development of make-to-order work instructions, for example, requires these kinds of measurements to ensure the controlled flow through the value stream.

Similar measurements will be very helpful in many of the support departments, particularly those that are in the direct flow, from order through to shipment and cash collection.

How Does this Relate to Accounting and Control

In this chapter we have stressed the importance of cell performance measurements to enable cell operators to monitor their own work throughout the day and ensure they meet the needs of the customers. While this is the primary reason for the measurements, the cell-level measurements are also one of the principle control mechanisms within the value streams.

As we move away from traditional, transaction-based cost accounting, inventory control, and production control processes, we need another way to make sure the processes are under control. The cell-level performance measurements are one of the methods we use to ensure this. We can remove wasteful transactions only when we know the processes are under control and consistent.[4] To do otherwise would be to risk the financial control of the business; and we will never compromise financial control.

If you are a financial controller or other financial person within the newly lean operation, you will be monitoring the cell level performance measurements as one of your principal methods of ensuring financial control of the

---

4. Chapters 5, 12, 15, and 20 deal with the elimination of wasteful transactions from the business processes.

business. The finance people also spend a considerable amount of time on the shop floor and in the other parts of the company that support the value streams. They need to review the performance measurements regularly.

Finance people will use the value stream performance measurements[5] to assess the level of business control. Finance people will also be active members of the value stream continuous improvement teams. The continuous improvement processes are also primary control mechanisms of the business.[6]

SUMMARY

Most companies embark on lean manufacturing by introducing pilot lean manufacturing cells. This is the first step in the maturity path for lean manufacturing. At this early stage of lean there are a number of changes required in the accounting, control, and measurement systems. These include:

- New performance measurements for the lean production cells.
- The elimination of many of the wasteful transactions within the cell.
- A method of measuring and understanding the financial impact of the implemented lean improvements.

In this chapter we have identified the BMA Starter Set of performance measurements for lean manufacturing cells. These measurements are not intended to be the perfect measurement system, but they have been tried and tested in many lean operations and create a very good starting point for a lean measurement system. These measurements are given in Table 3.2.

The purpose of these measurements is to provide the cell team-members with the information they need to meet the customers' needs today, to get done today what needs to be done. These are action-oriented measures. If things go wrong, these measurements trigger action to correct the problems.

Managers, supervisors, and support people within the value stream use these measurements throughout each day to ensure that the cells and the value stream operate to meet customers' takt time. This requires managers and supervisors to use the performance measurements frequently throughout the day and the week to visually monitor production and to solve problems. Problems preventing the cells and the value stream from meeting customer needs must be solved very quickly. These problems are identified quickly through the performance measurements.

These cell level measurements are just one set of measurements used to ensure that the company's operational processes are under good control. If the processes are under control, then the elaborate and wasteful financial control systems can begin to be eliminated. This leads to a lean accounting system with very few transactions.

---

5. See Chapter 8 for further discussion of value stream performance measurement and finance.

6. See Chapter 12 for further discussion of the continuous improvement process as primary control.

Table 3.2

Cell Performance Measurement	What Does It Measure?	Lean Principle
Day-by-the-Hour	Hourly production compared to the quantity required that hour.	Make to takt time.
First Time Through	Percentage produced in the cell right-firsttime without rework, repair, or scrap.	Make to standardized work the same every time.
WIP-to-SWIP	The amount of inventory within the cell compared to the amount of inventory designed to be in the cell.	Make to pull. Manufacture only when there is a kanban or other pull signal.
Operational Equipment Effectiveness	Combined measure of a machine's ability to make to quality, to make at the right rate, and to be available when required.	Make to takt time for a bottleneck or constraint machine.

CHAPTER 4

Financial Benefits of Lean Manufacturing

Lean manufacturing typically generates impressive operating benefits, but companies frequently find that financial benefits are not immediately forthcoming to the same degree. In this chapter, we look at measuring and managing financial benefits from an operations perspective to predict the impact of lean improvements on the financial results. Many teams are unable to answer this question satisfactorily as traditional accounting does not provide the necessary information. The approach to measurement developed in this chapter provides a way for the team to communicate to upper management what the impacts of lean are likely to be. It also provides a structured method for evaluating the financial benefits from alternative strategies for taking advantage of the increased operating capability. The chapter is organized into four sections:

- The Problem
- Creating the Box Score
- Managing Capacity
- Making Money from Lean Manufacturing

THE PROBLEM

When lean is introduced in a company, executives and employees expect to see tangible financial improvement. Often, there is no short-term financial improvement; and sometimes the opposite occurs. This causes comments such as the following from dismayed executives: "We see wonderful results in operations, but they don't show up in the financial statements. If lean is so great, why doesn't it hit the bottom line?"

The problem stems from differing perspectives of operations and finance.

A language needs to be created that bridges these two groups. The operations people see results such as the following:

- Reduced lead times
- Improved quality—reduced scrap and rework
- Improved on-time delivery

- Reduced floor space
- Increased inventory turns

They rightly claim that achieving these results enables the company to satisfy customers better and thereby achieve increased growth and profitability. Often lean enables the company to reduce its backlog, and the results are reflected in increased customer satisfaction.

The financial view of the same set of data is radically different. Their perspective is that the lean changes provide the potential for financial improvement, but unless costs are reduced or revenue is increased, the financial picture will not change. It does not matter that operations can process an order through to delivery in one-quarter of the time. Here are some typical financial results from the early stages of lean:

- Revenue stays the same, although there may be some reduced backlog that brings revenue in quicker.
- Costs stay much the same, although overtime and scrap costs may reduce a little.
- Operating profits may go down owing to the impact of reduced inventory on cost-of-sales.
- Cash flow from operations may increase owing to inventory reduction.
- Other financial indicators have not improved, or have worsened.
- Sales per employee have stayed the same.
- Average cost per unit sold has increased due to increased costs.

From an operations point of view, the financial results do not make any sense at all. How can good things be happening, while the financial results, which are supposed to reflect what is going on in operations, show bad things happening?

Faced with the immediate mediocre financial results, the typical senior finance manager concludes that lean is not working. It is the unusual manager who can view the long-term benefits of these lean efforts. This manager sees beyond the unimpressive short-term results and looks to the long-term financial opportunities that lean operating creates.

However, most managers need a way of bridging the operational and financial views of lean. In the interest of providing a communication vehicle that bridges these two views, we have developed a way to display both the operating and financial views in one report. We call this the *Box Score*. The Box Score provides a three–dimensional perspective. It presents the key operations and financial results, together with information on how the value stream's resources are used, in a way that both perspectives can be viewed at the same time. These three perspectives enable managers to plan and evaluate lean results that have an impact on both the financial and the operational results positively.

CREATING THE BOX SCORE

The box score provides a framework for evaluating the operating and financial effects of lean and provides a structured way to view and speak about the different ways that lean creates value. In this section, we will discuss this framework in the context of a specific company, Electronic Components, Inc. (ECI). Subsequent sections will teach you how to complete the box score using ECI as an example.

Table 4.1 presents the box score report without any data.

Note the three categories of data listed down the left-hand margin: Operational, Resource Capacity, and Financial. We will discuss the operational and financial first.

Operational

Six items of data are included. You will read more about them in Chapter 8, "Value Stream Performance Measurements." We will include the definitions here to reinforce your understanding.

- *Dock-to-Dock Days* is the amount of time from material receipt to shipment of the finished product to the customer, hence its name, Dock-to-Dock days. It is calculated by dividing the number of items of a control part in the plant (raw material, work-in-process, and finished goods) by the average rate at which the end products are manufactured in that value stream in products per day. A control part is used in each step of production and leaves the value stream in the form of a finished item. Typical control parts are printed circuit boards, castings, and engine blocks.

- *First Time Through* is a measure of quality. It is calculated as the percent of total units that pass through the value stream on the first pass without being repaired, reworked or scrapped. It is often called First Pass Yield. Because we are measuring this for the value stream, it is the product of the measure at each evaluation point in the entire value stream.

- *On-Time Shipment* measures the extent to which the right products have been shipped on the right date and in the right order. It is calculated as the percentage of the scheduled customer order volumes actually shipped on schedule.

- *Floor Space* is the square footage of space the value stream takes up, including the production footprint and the space dedicated to raw material, work-in-process, and finished goods inventories.

- *Sales per Person* is a measure of both the value created and the productivity of the value stream. It is calculated by dividing the revenue shipped and invoiced from the value stream, during a given period, by the average number of full-time equivalent employees, including first-line management, in the value stream during the period.

Table 4.1: Value Stream Box Score

Lean Value Stream Box Score

Value stream: | Electronics controllers

		Current state	Future state	Change	Long term future state—Alt#	Change from current state
Operational	Dock-to-dock days					
	First time through					
	On-time shipment					
	Floor space					
	Sales per person					
	Average cost per unit					
Resource capacity	Productive					
	Non-productive					
	Available					
Financial	Inventory value					
	Revenue					
	Material costs					
	Conversion costs					
	Value stream profit					

- *Average Cost per Unit* is the total value stream costs for a period, divided by the number of units shipped during the period. Costs included are all production labor, production support, operations support, engineering support, facilities and maintenance, production materials, and other costs consumed by the value stream.

Table 4.2 is an example of the calculation of the value stream costs for a sample month. Note that the value stream costs include all the costs used in producing controllers made during the month:

- Raw materials used in production
- Outside processing costs
- Employee costs, including wages and employee benefits
- Machine costs, depreciation expense, and utilities if metered
- Other costs, such as tooling, consumables, allocated overhead, and so forth.

Also, it is important to note that the costs included are not only those incurred by the "touch" manufacturing departments, but also include employee costs incurred in supporting production of the controllers, that we would normally call Indirect costs.

- Customer service takes the orders and receives customer calls related to the product.
- Purchasing schedules production and procures the raw materials.
- Shipping ships the controllers to customers.
- Quality Assurance performs quality inspections, inventory reviews and improvement projects for the value stream.
- Manufacturing Engineering gets involved in improvement projects.
- Accounting pays supplier invoices, does the payroll, and invoices customers for shipments.
- Information Systems maintains the computer systems used by the value stream.
- Design Engineering performs improvement projects.
- Technical Support performs improvement projects.

Table 4.3 shows the number of employees in each function and their average cost per employee for the month.

In the case of ECI, functions that are expected to reside in the value stream over the long run are included in the cost of the value stream, though the people are not assigned to value stream organizationally. So people who spend most of their time either working in or supporting the value stream, are included. On the other hand, those functions that are never expected to be included in the value stream should be excluded. We will have more to say

Table 4.2: ECI Value Stream Costs per Month

Company Electronic Components	Location Nirvana, CA	Value stream Controllers	Type Current	Date			
	Material costs	Outside process cost	Employee costs	Machine costs	Other costs	TOTAL COST
Customer service			$11,921			$11,921
Purchasing			$14,902			$14,902
SMT cell	$358,512		$16,704	$16,956	$20,000	$412,172
Hand load & wave cell	$25,608		$22,968	$2,016		$50,592
Test & rework cell			$16,704	$3,528		$20,232
Assemble & burn-in cell	$128,040		$10,440			$138,480
Shipping			$2,088			$2,088
Quality assurance			$7,978			$7,978
Manufacturing engineering			$7,978			$7,978
Accounting			$7,978			$7,978
Information systems			$3,989			$11,749
Design engineering		$7,760	$3,989			$11,749
Maintenance and other support			$11,967			$11,967
TOTAL	**$512,160**	**$7,760**	**$139,606**	**$22,500**	**$20,000**	**$702,026**

Table 4.3: ECI Value Stream Resource Unit Costs

	# of Employees	Cost per employee	Overtime
Customer service	4.00	$2,980.33	
Purchasing	5.00	$2,980.33	
SMT cell	8.00	$2,088.00	
Hand load & wave cell	11.00	$2,088.00	
Test & rework cell	8.00	$2,088.00	
Assemble & burn-in cell	5.00	$2,088.00	
Shipping	1.00	$2,088.00	
Quality assurance	2.00	$3,989.00	
Manufacturing engineering	2.00	$3,989.00	
Accounting	2.00	$3,989.00	
Information systems	1.00	$3,989.00	
Design engineering	1.00	$3,989.00	
Technical support	3.00	$3,989.00	
TOTAL	**53**	**# People**	**$0**

about value streams and value stream costing in Chapters 7 and 9. The costs included for the month are the total costs of the production of controllers for the month. It is important to note that this means that, rather than including some of the costs in work-in-process and finished goods inventories, they will be included in the expenses of the month in which they are incurred.

Let us look at the financial information included in the box score.

Financial Information in the Box Score

Five items make up the financial data to be included in the box score. These are the items that are most often the concern of both accounting and finance and the senior officers of the company.

- Inventory value is the end-of-period cost of inventory belongs to the value stream, using the amounts in the books of the company.
- Revenue is the invoiced amounts for shipments from the value stream during the period, as recorded in the company's books.
- Material cost is simply the amount the company spent for production materials during the period. In the mature lean company in which inventories are level and low, this amount is equal to the materials cost included in cost of sales for the period. This is because materials are purchased and used in production for products sold during the same

accounting period. For companies at the start of their lean journeys, we will use the same convention.

- Conversion costs include expenses incurred, during the period, to run the value stream. In the mature lean company, which is organized by value stream, all of these resources will be in the value stream itself and there will be very few support services shared among two or more value streams. This is the ideal situation in which there are no costs allocated across value streams. However, as discussed above in the description of Average Cost per Unit, we recognize that in the initial stages of lean, few companies will have organized by value stream and, therefore, it will be necessary to allocate significant support costs to account for the true costs of running the value stream. For the most part, the costs can be taken directly from the payroll records and accruals for employee benefits. Depreciation should be taken from the journals.

  When inventories are level and low, these amounts equal the conversion costs included in cost of sales in the company's financial statements. At the initiation of lean this will most likely not be the case, and companies find that the levels of inventories affect their book profits. These profits increase as inventories rise at the end of a period and fall as inventory levels fall. For this reason we do not use this method of calculating costs in Lean Accounting. We do not believe that it serves the lean process to measure costs in such a way that costs rise when inventories decline and decrease when inventories increase. That is exactly contrary to what lean is trying to accomplish. We will have more to say about this later in Chapter 9, "Value Stream Costing," but for the purpose of calculating conversion cost for the box score, the use of the total costs for the period will eliminate the effects of changing inventory levels on the conversion costs for the period.

- Value stream profits are simply the difference between revenues and costs of sales (in this case, the sum of material costs and conversion costs). It is essentially equivalent to cash flow.

  In traditional financial accounting, profits differ from cash flows. The reason for this difference is due to the accounting convention of matching expenses for items sold with the revenue received to arrive at gross profits. This causes cash outflows for items in production, but not yet sold, to be included in cash expenses, but not in cost of sales. Similarly, the cost of items sold from inventory, in excess of the purchases for the period, are included in cost of sales, but not cash flow. Other non-cash transactions are included in gross profits, but not cash flow. Examples are sales awaiting receipt of cash in accounts receivable; invoices received waiting for cash payment in accounts payable; and hours worked waiting for payment to workers in accrued payroll. All of these are included in the company's accounting records as working capital accounts.

Because lean is about increasing the flow of cash, increased cash flow is an important financial benefit of lean. The expensing of costs of production as incurred makes Value Stream Profit essentially equivalent to period cash flow.

Using the Box Score in Planning

The box score has two important purposes. The first is as a planning tool at the outset of lean to judge the effectiveness of lean from a business perspective. In this regard it answers the question whether the lean initiatives planned are a sensible thing to do and under what conditions they would be so. The second is to monitor how to progress toward achieving the plans. We will deal with the former here.

You will note that in Table 4.1 there are four columns to the right of the items measured:

- *Current State* provides the status of the items measured prior to completion of any planned initiatives. This provides the base case against which any improvements will be compared.

- *Future State* provides the status of measured items if the planned initiatives provide the expected benefits. Usually the time horizon is six months or less.

- *Change from the Current State* simply shows the difference between the Current and Future States.

- *Long-Term Future State* provides an estimate of the business benefits that are expected to accrue over the long term as a result of the lean initiatives and strategic actions undertaken to take advantage of the opportunities afforded. Usually several scenarios are developed to assess and select the most attractive from a business perspective.

The aim is to maximize the benefits to the business from lean. Let us develop the Operations and Financial sections of the box score for ECI and then launch into a discussion of Resource Capacity.

The ECI Current State

The diagram below shows the current state electronics components value stream for ECI.

Production is based on a weekly schedule produced by Customer Service, based on a forecast from the customer. Shipments are scheduled daily based on firm orders. During an average month ECI ships 2,134 boards to customers. Leadtime for the process is 20.5 days and processing time is 30.3 minutes of the leadtime. There is a great deal of room for improvement.

The production process is straightforward:

- Standard components are loaded into boards using a surface mount machine (SMT)

- Specialized components are loaded by hand into the boards

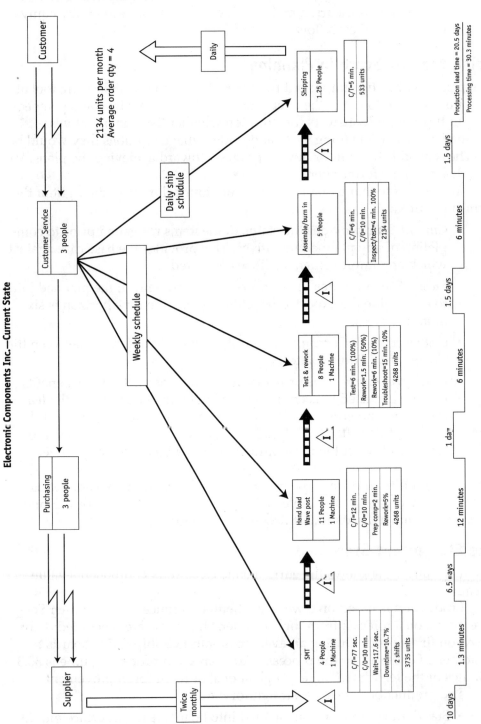

Figure 4.1: ECI Current State Map for the Controllers Value Stream

Table 4.4: Box Score for the Current State—ECI Controllers Value Stream

Lean Value Stream Box Score

Value stream: Electronics controllers

		Current state	Future state	Change	Long term future state—Alt#	Change from current state
Operational	Dock-to-dock days	20.5 days				
	First time through	48% FTT				
	On-time shipment	90%				
	Floor space	34,000 sq feet				
	Sales per person	$25,230				
	Average cost per unit	$328.27				
Resource capacity	Productive					
	Non-productive					
	Available					
Financial	Inventory value	$58,502				
	Revenue	$1,292,640				
	Material costs	$512,160				
	Conversion costs	$189,866				
	Value stream profit	$590,614				

- Every board is tested and defects are reworked
- The final product is assembled and undergoes a burn-in test
- The final product is shipped.

There are several things wrong with the process as it stands:
- There is a push system with a great deal of inventory
- The process cycle times are unbalanced
- There is a great deal of inspection and rework
- Delivery times are unstable and production is rushed

The box score for the current state reflects these problems.

ECI Future State

Figure 4.2 depicts the value stream map for the electronics components planned future state:
Some changes from the current state are obvious:
- Flow time through the value stream was reduced from 20.5 to 4.5 days

A kanban system was implemented to pull customer requirements through the value stream, rather than scheduling each work center and pushing.
- The cycle time in the Hand Load/Wave Post cell was reduced to 6 minutes from 12 minutes by redesigning the cell thereby permitting the work to flow smoothly
- Quality was improved dramatically, reducing the reject rate in the Test and Rework cell from 50 percent to 3 percent, by implementing self-inspection and continuous improvement in the SMT and Hand Load/Wave Post cells.
- Agreements with suppliers were renegotiated, provided key suppliers deliver daily to the supermarket in front of the SMT cell in response to a kanban order from the cell, rather than twice weekly resulting from a material requisition from the MRP system.
- The SMT cell was able to reduce its operating time from two shifts to one shift as a result of the initiatives. Consequently, the number of people in the cell was reduced from eight to four. The four people freed up were deployed to other value streams.

Operating results of these lean initiatives were impressive:
- Dock-to-Dock days went from 20.5 to 4.5 days
- First Time Through improved from 48 percent to 96 percent
- On-Time Shipment went from 90 percent to 99 percent
- Floor Space consumed went from 34,000 square feet to 17,000

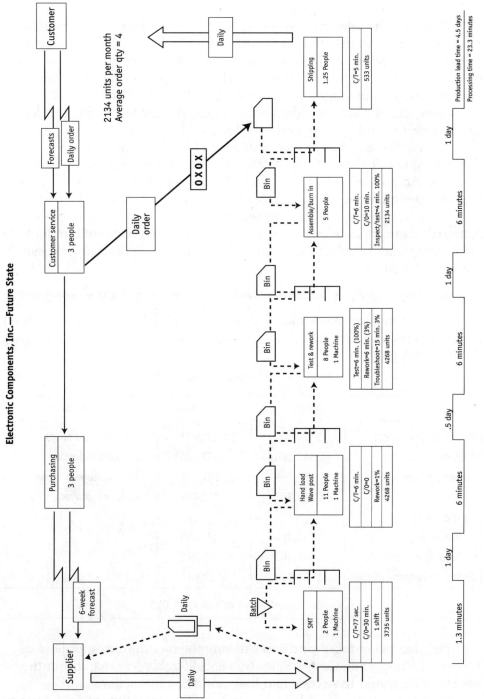

Figure 4.2: Future State Map for the Controllers Value Stream

However, an improvement in financial results has not happened, as shown in the company's income statement. In fact, despite the impressive operating improvements, costs have gone up rather than down, resulting in a $1,055 reduction in gross profit.

With that, the sales vice president of ECI complained that he could not raise prices to cover the increased costs caused by lean. The financial vice president complained of the under-absorption of fixed costs caused by the reduced production and wondered aloud how he was going to explain the sudden drop in profitability to the banks and equity investors. The CEO demanded that the vice president of operations fix the problems with lean so that profit would be increased, not decreased.

The sad thing is that profits went down for ECI because of the way the company was calculating Cost of Sales. The method is required by Generally Accepted Accounting Principles (GAAP), so that product costs are matched in the same period as the revenues from sales of those products. The costs that remain are in inventory, to be matched with sales of a subsequent period. Although there are different ways to calculate cost of goods sold under GAAP, many companies calculate the number the same way, by deriving it from the following formula:

Beginning Inventory + Purchases of Materials + Conversion Costs – Ending Inventory.

ECI's ending inventory had decreased by $44,505 due to lean initiatives, and that in itself caused cash flow to increase. At the same time, it had a negative effect on profit, as shown in Table 4.5, below:

Table 4.5: Impact of Inventory Reduction on Cost of Sales

	Period one	Period two	Comment
Beginning inventory	$ 58,502	$ 58,502	Reduced purchases
Material purchases	512,160	477,160	$35,000 reduction
Conversion costs	189,866	181,416	SMT employees on second
	760,528	717,078	shift redeployed
Cost of sales			
Materials	512,160	477,160	
Conversion costs	189,866	225,921	
Ending inventory	$ 58,502	$ 13,997	
Increase in cost of sales: $1,055			

Because ECI reduced purchases during the month from suppliers by $35,000, the impact on Cost of Sales was considerably less than the entire $44,505, as it would have been had they not taken this action.

So management of ECI is in a quandary. The operating and the financial results seem to be telling different stories.

To eliminate the problems of traditional accounting caused by the way companies calculate Cost of Sales for financial statement purposes under GAAP, we eliminate the effects of inventory changes by including all spending for materials and conversion costs for the purpose of managing the value stream. The results now eliminate the negative impacts of inventory reduction on cost. This is shown in the future state box score in Table 4.6.

Note that the financial picture is much improved from that shown in the company's financial statements. The decrease in materials purchases caused by the inventory reduction of $44,505 has directly affected the value stream profit. Furthermore, the reduction of conversion costs to $8,450 also is reflected. These reductions in the operating costs are reflected in the cash flow impacts of lean. Instead of showing a decline in profits under traditional accounting, we show an increase of $43,450! What is not reflected, however, is what the lean improvements have done to the conversion costs beyond the elimination of one shift in the SMT cell.

To gain insight into these deeper impacts, we need to get behind the conversion cost numbers in the future state. Although the volume of resources used has not changed between the current and future state, the way they are used has changed dramatically, as shown in Figure 4.3, below.

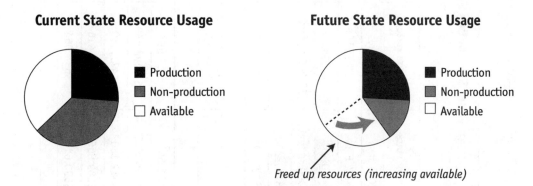

Figure 4.3: Increased Available Capacity Due to Lean

The resource usage has shifted from non-productive in the current state to available in the future state. Lean has freed up large amounts of resource capacity. As ECI is still writing the same checks, the accounting system treats these expenditures as required to create the products sold during the period, but in reality they were not all required! A significant number of these resources are now available (in the future state) to be employed elsewhere—to provide for growth or to be eliminated if there is no better use. And this information, added to the box score, provides the bridge between operations and finance that allows the whole company to focus on how these resources are to be used now that they have been freed up by lean, transforming the problem from an operations issue to a strategic issue. However, first ECI needs to learn how to calculate just how much resource capacity has been freed up by lean.

Table 4.6: Box Score for the Future State—ECI Future State Value Stream using Lean Accounting

Lean Value Stream Box Score

Value stream: Electronics controllers

		Current state	Future state	Change	Long term future state—Alt#	Change from current state
Operational	Dock-to-dock days	20.5 days	4.5 days	16 days		
	First time through	48% FTT	96% FTT	48%		
	On-time shipment	90%	99%	9%		
	Floor space	34,000 sq feet	17,000 sq feet	(17,000) sq feet		
	Sales per person	$25,230	$26,380	$1,150		
	Average cost per unit	$328.27	$308.61	($19.66)		
Resource capacity	Productive					
	Non-productive					
	Available					
Financial	Inventory value	$58,502	$13,997	($44,505)		
	Revenue	$1,292,640	$1,292,640	$0		
	Material costs	$512,160	$477,160	($35,000)		
	Conversion costs	$189,866	$181,416	($8,450)		
	Value stream profit	$590,614	$634,064	$43,450		

MANAGING CAPACITY

Lean forces a basic question of just how much capacity in terms of available people and machines the company needs to achieve its goals. This is due to the significant amount of capacity freed up by the lean initiatives. The challenge for the lean company is to plan for its use during the planning phase of lean, that is, at the time the value stream maps are being prepared. The lean company has only two choices: use the capacity to grow the business, or eliminate the free resources. Far too many companies implement their lean programs, find that there is a great deal of free capacity, and, not knowing what else to do, eliminate the resources that have been freed up. That can spell the end of lean. So the message is to evaluate alternatives for using the capacity to grow the business.

In this section, we discuss how to calculate how much capacity has been freed up by your lean initiative and how to add this information to the box score. A more detailed description is provided in Chapter 21. We have organized the section to discuss the following:

- What we mean by resource capacity
- Analyzing the capacity freed up

What We Mean by Resource Capacity

Capacity is the ability to do work as provided by resources. For our purposes we are concerned with two categories of resources:

- People, and the hours available to work during a period of time, such as a shift, a day, a week or a month.
- Machines, and the hours available to do work during a period of time.

We are concerned with what people and machines do with the time available. For ECI there are 7.5 hours available in a shift for employees, after subtracting two 15 minute breaks, and for the machines, there are 8 hours available. The company works one shift per day for 20 days during the month, and so we say that people are available 150 hours per month and machines 160. We do not consider the time that they might have been working as available then, only the time that, by company policy, was work time.

Most cells are either labor or machine intensive, i.e., certain machines do not need an employee tending them all the time. Those employees are free to do other things. So if we want to know how the resources were employed, we have to know how both people and machines were used. On the other hand, other cells are more labor intensive. Machinery in the cells is only used when the people in the cell are employed. So we can know what the machines do by knowing what the people do.

The ECI value stream we are studying is machine intensive, so we are concerned equally with both labor and the machines.

Now, as we said above, we are very concerned with what the people and the machines do during a period, for example, one month. Not only are we concerned with what they do, we are also concerned with the value of what they do. So we divide the work done into three categories:

- Productive: labor or machine time spent creating product at the pull of the customer.
- Non-productive: all other uses of time, for example, including as non-value adding, time spent on changeovers rework/remake, material movement, inspection, repair, maintenance, waiting for resources, scheduling, planning, procurement, management, administration, etc.
- Available: machine and labor time left over after productive and non-productive time has been accounted for.

As lean changes the use of resources from nonproductive to available, we are quite concerned with understanding the nonproductive work in the current and future state.

Analyzing the Capacity Freed Up

As a result of performing the analysis in Chapter 21, the following resource capacity has been freed up, shown in Table 4.7.

In total, 19.5 equivalent people and one SMT machine for one shift were made available by the lean initiative. These costs are not reflected in the financial statements or the future state box score, because the company is still paying for the services of these resources. So, from a purely financial perspective, there is no change. However, as we have seen, the effects on the use of resources are huge.

Note that in the SMT cell, by reducing the changeover and thereby being able to reduce the number of shifts from two to one, the number of people required was reduced by four and the machine was required only for one shift. In addition, due to the other lean initiatives, the requirement to run the cell was reduced to 2.5 from 4.

To exploit this available capacity, the company must decide whether it will use the available resources to expand the business, or eliminate the capacity—or some combination of both.

Management has a decision to make concerning the use of the 2,325 hours per month (15.5 equivalent people) that have been made available, plus the disposition of the people from the second shift on the SMT. This will be dealt with in the next section.

MAKING MONEY FROM LEAN MANUFACTURING

As noted above, management has two choices for the use of the capacity freed up by lean: the first is to use it to grow the business and the second is to dispose of it and, thereby, reduce the costs of manufacturing. One of the features of the former is that, if the capacity can be used, it produces great benefits to the bottom line—the only costs incurred for the additional business are the

Table 4.7: Summary of Freed-Up Resources in the Planned Future State

Summary of Freed Up Resources				
Value stream: Controllers				
	Available hours in the current state	Available hours in the future state	Freed up hours	Equivalent resources	Comment
SMT					
People	481.4	867.5	386.1	2.5 people	Reduced changeover time. Eliminated downtime and material moves.
				4 people	In addition there is potential to eliminate one shift; people no longer need to tend the machine.
Machines	25.3	190.1	164.8	1 machine-shift	Reduced changeover time and eliminated downtime. Reduced to one shift from two.
Hand load/wave post	-43.8	543.9	587.7	4 people	Eliminated changeover time. Eliminated material moves.
Test and rework	360.9	747.4	386.5	2.5 people	Cut defects by two-thirds.
Shipping	54.2	98.7	44.5	.3 person	Reduced shipping time from 15 to 10 minutes.
Customer service			487.7	3.2 people	Eliminated expedites. Reduced customer complaint calls due to better service.
Purchasing			395.8	2.6 people	Implemented kanbans—eliminated production schedules. Reduced POs due to master POs. Eliminated suppliers and certified remaining.
Accounting			58.3	.4 people	Eliminated invoices due to purchasing initiatives.
				19.5 people	

cost of the materials and other truly variable costs. Because the costs of the labor are already being paid for to produce the existing business, there is no incremental expense. So this alternative produces benefits that far outweigh the other alternative of eliminating the resources.

Let us follow the ECI lean team as they evaluated these alternatives.

Alternative 1: Eliminate the Resources

The impact on the value stream from this alternative is shown in Table 4.8. The cost per month for one employee including employee benefits was $2,135. So the team developed the box score in Table 4.8 under this alternative.

Note that value stream profits will have increased by $76,633, Sales per Employee will have increased by a whopping $13,356 as a result of reducing the payroll by 19.5 people—$41,633, and Average Cost per Unit will have decreased by $35.21 as a result of applying this alternative.

Alternative 2: Grow the Business

Under this alternative, the team considered several possibilities.

How can we use the freed-up resources?

Reduce expenses, sales flat	Increase revenue without increasing expenses (using freed capacity)	
• Sell or lease-out space • Close down a plant • Avoid future planned capital investment • Sell the machines and equipment • In-source outsourced items • Layoff the people	• Sell more product • Introduct new products • Build new markets • Rent space to subcontractor • Avoid future planned costs • Sell excess capacity • Add more value to products	• Work off backlog and win more business as result of crunched lead times • Use floor space to expand without incurring new lease/building expense

Invest in lean

Figure 4.4: Alternative Uses of Freed-Up Capacity for the Electronics Value Stream

The team realized that they could not evaluate all the possibilities solely from a manufacturing perspective; so they included sales and marketing, engineering, finance, procurement and human resources, as well as the CEO. They reasoned that all these resources would be required to evaluate the amounts of business that could be generated to employ the resources freed up. Various possibilities were evaluated.

They decided to increase the sales of controllers by accelerating a marketing plan that was currently in the works and sublease freed-up floor space to a subcontractor that had been having difficulty delivering on time. Since the new components had similar characteristics to the ones being manufactured in the value stream, they believed that they could be manufactured in the value stream without modifying the processes and without going to two shifts. So they could still eliminate the four people on the second shift in the SMT process.

Reviewing the available capacity at the completion of the future state, the team saw that the additional through-put would be limited by the capacity

Table 4.8: The Long Term Future State Box Score Assuming that Freed-Up Capacity is Eliminated

Lean Value Stream Box Score

Value stream: Electronics controllers

		Current state	Future state	Change	Long term future state—Alt#1	Change from current state
Operational	Dock-to-dock days	20.5 days	4.5 days	16 days	4.5 days	16 days
	First time through	48% FTT	96% FTT	48%	96% FTT	48%
	On-time shipment	90%	99%	9%	99%	9%
	Floor space	34,000 sq feet	17,000 sq feet	(17,000) sq feet	17,000 sq feet	(17,000) sq feet
	Sales per person	$25,230	$26,380	$1,150	$38,586	$13,356
	Average cost per unit	$328.27	$308.61	($19.66)	$293.06	($35.21)
Resource capacity	Productive	20%	17%	-3%	25%	5%
	Non-productive	62%	36%	-26%	52%	-10%
	Available	18%	47%	29%	23%	5%
Financial	Inventory value	$58,502	$13,997	$44,505	$13,997	$44,505
	Revenue	$1,292,640	$1,292,640	$0	$1,292,640	$0
	Material costs	$512,160	$477,160	($35,000)	$477,160	($35,000)
	Conversion costs	$189,866	$181,416	($8,450)	$148,234	($41,633)
	Value stream profit	$590,614	$634,064	$43,450	$667,247	$76,633

Table 4.9: Analysis of Freed-Up Capacity in the Future State

Future State Value Stream Cost Analysis by Capacity Category

		Totals	SMT	Hand load / wave post	Test and rework	Assemble and burn-in	Shipping	Customer service	Purchasing	Quality assurance	Accounting	Design engineering	Information systems	Manufacturing engineering	Technical support
EMPLOYEES	Cost	$139,624	$14,704	$22,968	$16,704	$10,440	$2,088	$11,928	$14,902	$7,978	$7,978	$3,989	$3,989	$7,989	$11,967
	Productive		0%	52%	0%	28%	0%	0%	0%	0%	0%	0%	0%	0%	0%
	Non-productive		28%	18%	38%	67%	71%	90%	1%	99%	71%	80%	91%	64%	83%
	Other		0%	0%	0%	0%	0%	0%	0%	0%	0%	0%	0%	0%	0%
	Available capacity		72%	30%	62%	5%	29%	10%	80%	1%	29%	20%	10%	36%	17%
MACHINES	Cost	$22,500	$15,956	$2,016	$3,528		$—	$—							
	Productive		25%	58%	0%		0%	0%							
	Non-productive		16%	3%	80%		0%	0%							
	Other		0%	0%	0%		0%	0%							
	Available capacity	0%	59%	39%	20%		0%	0%							

remaining in the cell having the lowest available capacity in the future state. An analysis of the freed-up capacity in the future state is in Table 4.9.

The table shows that the cells having the lowest available capacity in the planned future state would be:

- Employees in the Assembly and Burn-in Cell with 5 percent

- Employees in the Quality Assurance Cell with 1 percent

- Machines in the SMT cell after elimination of the second shift. Note that the table shows the Available Capacity at 59 percent before elimination of the second shift

As employees from other cells were trained to supplement the resources in the Assembly and Quality cells, the truly limiting resource was the SMT machine in the SMT cell. There was no substitute for that resource.

The SMT cell had about 30 available hours on the machine. The average unit would take 77 seconds to pass through the cell, so the maximum additional volume that could be run on the cell would be 1400 circuit boards per month. This translated to 800 completed controllers, because each controller contained, on average 1.75 circuit boards. It was believed by marketing and sales that they could achieve an additional volume of 700 per month within a three-month period. So the final plan was as follows:

- Eliminate the second shift on the SMT and reduce the work force by four, reducing monthly costs by $8,450.

- Sublease the 17,000 square feet to a subcontractor at $1.70 a square foot, adding $25,500 per month to revenues.

- Increase sales of controllers manufactured in the value stream by 700, drawing from the planned market expansion.
  - Additional revenues at $600 per unit would be $420,000 per month
  - Additional material costs would be $240 per unit, or $133,000 per month.
  - There would be no incremental conversion costs.

The box score in Table 4.10 shows the results of Alternative #2.

Comparing the long-term future states under alternatives 1 and 2, shown in Table 4.11, it is clear that alternative 2 provides a significantly greater financial payoff to ECI.

Under Alternative 2, the growth scenario, Value Stream Profit increased by $244,317, a 32 percent increase, on a 34 percent increase in sales. Sales per Employee under Alternative 1 was greater than Alternative 2 due to large numbers of employees eliminated in that scenario.

The management of ECI chose Alternative 2 because of the significant contribution that would bring to ECI.

The significance of the difference between these two alternatives is typical across companies implementing lean. Seldom is it more beneficial to reduce the resources that are made available by a lean initiative, and yet this is the only alternative that far too many company managers see.

Table 4.10: Long Term Future State Assuming Freed-Up Capacity is Used to Grow the Business

Lean Value Stream Box Score

Value stream: Electronics controllers

		Current state	Future state	Change	Long term future state—Alt#2	Change from current state
Operational	Dock-to-dock days	20.5 days	4.5 days	16 days	4.5 days	16 days
	First time through	48% FTT	96% FTT	48%	96% FTT	48%
	On-time shipment	90%	99%	9%	0.99	9%
	Floor space	34,000 sq feet	17,000 sq feet	(17,000) sq feet	17,000 sq feet	(17,000) sq feet
	Sales per person	$25,230	$26,380	$1,150	$35,475	$10,242
	Average cost per unit	$328.27	$308.61	($19.66)	$291.66	($36.61)
Resource capacity	Productive	20%	17%	-3%	41%	21%
	Non-productive	62%	36%	-26%	25%	-37%
	Available	18%	47%	29%	33%	15%
Financial	Inventory value	$58,502	$13,997	$44,505	$13,997	$44,505
	Revenue	$1,292,640	$1,292,640	$0	$1,738,140	$445,500
	Material costs	$512,160	$477,160	($35,000)	$645,160	$133,000
	Conversion costs	$189,866	$181,416	($8,450)	$181,416	($8,450)
	Value stream profit	$590,614	$634,064	$43,450	$911,564	$320,950

Table 4.11: Comparison of Alternative Uses of Freed-Up Capacity

Long Term Future State			
Value stream: Electronic Controllers			
	Alternative 1	**Alternative 2**	**Difference from alternative 1**
Sales per employee	$38,586.27	$35,472.24	($3,114.02)
Cost per unit	$293.06	$291.66	($1.40)
Revenue	$1,292,640.00	$1,738,140.00	$445,500.00
Value stream profit	$667,246.50	$911,564.00	$244,317.50

At the completion of executing Alternative 2, available capacity in the SMT and Test and Rework cells was limiting to further growth, as is shown in Table 4.12.

SUMMARY

This chapter presented a way to think about the effects of lean on the financial results of a business. It presented a Box Score as a way of viewing operating and financial effects together and to evaluate alternative courses of action. It also presented a way to view the capacity freed up by a lean initiative, so that company managers can develop appropriate plans for deployment. Finally it presented sets of generic strategies for the deployment of the capacity freed up. The analytic approach presented here should be used by lean teams to evaluate the financial benefits of all lean programs and *kaizen* events. It should be reviewed periodically to assess whether the actual results have borne out the plans at the outset of the program. Finally the review should be performed at each major phase of lean expansion to ensure proper focus on the alternative uses of the capacity that will be freed up as a result of that phase's improvements.

Table 4.12: Available Capacity at the Completion of Long Term Future State Alternative 2

Long Term Future State Value Stream Cost Analysis by Capacity Category

	Totals	SMT	Hand load / wave post	Test and rework	Assemble and burn-in	Shipping	Customer service	Purchasing	Quality assurance	Accounting	Design engineering	Information systems	Manufacturing engineering	Technical support
EMPLOYEES														
Cost	$139,624	$16,704	$22,968	$16,704	$10,440	$2,088	$11,928	$14,902	$7,978	$7,978	$3,989	$3,989	$7,989	$11,967
Productive		0%	53%	0%	66%	0%	0%	0%	0%	0%	0%	0%	0%	0%
Non-productive		34%	18%	48%	30%	71%	90%	1%	99%	71%	80%	91%	64%	83%
Other		0%	0%	0%	0%	0%	0%	0%	0%	0%	0%	0%	0%	0%
Available capacity	0%	66%	29%	52%	4%	29%	10%	80%	1%	29%	20%	10%	36%	17%
MACHINES														
Cost	$22,500	$16,956	$2,016	$3,528		$—	$—							
Productive		66%	75%	0%	0%	0%	0%	0%	0%	0%	0%	0%	0%	0%
Non-productive		32%	3%	99%	0%	0%	0%	0%	0%	0%	0%	0%	0%	0%
Other		0%	0%	0%	0%	0%	0%	0%	0%	0%	0%	0%	0%	0%
Available capacity	0%	2%	23%	1%	0%	0%	0%	0%	0%	0%	0%	0%	0%	0%

CHAPTER 5

Eliminating Wasteful Transactions

An important process for becoming lean is to eliminate the transactions, systems, and controls that supported the company's batch manufacturing process, but are no longer needed. For example, traditional manufacturers use work order scheduling and detailed tracking of labor and materials charged to the work order. Thus, management can be kept apprised of the progress of any job against the financial budget and schedule. Such detailed tracking is required for controlling a manufacturing process that can take weeks and months to produce a product. Lean manufacturers, on the other hand, take only days or weeks to manufacture a product and rely on kanbans and other pull methods to control the flow of the product through the plant, based upon the demand from the customer. Continuing to use the old tracking system in the face of these new manufacturing realities creates waste; so companies that are becoming lean need a way to judge when it is appropriate to remove unnecessary systems, transactions, and controls.

Companies going lean may even find that transaction volumes increase dramatically. Some areas where this can happen are:

- Purchase orders, receiving reports, and invoices for daily deliveries from suppliers
- Work order volumes and batch tickets to deal with a larger number of small batches and single-piece part flow
- Increased shipping documents and customer invoices to process daily shipments to customers.

So a lean company needs to manage and control lean in a way other than by creating paper or computer transactions every time material is moved or altered during the production process. Otherwise, the job of creating and processing transactions to control manufacturing is likely to mushroom, even as manufacturing itself becomes lean. That is why we say that transactions are to Lean Accounting as inventory is to lean manufacturing. Transactions are pure waste and for the most part are in place to bring control into a manufacturing process that is out of control.

In Chapter 2 we discussed the maturity path for Lean Accounting, noting that as lean progresses, most of the detailed transaction controls required for a traditional manufacturing system become unnecessary. We have included the high-level view from Chapter 2 below:

LEAN MANUFACTURING	LEAN MANUFACTURING ATTRIBUTES	LEAN ACCOUNTING
Pilot Lean Production Cells	• Successful lean cells in place • Extensive training in lean principles • Flow, pull, kanban • Quick changeover and SMED • Standardized work • Quality at source and self-inspection	Getting Started with Lean Accounting
Lean Manufacturing Widespread	• Widespread manufacturing in cells across the plant with standardized work and single-piece-flow • Extensive use of visual systems • Continuous improvement teams trained and established • Initial supplier certification program and kanban pull from some suppliers • Manufacturing managed by value stream • Processes under control; typically some use of SPC • Work-in-process and finished goods inventory relatively low and consistent	Managing by Value Streams
Lean Thinking Applied Throughout Organization and Partners	• Company organized by value streams • Extensive cooperation with customers, suppliers, and partners • Continuous improvement is a way of life • Lean thinking applied throughout the entire organization	Lean Enterprise

This chapter deals with the questions of when it is appropriate to eliminate transactions that are no longer needed without losing control of the business, and what is the process that determines what can be eliminated? The questions are addressed at each phase of the maturity path. This chapter deals with the kinds of transactions that normally can be eliminated in the Getting Started phase, when the company is piloting lean cells, but lean has not been implemented across a value stream or plant. In Chapter 12, "Eliminating More Wasteful Transactions," we will deal with the kinds of changes that can be implemented when lean manufacturing is widespread and the company is operating by value stream. Finally, in Chapter 17, "Expanding Value Streams Outside Our Four Walls," we will deal with this topic from the perspective of the fully lean company that has spread lean beyond the plant to include sales and marketing, suppliers, and customers.

This chapter deals with issues of getting started. It is organized into three sections:

- The "what must be in place" Method
- Cell Transactions
- Labor Tracking, Material Costs, Inventory Tracking

WHAT MUST BE IN PLACE?

Companies frequently ask how they will know when they no longer need the transactions that support their existing systems. The answer is that as their lean process makes the transaction unnecessary to the control of the manufacturing process, they can eliminate the transaction for it. With respect to any particular transaction type, the appropriate question then is, "what must be in place, from a lean manufacturing point of view, to allow as good, or better, control than already exists under the current system." Although all companies are different in this regard, there are enough similarities to develop rules of thumb.

To put the issue in perspective, we present two scenarios of companies below. One is typical of manufacturers prior to adopting lean manufacturing and the other is a mature lean manufacturer. The question posed is how many, and what kind of, transactions are required to control the process.

HOW MANY AND WHAT KIND OF TRANSACTIONS ARE NECESSARY?

BEFORE
- Production lead time is about six weeks.
- Frequent expediting.
- WIP inventory varies considerably.
- Production costs vary considerably.

AFTER
- Production lead time is 2.5 days.
- Predictable cycle time; one every six minutes.
- WIP low and consistent.
- Process and cost under control.
- Effective operational performance measurements.
- Continuous improvement team constantly working to improve the value stream.

The lean scenario requires a lot fewer transactions to control the processes. This is due to the difference in production lead times between the two scenarios. When a product takes six weeks to pass through the production process, it spends much of the time in work-in-process inventory. In this scenario, management spends a great deal of time expediting customer orders. The only way management can know where these expedited orders are in the process is by tracking them through the process. This requires a large number of transactions. On the other hand, when manufacturing takes less than three days to process orders, there is no problem in determining the status of a customer order, due to the short time taken to fill it. Consequently, it is unnecessary, and wasteful to maintain a system to track orders under these conditions.

However, between these two extremes the degree of transaction control is less obvious. To answer that question we must define what we mean by lean at each stage of the maturity path. Let us look at a typical progression for a company in its initial stages of lean, when lean pilots are in place, but lean production is not yet widespread throughout the plant. A similar table for your own company provides a basis for evaluating what must be in place for you to remove operations transactions. The table on the following page shows the status of lean maturity at two points in time: when the company is just starting lean but before any lean initiatives have been completed, and after the company has implemented its first round of pilot cells. It calibrates the status in terms of key dimensions of lean.

Your table may look different, but it is important to note the strides that the company has taken from its initial state. The progress made implementing lean manufacturing up to that time determines which operating transactions can be eliminated after pilot cells have been implemented. Our assessment of this progress will draw from the example above. However, before we evaluate what can be eliminated at this stage, we need to review the transactions at the cell level during the first phase of the lean manufacturing maturity path. Then we can ask the question, "what must be in place, from a lean point of view, to enable elimination of the transaction and still retain the control of the process?"

CELL TRANSACTIONS

When you are in the first stage of lean you find that you have created isolated cells here and there across the factory and still need the existing transactions systems to manage the factory. The most transaction-heavy operational processes are the following:

- Work in Process Tracking and Labor Reporting—tracking production job in detail using work orders
- Material costs—tracking all materials used in detail to work orders
- Inventory Control and Valuation—Detailed tracking of all inventory, from receipt through to use or disposal. Every material movement has a transaction. Transactions are posted at standard cost.
- Inventory Record Accuracy—Full annual inventory count

As these processes are the most transaction-heavy, they are the ones to focus on during each stage of lean so that the unnecessary transactions are eliminated.

DIMENSION	MAKING A START WITH LEAN	LEAN PILOTS IN PLACE
Cycle Time	• 12 weeks • Just beginning to understand lean concepts	• 4 weeks • Value streams mapped • Flow started in pilot cells • Bottlenecks reduced
Inventory Levels	• 3 turns • High raw, WIP and finished goods inventories • Inventories high but not the right stuff	• 5 turns • Kanbans used in pilot cells • Supermarkets and FIFO lanes used
Kanban and Pull	• MRP • Push system • Very little or no kanban pull	• Kanban introduced in cells • Kanban with some suppliers • Pull system used in pilot cells • Pull bottlenecks minimized
Standard Work	• Work instructions and routings for standard costing employed	• Standard work used in pilot cells • 5S started • Lines balanced • Elimination of subassemblies started
Supplier Quality	• Many suppliers, but few certified • No measurement system • Frequent supplier delivery problems • Receiving inspects most incoming material • Inspection shows erratic supplier quality • Scrap and rework issues • Only 75% on-time delivery to the next operation	• Core supplier identified • Number of suppliers decreased • Supplier certification program developed • Some suppliers certified • No longer inspect receipts from certified suppliers • Cell Quality • Large batches • Formed cells • Pull system used in the cells • Smaller batches • Operators cross-trained and certified • Better quality and less rework
Performance Measures	• Using detailed labor reports for efficiency • Using machine utilization measures • Measures are primarily accounting	• Start using lean performance measures (e.g.: scrap, day by the hour, First Time Through, etc.)

Continued on next page

Continued from previous page

DIMENSION	MAKING A START WITH LEAN	LEAN PILOTS IN PLACE
Visual Systems	• No visual systems—basically, paper, paper, and more paper • Using MRP work orders and ad hoc reports	• Measures are vital and visible • Measure boards in cells • Measures posted real-time • Display is simple to understand
Engineering Data	• Multiple level bills of materials • Routings and bills of materials inaccurate	• Bills of materials and routings are simple and accurate • Engineering responsible for keeping BOMs and routings accurate
Organization and Control	• Organized by functional department • Use department continuous improvement teams with only limited results.	• Identified the value streams • Started educating on value streams • Formed some value streams • Continued movement toward value stream organization—buyer/planner located in value stream

LABOR TRACKING

Before companies implement lean manufacturing, they typically record all labor incurred in each step of the production process on a work order. This document travels with the job through the production process and is the record of the work performed to date. The labor hours accumulated on the work order provide the basis for determining how much the product costs.

For the reasons stated in the "before" and "after" lean scenarios presented above, work orders becomes less important as a means of determining the status of customer orders as lean is implemented. For the same reason, work orders become less important as a costing document as the production lead time gets shorter, in-process inventories decrease to a very low level, and production cycle times become more predictable. Under these conditions, the cost of the product is determined more by the flow of the production than by the resources added to an individual item. Therefore, as lean is implemented, we want to move from tracking labor by each job step on production work orders to the elimination of work orders entirely. So an important lean accounting goal is to stop tracking labor hours. Still, we cannot make the change all in one step, particularly when we are just implementing cells on a pilot basis. The existing accounting system cannot be applied to turn off labor tracking cell by cell on a piecemeal basis. Consequently, we have to apply our changes in the accounting system to the whole factory, or not all. There is a logical progression in doing this and the key is to decide what must be in place in order to take the next step. Let us look at the progression for labor tracking:

Number	Actions	What Must Be in Place
1	• Eliminate job step tracking. Track only starts and completions	• Accurate labor routings and bills of materials
2	• Eliminate detailed labor tracking. • Automate the assignment of labor through backflushing using standard labor costs and actual production	• Accurate labor routings and bills of materials
3	• Back-flush or prorate the overhead • Eliminate detailed tracking and variance reporting	• Cell level performance measures in place in pilot cells and day by the hour reporting in all work areas
4	• Apply labor and overheads as summary direct costs to the value stream. Do not apply these costs to specific products or production jobs.	• Implementation awaits further lean progress—discussed in Chapter 12
5	• Eliminate work orders or other production tracking documents	• Elimination awaits further lean progress—discussed in Chapter 12

Note the progression. The first step is to retain the work orders, but eliminate job step tracking—only the tracking starts and stops. The implication is that there is control of the steps performed between the start and the completion points. The absolute requirement for this is that the information in the bills of materials and routings for products made are accurate and up-to-date. In an ideal world we would want one hundred percent accuracy, but eighty percent is satisfactory, as it provides the needed confidence that ensures that the labor hours included in the standard costs are accurate.

The second step is to change the way costs are applied to the work order. Note that we still have work orders, but we no longer track costs to each work order. We apply costs through a method known as backflushing. The logic here is that, once we know that we have made a product on a work order, we also know that it took us a standard number of hours to make the parts at a standard rate per hour. So knowing a work order has been completed, the costs can be applied at the standard cost. Overtime will still have to be recorded, however.

Finally, we need to get rid of variance reports at the earliest stage possible. In Chapter 3, we showed how measuring factory performance, based on variances between actual cost and standard cost, causes a focus on maximizing efficiency in the use of individual resources, at the expense of accomplishing lean goals. In traditional factories it is common to measure how efficiently labor and machines are being used. The so-called efficiency and volume variances compare the cost of production at actual versus planned volumes. At lower actual volumes, these variances show negative performance. By means of these variances, management can get a handle on how efficiently its factory has performed during the period—usually a month—then investigate reasons for out-of-line performance and make appropriate changes. These variances are useful in controlling a traditional, mass-production factory, and assuring maximum use of expensive machinery. However, their application is detrimental to the success of a lean factory because it creates a strong incentive to make excess inventory, which contradicts the lean goal of eliminating inventory. So, for a lean company, it is important to discontinue measuring factory performance using variances from standard cost. To get rid of these variances, however, we must have in place lean control tools that accomplish the objectives intended by the variance reports—only better. At the minimum, day-by-the-hour reporting, discussed in Chapter 3, should be in place in all work centers to ensure that machinery and people are employed at the rate required by lean production, the takt rate for each work cell.

Until the company advances further with lean, not much more can be accomplished in eliminating work orders entirely. We shall discuss this further in Chapter 12.

MATERIAL COSTS

The goal here is to shift from multiple postings of materials, accumulating product costs, to expensing materials to the value stream as they are received. Before the lean transition, we assume that the company uses a costing system to track the costs and materials used on each production order. Actual quantities of materials used are posted to a work order at each operation. Variance reports monitor actual material costs against standard costs for the unit manufactured.

As in the case of labor tracking, when cells have been implemented across the plant, we can eliminate detailed posting of material used to work

Number	Actions	What Must Be in Place
1	• Eliminate detailed labor tracking. • Automate the assignment of materials through backflushing using standard material costs and actual production. • Keep track of scrap and rework.	• Accurate labor routings and bills of materials • Accurate records for scrap and rework
2	• Apply material costs directly to the value stream at the time of received. There is very little inventory in the plant and the cycle times are so short that they are used as they are received.	• Elimination awaits further lean progress—Discussed in Chapter 12
5	• Eliminate work orders or other production tracking documents.	• Elimination awaits further lean progress—Discussed in Chapter 12

orders. Material used is charged to the job using the standard cost of materials multiplied by the number of units completed, using the backflushing technique discussed above for labor tracking. The ability to use this method is predicated on accurate bills of materials and material routings for the products manufactured. Furthermore, it will be necessary to maintain accurate records of material scrapped and used in rework, so that these costs can be added to the standard costs charged.

INVENTORY TRACKING

Number	Actions	What Must Be in Place
1	• The annual physical inventory is replaced with cycle counting. Cycle counting is used as a way to discover the root causes of the errors created in the inventory balances. In this way, the company is gradually eliminating the error causing problems in its processes.	• Accurate labor routings and bills of materials • Accurate records for scrap and rework
2	• Kanban control of inventory in the cells eliminates the need for cycle counting, inasmuch as there is visual control of all work in process and raw material inventories of the lean cells.	• Elimination waits further lean progress—discussed in Chapter 12
5	• Inventory tracking has been largely eliminated from the computer system.	• Elimination awaits further lean progress—discussed in Chapter 12

We need to track inventory so that we can prepare financial statements at the end of an accounting period. For a company that is in the early stages of lean, in which pilot lean cells are in place but lean has not been expanded to an entire value stream, there is a need to relieve raw material and work-process inventories as materials move through the value stream. The traditional company keeps detailed track of all movements of raw materials, work-in-process, and finished goods. Transactions are entered for receipts, issues, adjustments, and miscellaneous usage of materials. All this is pure waste and can largely be eliminated during the early stages of lean by using backflushing, as discussed in the section, "Labor Tracking," above.

However, that leaves the problem of assuring the accuracy of the inventory balances. Once there is some assurance as to the accuracy of the bills of materials and routings on which the backflushing is based, samples of the accuracy of this process can be conducted rather than counting the entire inventory. This is known as cycle counting and its purpose is to test the accuracy of the processes that create the inventory balances. As it is only conducted on a sample basis, it is not a good way to correct the inventory that has been created with flawed processes. However, cycle counting combined with an effective continuous improvement program is a very effective way to uncover the causes of these errors, and correct them. Many companies count the same parts in each cycle so that they can measure the effectiveness of improvements made.

Summary

This chapter has dealt with appropriate transaction elimination strategies during the early stages of lean, when pilot cells are being implemented. Through backflushing labor and material, significant reductions of transactions can be achieved. What must be in place are accurate bills of materials and routings, as well as scrap, rework, and overtime records. In Chapters 12 and 17, we will deal with the greater elimination that is possible during more advanced stages of lean.

CHAPTER 6

Lean Financial Accounting

In Chapter 5, we dealt with the issue of eliminating operations transactions as lean manufacturing is implemented. This chapter elaborates on this theme, specifically for financial transactions. Throughout, we discuss themes that underlie Lean Accounting.

The first is that all transactions are waste and a large part of realizing the benefits of lean is to consciously eliminate support transactions and functions as lean makes them unnecessary. We say "consciously" because, without a concerted focus, wasteful support functions and transactions will clog the flow of the product through the value stream.

So, a second theme is to eliminate the need for transactions by creating financial control directly from operational control. We seek a single control system that stems from operational control.

A New Perspective on Internal Accounting Control

Internal accounting control refers to the overall operating framework of policies, practices, systems, management philosophy, values, and actions that ensure the organization achieves essential objectives, protects assets, manages risks, and meets legal requirements. Traditionally, companies relied on detailed inspection of transactions to ensure proper authorization, accuracy in recording, and in reporting all transactions with suppliers and customers. These include orders, revenues, receivables and receipt of cash with customers and purchases, accounts payables, and cash disbursements with suppliers.

Most financial control systems rely on inspection of transactions produced in the operational processes to ensure that they are accurate and consistent with company policy. One of the principles of accounting control is that the costs of control should be proportional to the risks being controlled. The relevant risk relates to the joint probability of a material error occurring and then escaping detection. To counteract this risk, companies instituted systems of multiple approvals and inspections of all transactions with outside companies, regardless of the size of the transaction or the risk of error.

The emphasis in lean on standardization of work, on reducing the number of suppliers, and of insisting on perfection, flow of the work, and empowerment of people to fix problems has enabled a change in the paradigms related to control. This change is depicted in the diagram below.

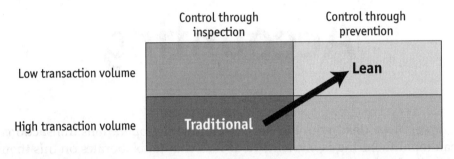

Figure 6.1: Changing Transaction Controls in the Lean Finance Function

Just as the strong visual control framework eliminates the need for transactions to control the work on the shop floor, the emphasis on daily delivery to the shop floor requires suppliers to reliably deliver exactly what is ordered with 100 percent quality. The resulting certification of a few key suppliers who deliver under blanket purchase orders reduces the risk of errors in deliveries, as well as the number of the suppliers. Major reductions in invoice volume result from providing shop floor personnel with credit cards to purchase small items rather than requiring separate purchase orders and invoices for each purchase. The lean environment thus pushes the control out of the accounting department and onto the shop floor where transactions are initiated, and builds control into the process rather than attempting to inspect control after the fact.

ELIMINATING WASTE FROM THE FINANCIAL

ACCOUNTING PROCESSES

However, we are interested in the waste that can be eliminated during the initial stage of lean, prior to the certification of suppliers and before kanban control of inventory and procurement is widespread. Waste must be eliminated to free up accountants from routine transaction audits and administration, so that they can get involved in the lean improvements that will be underway once value streams are put into place. Since the real control is on the shop floor in a lean value stream, accountants should assist the shop floor personnel in implementing these controls and should be involved in the assurance that the controls are in place and operating as planned. The diagram below shows the desired shift from using accounting personnel primarily to perform bookkeeping to using them, as described above, as part of the lean control process.

- There is an important role for the finance and accounting people within a lean organization
- They become change agents on the lean team
- To take this role their time must be freed up
- The elimination of wasteful bookkeeping activities achieves this

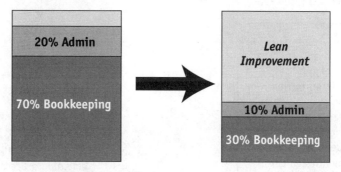

Figure 6.2: Changing the Role of the Accounting Personnel

In each of the accounting processes, waste can be eliminated even before any significant lean manufacturing has begun by examining each process, each report, each sign-off or approval, each transaction type, and asking a series of questions:

- Why is that report or process or sign-off necessary?
- Do we really need to continue requiring that transaction or can we accomplish our goal a simpler way?
- If we eliminate the approval or report, what is the risk of errors for some or for all transactions?
- Do we know of companies that have eliminated these controls? What have been their results?

On the next few pages we will look at some of the high-transaction accounting processes and see how this thinking can be applied to them. These processes are listed in the table below.

The approach used is to work out how to eliminate the need for each process by eliminating the reason for its existence. In general, we do not want to get better at doing wasteful things, such as inspecting transactions. We seek ways to eliminate the need for each transaction.

We have already addressed the reductions in authorizations. We will now work on two other specific processes in which significant reductions in transactions can be made during the early stages of lean. These are the Accounts Payable Process and the General Ledger and Month-End Close Process.

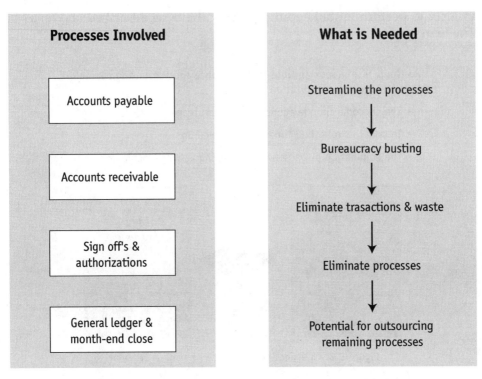

Figure 6.3: Eliminating Waste from the Financial Accounting Processes

The Accounts Payable Process

This type of processing occupies a large amount of the time of the traditional accounting department. The most time-consuming is the inspection of all invoices received from suppliers and matching them with purchase orders and receiving reports. This matching ensures that the company is being billed only for what has been ordered and received, within the price and quantity terms of the purchase order. For companies with thousands of suppliers, this is a full-time job for many accounting clerks. Shown below, Figure 6.4, depicts the flow from a manual three-way match, (described above) to the complete elimination of invoices. This is accomplished by paying for the materials automatically, as they are used, via electronic transfer of funds from the backflush from the bill of materials into the suppliers' bank accounts. Under these conditions, there is no need for accounts payable at all. The cash disbursement process is totally automated.

The first step in such a progression is to understand the supplier base, to simply ask, "who are my key suppliers?" Alternatively, put another way, "which suppliers make up eighty percent of the total dollar value of purchases? How many do we have for each major item purchased? Which of these can be qualified to be key suppliers for the item?" Efforts can then be made to certify these suppliers and to create blanket purchase orders that specify terms for supplying all (or most) of the item requirements.

- Manual three-way match for all payments

- Introduce supplier certification

- Blanket purchase orders

- Voucher on receipt—eliminate invoices

- Introduce purchase credit cards

- Automatically voucher on receipt

- Voucher on backflush *or*

- Pay on monthly statements

- Automatically pay on backflush using EFT

Lean Thinking:
Very few transactions, payments under control,
cooperative supplier relationship.

Figure 6.4: Creating the Lean Accounts Payable Process

At the same time, the remaining twenty percent of the purchases should be analyzed. Most likely, these make up the suppliers that create the greatest numbers of transactions (purchase orders and sign-offs, invoices, receiving reports, and three-way matches). The vast majority of these transactions can be eliminated simply by paying for these purchases by credit cards issued to employees, thereby replacing thousands of transactions with one single transaction.

Most of these initiatives can be started during the initial stages of lean and can work in parallel with the supplier certification process. The result will rely on close working relationships with a small number of suppliers that deliver key items daily to the lean cells in exactly the correct amounts and with high quality. Under these conditions, invoices become unnecessary, because the invoices that need to be paid constitute the parts used for one day's production. Those items are spelled out in the bills of materials of the backflushed finished items.

Accounts Receivable Process

The logic that applies to accounts payable also applies to accounts receivable. In a traditional accounts receivable function, acknowledgements are sent to customers on receipt of a purchase order. This usually occurs in the Customer Service or other department that receives and processes customer orders. The Shipping Department notifies the Accounts Receivable Department that the order has been shipped, and the department then prepares an invoice and mails it to the customer for each shipment made. The department collects cash from late-paying customers by making telephone calls and coordinating with collection agencies. This is by far the most time-consuming function of the typical Accounts Receivable Department.

The goal is to simplify these functions by shifting from a transaction-intensive and procedurally complex process to one with minimum transactions and built-in controls. The steps to achieving this goal are:

- Reduce the volume of purchase orders received by encouraging blanket purchase orders from key customers.
- Take steps to become certified suppliers to key customers.
- Eliminate the involvement of Accounts Receivable in invoicing by invoicing automatically from the shipment, including the invoice with the shipping documents.
- If the key customers are also on the lean journey, encourage payment of the invoice upon receipt of materials, in return for providing daily delivery to their facility based upon receipt of kanban orders.
- For those customers for which the company has been designated as a certified supplier, encourage the elimination of invoices altogether, using the shipper information to post the accounts receivable record.
- Encourage automated wire transfers into the company's bank accounts for materials delivered, with payment made based upon the customer's usage of the products shipped.

During the lean pilot phase, it is practical to initiate the first three steps listed above. The use of blanket sales orders requires coordination between the Sales, Order Processing, and Accounts Receivable departments. This step sets the stage for Step 3, Invoicing from the Shipping Department, because the billing information can be taken from the blanket sales order data on file. The process for becoming a certified supplier can be initiated at this stage. We will have more to say about the accounts receivable simplification process in Chapter 14 dealing with the elimination of financial transactions in the later stages of lean.

The General Ledger and Month-End Close Process

The process of closing the books every month to create financial statements can be extremely time-consuming for an accounting department. The number of departmental units and the number of the accounts in the company's chart of accounts determine how much time is spent on this. Each of these accounts requires analysis to ensure the correct posting of items into the account and, thereby, ensuring that the items in the financial statements will be properly classified. Charts of accounts have a way of growing over time as new accounts are added to collect costs for a given purpose. However, these accounts are seldom eliminated after the reasons for their establishment have been satisfied. Consequently, the numbers of accounts grow over time, but there is great reluctance to eliminate an account in case someone asks a question about the information contained in the account, requiring a great deal of work to find the answer. Of course, the real issue is of the relevance of the question asked. Is the report or analysis really necessary? How valuable is the report or information provided by these collections of accounting data relative to the effort to maintain the accounting structure to create such data? In many cases, the managers requesting the reports or the information have no idea of the effort required to create them. Typically, the reports and account structure created to satisfy one manager's need for information remain long after that manager has moved on. This leaves a pile of unread reports and a great deal of wasteful activity associated with maintaining the system necessary to create these reports.

Not only is the account structure wasteful in itself, but it is no longer needed to manage the lean company. The traditional company relies on the reporting actual costs versus budgeted amounts by department, as the cornerstone of the accounting control process. Managers are held responsible for making budgeted numbers. The accounting structure is built on department organization. Costs incurred by a department are charged to the expense account within that department. While useful in promoting department efficiency, the system has the unfortunate effect of optimizing the parts at the expense of the whole in a lean company, which should be focusing on value streams that cross many departments, not just one. It is not so much interested in the cost of an item to an individual department as to the value stream as a whole. Yet traditional companies keep their accounts by functional departments. Value streams do not exist in the current account structure. So the lean company will want to consider recasting its chart of accounts from functional departments to value streams. The initial stages of lean, when value streams are being established, is the time to think about this new way of looking at the business and what it means for the way financial information is reported, collected, and measured. We will say more about this in Chapter 7, which deals with the changes that take place with the shift to value stream management. For now, however, we leave it with you as something to think about during the initial stages of lean.

Figure 6.5 depicts the flow of steps from traditional account closing to fully lean.

We are concerned in the early stages of lean with just the first three steps and will discuss the other steps in Chapter 14.

- Lengthy and late close every month

- Simplify and standardize the month-end process

- Reduce cost centers, simplify the chart of accounts, eliminate the accruals and adjustments

- Move to quarterly closes

- Expand sales & operations planning to provide relevant month-end information ahead of time

- Automate the month-end and quarterly close

- Outsource if necessary

Lean Thinking:
Move from lengthy & wasteful month-end closes
to simplified & automated quarterly closes.

Figure 6.5: Creating Lean General Ledger and Month-End-Close Processes

SUMMARY

This chapter has provided an overview of the changes the finance organization will undertake as the company moves toward lean. It is possible to eliminate much of the current work of the department as waste. However, it will entail a major shift in the way the finance department thinks about its work and also a change in the nature of the work itself—from inspectors and auditors of the work of operation to full partners as members of the lean team.

CHAPTER 7

Managing by Value Stream

WHAT IS A VALUE STREAM?

A value stream represents all the things we do to create value for the customer. The first principle of lean thinking relates to customer value.[1] We focus on creating large amounts of value for the customer. The second principle of lean thinking is that we always work by value stream.

A typical value stream fulfills customer orders through a process as shown in Figure 7.1

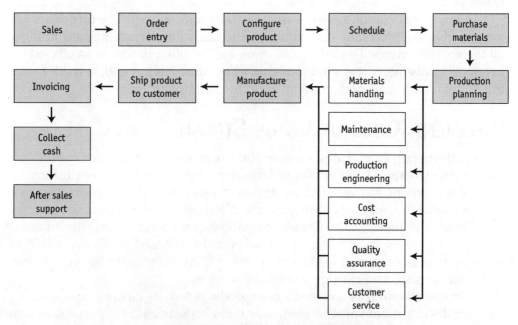

Figure 7.1: Typical Value Stream Structure

1. Womack, James P and Jones, Daniel T., *Lean Thinking: Banish Waste and Create Wealth in Your Corporation*, New York: Simon & Schuster. 1996), pp. 16–19.

The value stream involves far more than just the manufacturing processes. In the diagram above, manufacturing is shown as just one step in the whole process of serving the customer and creating value. However, many processes support the manufacturing steps. Some companies make the mistake of defining their value streams too narrowly; they include only the production steps. It is important to include all that is required to create value for the customer in your value stream.

It is often important to include more than just what occurs within the production plant. Organizations with finished goods warehouses usually include these in the value stream. The warehouse may be outside the immediate control of the plant people, but it contributes to both customer value and waste. Similarly, if the operation pulls materials from another plant in the same organization, then this supplier from within is often included as a part of the value stream. If you work through distributors, it may be necessary to include the distributors as a part of your value streams and see the flow right through to the end customer.

Organizations that are mature with lean manufacturing and lean thinking extend their value stream understanding beyond their own four walls; they include suppliers and customers into their value streams. This enables them to understand, for example, how customers use their products to create value for their own customers. By understanding the complete flow of the broader value stream of which they are a part, they are able to work with their customers, suppliers, and other third party organizations to eliminate waste and improve the entire flow.

A lean organization needs to manage the value stream. The company may be divided into many departments, and the value stream flows through all these departments. Departmental organization often becomes an obstacle to lean improvement. It is vital to identify the value stream and to work for the improvement and perfection of the value stream.

DIFFERENT KINDS OF VALUE STREAM

In manufacturing companies, most of the value streams are order fulfillment value streams. They obtain orders from customers and ship product to fill these orders. However, there are other kinds of value streams. Figure 7.2 is a useful first step in identifying the different kinds of value streams.

Order fulfillment value streams provide current products to current customers. Often there is no need for any sales and marketing in the order fulfillment process, because the value stream flows from order entry through to the collection of cash, and perhaps after sales service.

A value stream that addresses new products to new customers is a new product development value stream. This includes marketing processes, design engineering, production engineering, target costing, etc. Although this is not a production value stream, the same lean issues apply—value, flow, waste, teamwork, accountability, and the pursuit of perfection.

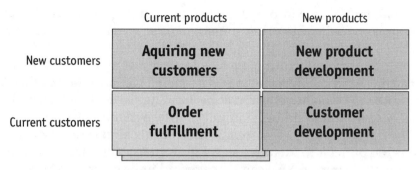

Figure 7.2: Categories of Value Streams

Value streams that deal with the acquisition of new customers for current products, and new products for current customers fall into the realm of sales and marketing. These processes are different from order fulfillment and may, in some organizations, be handled as different value streams.

This diagram is overly simple, but it is a good starting point for identifying the different kinds of value streams within your organization. The diagram can be expanded to include service value streams for companies that provide service in addition to physical products.

WHY DO WE FOCUS ON VALUE STREAMS?

We focus on value streams because this is where the money is made. We create value for the customers through the value streams, and thereby, we make money for our company through the value streams. We create value and make money through the combined efforts of people from many different departments. A primary purpose of lean thinkers is to focus relentlessly on the value stream processes. As we perfect the value stream processes we create more value for the customers and make more money.

The value is created within the value stream processes; this is also where the waste is. We focus on the value streams, because we can then identify waste and develop action plans to eliminate it. A lot of time is wasted when companies make improvements to one department or process, which have no overall impact on the business. It is only when we address the waste within the entire value stream that we can direct our improvement efforts correctly. We must map the value streams, identify the waste and any obstacles to the flow,[2] and initiate improvement efforts to eliminate waste and increase flow through the value stream. Only then can more value be created and more money generated.

Some of this is a matter of what we see. If we do not have a clear picture of how materials, information, and cash flows through the organization, it is

---

2. There are three kinds of flow through a value stream. There is the physical flow of materials, the flow of information, and the flow of cash. Lean improvement must increase the flow of all three.

difficult to identify where improvement efforts must be deployed. We focus on value streams and create value stream maps so we can see the flow and identify the obstacles to flow through the value streams.[3]

Prior to lean manufacturing, most companies were organized by production departments. These departments, sometimes called centers of excellence, were designed to be highly efficient at performing particular steps in the process. These may be welding, stamping, surface-mount insertion, assembly, burn-in, heat treatment, etc. An organization of this kind cannot see the flow—it is too difficult to identify. As we move into value streams the flow becomes much clearer, and we can manage and improve the process.

We focus on value streams because this focus is the best way to see the flow of materials, information, and cash through each organization. It is the best way to understand and increase the value we are creating for the customer, and it is the best way to grow the business, increase sales, and generate more profit.

Why Should We Manage the Business Through the Value Streams?

The three primary issues when managing a business throughout the value stream are focus, accountability, and simplicity.

Focus

Lean companies create a team of people who work together to maximize the value created by the value stream, to continuously improve the value stream, to grow the business, and make more money. The most important question is "who is responsible in this family of products for growth of sales, for increasing the value, for improving the processes, and for making more money?"

If the answer to this question is that sales and marketing are responsible for increasing sales, that the lean champions are responsible for making improvements, that the plant managers are responsible for increasing the efficiency and productivity of their plant, that Engineering is responsible for adding new products and improving the designs of current products, and that Quality Assurance is responsible for quality, and so on, then no one is focusing on that family of products. If this is the case, it is not surprising there is little growth.

We are not deriding the traditional manufacturing company organization. There are many companies that have done very well using it, but if you want to be a lean organization, you need to manage the business through the value streams, because the primary importance in lean is the focus on the flow of the product from the customer order to its final delivery. The value stream is designed to maintain the focus on flow.

---

3. This is why *Learning to See* has this title. It is a book about value stream mapping and creating lean improvement. To do this, we must first be able to "see" the issues correctly.

In their seminal book *Lean Thinking*,[4] Jim Womack and Dan Jones summed up this way of thinking:

"As you get the kinks out of your physical production, order-taking, and product development, it will become obvious that reorganizing by value stream is the best way to sustain your achievement."

Accountability

The value stream team needs to be accountable for the outcome of its work. We clearly identify the value streams and the value stream team. This team, and in particular the value stream manager, is responsible for the operational improvement, growth, and profitability of the value stream. A useful way to look at this is to imagine the company made up of several small, entrepreneurial companies. Each one responsible for making its value stream a spectacular success.

Table 7.1: Example of a Value Stream Box Score

		Current State	Future State	Long Term Future
Operational	Sales per person	$131,429	$131,429	$235,936
	On-time delivery	82%	96%	96%
	Dock-to-dock time—days	23.60	4.50	4.50
	First time through	90%	90%	90%
	Average cost per unit	$4.94	$4.94	$4.73
	AR days outstanding	30	30	30
Capacity	Productive capacity	25%	22%	29%
	Non-productive capacity	30%	8%	11%
	Available capacity	45%	70%	60%
Financial	Annual revenue	$1,840,000	$1,840,000	$3,303,100
	Annual material cost	$772,800	$772,800	$986,832
	Annual conversion cost	$317,752	$317,752	$317,752
	Value stream profit	$749,448	$749,448	$1,998,516
	Value stream cash flow	$749,448	$1,813,672	$3,062,740

The value stream team is responsible for the improvement of the value stream performance measurements[5] and the financial improvement of the value stream. This can be summarized using a value stream box score.

---

4. Womack & Jones, *Lean Thinking*.

5. See Chapter 8, *Value Stream Performance Measurements*.

The value stream team is not only responsible for the short-term improvement of their value stream, but also for the long term. This requires the team-members to think strategically about the changes they are instigating. The box score is used not only to report current information, but also to show the expected results from the team's long-term strategy.

Simplicity

One book on lean and world-class manufacturing[6] has the subtitle *"the lessons of simplicity applied."* Lean organizations are always striving to simplify all operations. It is, of course, very difficult to make processes simple. You must eliminate the root causes of variability and bring the processes under control.

An example of simplicity at work is a kanban pull system. A kanban is literally a signal from a downstream process in a production line that indicates to an upstream process that it needs to have parts replenished. At that moment the upstream process knows that it must provide the downstream process with exactly the number of parts requested. It provides the signal for the upstream process to begin making parts. Usually the instructions of what to make and how many are contained on a kanban card. So, the idea of kanban is very simple: when a replenishment kanban card is received, you immediately make more of the requested part that the card tells you to make. However, a production plant can only move from MRPII to kanban when the methods of lean manufacturing have been successfully applied. You must have small batches, reliable processes, effective machines, and regular production cycle times. Moving from MRPII to kanban is a move from the over-complexity of traditional manufacturing to the simplicity of lean operation.

Moving from a departmental organization to a value stream organization is a similar change. You move from a highly complex organization chart with hundreds of cost centers, thousands of transactions to track, and an organizational hierarchy consisting of managers and supervisors for each of the cost centers, to three or four value streams within the plant and a clear-cut line of responsibility.

This is simple not only because the people know where they should focus their work, but also because it simplifies performance reporting, organizational structure, accounting reports, and other infrastructure processes. A well-run value stream has a team of people working together to serve the customers, increase value, improve their performance measurements every week, and make more money. It is simple, clear-cut, and effective.

Continuous Improvement

Continuous improvement (CI) is achieved through the value streams. Lean organizations have CI teams assigned to each value stream. These are made up

---

6. Richard Schoenberger, *World Class Manufacturing*, Free Press, June 1986.

of people working in the value stream, but may also include some outsiders. The purpose of the CI team is to review the value stream performance measurements each week and initiate projects to improve these measurements.

There is a place in lean companies for top-down, breakthrough kaizen events, but as time goes on, the emphasis of improvement moves to the continuous improvement teams within the value streams. These teams are within the value streams because they must have a view of the entire flow of all processes. This way the focus will always be on improving the flow and increasing the value to the customers, and avoiding the pitfalls of making local improvements that do not benefit the overall process.

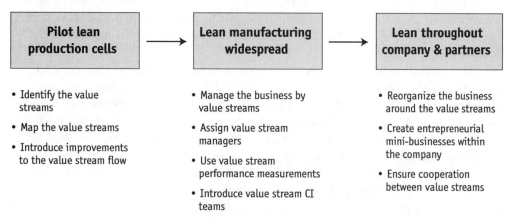

Pilot lean production cells	Lean manufacturing widespread	Lean throughout company & partners
• Identify the value streams	• Manage the business by value streams	• Reorganize the business around the value streams
• Map the value streams	• Assign value stream managers	• Create entrepreneurial mini-businesses within the company
• Introduce improvements to the value stream flow	• Use value stream performance measurements	• Ensure cooperation between value streams
	• Introduce value stream CI teams	

Figure 7.3: The Stages of Lean Manufacturing

THE MATURITY PATH TO LEAN VALUE STREAM ORGANIZATION

It is not necessary to redraw the company's organization chart in the short term. When lean manufacturing is first introduced into a company, there is no need to make organizational changes. At this stage, pilot (or trial) cells are implemented to explore how to make lean work in that plant. Normally, the pilot cells and other lean changes made at this stage can be achieved without major disruption to the company's departmental structure.

When you move beyond the early stage, it is necessary to manage by value stream. As lean manufacturing becomes widespread across the plant, it becomes important to assign particular people to each of the value streams. Ideally, this would include not only production people, but also support people, administrative people, sales and marketing, purchasing, quality assurance, cost accounting, and all the other people involved in the value stream.

Assigning people to value streams can be a difficult task. There may be three engineers and four value streams, for example, or we may have support people with particular specialties required by all value streams. In the long

term we use cross-training to bridge these gaps, but in the short term we may
have people working in more than one value stream.

Some people worry that a value stream organization will require more
people because, for example, there is only one production planner for the factory, yet this work now needs to be incorporated into the value streams. This
can be overcome in two ways. First, many of these administrative tasks can be
eliminated as lean manufacturing matures within the plant. For example, the
Production Planning Department becomes unnecessary when an effective
pull system is in place. Second, cross-training is used to provide these skills
in every value stream. The original production planner joins one value stream
and trains people in the other value streams. The production planner is also
cross-trained in, for example, inventory control, purchasing, and cost reporting. This way, the value streams contain all the required skills and no additional people are needed.

It is also common, in the early stages, for the department structure to
still be in place. The people still report to the functional boss, but they are
assigned to work with particular value stream teams. This matrix management is often the most convenient way to make changes without totally dis-
rupting the organization of the company. Having said that, companies that
make the radical change quickly are often rewarded by fast and radical
improvement. Once the team is in place and the complexities of the organization have been resolved, the people involved quickly focus on increasing
value, making improvement, and, as a result, making more money.

As lean thinking becomes embedded in the culture of the company, it
becomes increasingly obvious that reorganizing by value stream is the most
practical move. The value stream managers then take full responsibility for
the operation of the value stream and the leadership of the people within
the value stream. There are no other departments, except for the few
people who provide support or administrative functions outside of the
value streams.

Some lean organizations, particularly large and complex operations,
retain the departments and continue with a matrix organization. They find
that their size and complexity make it more convenient to retain the departmental structure, while the operations are managed by value stream. Small-
and medium-sized lean operations almost always take the step of redrawing
the organization chart to reflect value stream management.

PROBLEMS AND ISSUES

How to set up the value streams is not always a clear-cut decision when you
first start out with lean manufacturing. A number of issues and problems frequently arise. Some of these can be addressed and resolved, others cannot be
dealt with until a long-term solution can be found.

It is not necessary to solve all the problems in order to make progress. It
is a lean rule that we move ahead step by step. If you wait until every even-
tuality has been discussed and resolved, you will never get started! Value

streams are like this. Rarely can a perfect value stream be set up, but that should not deter you from setting up a good one.

People in More Than One Value Stream

Sometimes, it is not possible to have all the people in the value stream organized by value stream, just as in the lean factory it is not always practical to provide each value stream with a dedicated machine. Frequently, it is necessary for value streams to share large pieces of equipment, such as a stamping press that is expensive and difficult to move. In the parlance of lean manufacturing, such large machines are known as monuments. Monuments also exist outside the factory. For example, it is not unusual for the sales and marketing departments to be organized geographically or by market, rather than by the value stream product families. These service department monuments need to be treated the same way as physical monuments in the factory. The general rule is to recognize that you will not be able to achieve the perfect lean approach initially, but you can usually work out ways to limit the problems

If the sales people cannot be included in the value stream, perhaps marketing can. Marketing may be able to take on a product management role using the value stream product families. Perhaps certain sales and marketing people can be assigned to focus on the value stream products.

It will be necessary to introduce a closer liaison between the sales and marketing people and the production and product development people. This can be achieved using an effective sales and operations planning method. Chapter 13, *Operational and Financial Planning*, discusses this more fully. Target costing (described in Chapter 16) is also an important tool for integrating the true value stream when it is organizationally divided.

Monuments

A similar issue is a company with a series of monument machines. A monument is a machine that serves more than one value stream. A monument is typically a large, expensive piece of equipment with large batches, long lead times, and a slow changeover. In the long run, these monuments would be replaced by smaller, right sized machines, which are sized appropriately for the volume of work demanded by the required production rate of the cell or value stream. But, we often have to work around the monuments in the short term.

We have a client that does fabrication job-shop style, because it has 18 monument machines that cannot easily be assigned to value streams. At present this job-shop is treated as though it was its own value stream and is regarded as a supplier to the value streams, which assemble, ship, and sell the products.

This is a classic lean monument problem. It cannot be solved in the short term, so we work around it. Physically, the fabrication value stream manufactures to kanbans received from a downstream inventory called a supermarket. This supermarket inventory acts as a buffer between the fabrication monument machines that serve many value streams and the downstream value streams they serve. Organizationally the fabrication work center is treated like a value stream. It has its own value stream performance measurements, value stream manager, and reporting. The continuous improvement teams, however, include both assembly and fabrication value stream people. This ensures that improvement projects take account of the real, larger value stream.

Small Value Streams

Another common problem is the size of the value streams. Conventional wisdom says a value stream should contain between 25 and 150 people. If it is bigger than 150 people, you will not have the focused team required for the value stream to prosper; it will be an organization. If you have less than 25 people, you do not have enough people to run an effective operation. These are just guidelines; they have often been successfully violated.

It is important not to have too many value streams and to make sure that none of the value streams represent an insignificant part of the business. It is common to have three primary value streams, for example, and then have a fourth that contains all the odds and ends that do not fit well anywhere else. It is not necessary to solve all the problems up front. If you get the three primary value streams working well, you will learn more about the processes and be able to better address the products in the fourth value stream.

Competition between Value Streams

It is also important not create competition between the value streams. The value stream managers and team members should be striving to improve their performance measurements week-in and week-out. It makes no sense to compare one with the other. Every value stream is different. They have different issues and different outcomes. We want the value stream people to cooperate with each other. This cannot be achieved if undesirable competition has been created between them.

A healthy competition develops naturally between the value streams, and this friendly rivalry creates a positive atmosphere for improvement. It does not prevent the people from working together. We want the value stream teams to be good neighbors; helping each other out when there is a problem, pitching in when there is a heavy workload, and sharing improvements and successful ideas. A lean organization is a cooperative and flexible team.

What About the People who are not in the Value Stream Teams?

There are always some people within the plant or organization that do not fit into the value streams. These include:

- People whose work does not apply to any particular value streams—a human resources person, for example, or a financial accountant. Other examples would be the plant manager or the facilities people.
- People who support the value streams, but whose work is not easily split between each value stream—the IT people who keep the computers running, for example.

- People who do cross-value stream work. It is common to have a Quality Assurance manager outside the value stream, for example. This person's responsibilities might be to administer the ISO9000 process, certify the training of Quality Assurance people within the value streams, ensure consistency in quality methods across value streams, etc.

The end result is an organization in which the majority of people work in the primary value streams, and a few in vestigial departments that support the operation. These small departments may be organized in the traditional way, or they may be lumped into a single cost-of-doing-business department for budgeting and management purposes.

How Do We Identify the Value Streams?

The ideal value stream contains all the steps required to create value for the company's customer for a family of products. These products are a family because they all require similar steps through the value stream. In most cases, these similar steps relate primarily to the production processes.

Staple Yourself to an Order

The best place to start is with the order fulfillment value streams, because these are the most significant value streams for a manufacturing company in the early stages of lean. Walk through the process from beginning to end. And we mean walk, literally. Physically go through the steps in the process, as far as is practical. Gain an understanding of what happens from your company's first knowledge of a customer's need through to the collection of payment from the customer.

It is surprising how few people within a company have an understanding of the entire flow. There are many with a detailed knowledge of their section of the flow, but people with a broader understanding are difficult to find.

If the products your company sells are standard designs, then the order fulfillment process may begin with placing an order or pulling from a customer's kanban. However, if your products are designed or configured to order, there will likely be some quoting and engineering steps involved in the order-taking processes.

Draw a diagram of the entire process. This diagram may be in the form a value stream map or a more traditional process flow chart. The purpose of this diagram is not to give every last detail of the process, but to provide an understanding of the flow through the value stream, the delays encountered, the inventory at each point in the process, and the other relevant information.

Production Flow Matrix

The value streams in many production plants are obvious and well known to the operators and supervisors. Include the operators and supervisors in the process of defining the value streams. If the value streams are not clear, then it will be useful to draw a production flow matrix.

Using a simple spreadsheet, create a matrix of the products and the steps in the production processes. On the *y*-axis list all the products (or families of products) manufactured in the plant. On the *x*-axis list all the machines and/or production departments in the factory. Mark the matrix to show which products families use which production processes.

		Production Steps													
		Order entry	Scheduling	Stamping	Machining	Deburr	Heat treat	Outside processing	Inspection	Subassembly A	Subassembly B	Final assembly A	Final Assembly B	Pack & ship	Invoice
Product Families	112	X	X	X				X	X			X		X	X
	212	X	X		X			X	X		X	X		X	X
	212a		X		X	X	X			X		X		X	
	356	X	X	X				X	X			X		X	X
	356e		X		X	X	X			X		X		X	
	401	X	X	X				X	X			X		X	X
	402	X			X			X	X		X	X		X	X
	596	X			X			X	X		X	X		X	X

Figure 7.4: Example of a Production Flow Matrix

Sort the rows of the matrix to bring together the product families that have broadly similar production processes. The products with similar production flows will be the ones that need to be grouped together within the same value stream.

At this stage, ignore the current layout of the plant and ignore the existing departments within the organization. They are not relevant to this process at this time.

There is a more sophisticated approach to the use of value stream definition matrices. This is used for highly complex, mixed-model production processes. This method is described in the book *Creating Mixed-Model Value Streams*[7] and, while more time consuming, gives very good results.

---

7. Kevin Duggan, *Creating Mixed-Model Value Streams*, Productivity Press 2002.

Table 7.2: Example of a Value Stream Definition Analysis

Product Families		Order entry	Scheduling	Stamping	Machining	Deburr	Heat treat	Outside processing	Inspection	Subassembly A	Subassembly B	Final assembly A	Final Assembly B	Pack & ship	Invoice
	112	X	X	X				X	X				X	X	X
	356	X	X	X				X	X				X	X	X
	401	X	X	X				X	X				X	X	X
	212A		X		X	X	X			X		X		X	
	356E		X		X	X	X			X		X		X	
	212	X	X		X			X	X		X		X	X	X
	402	X			X			X	X		X		X	X	X
	596	X			X			X	X		X		X	X	X

Other criteria you may need to take into account include the production cycle time of the products and the physical size of the products. If 15 product families take similar production flows, but 7 of the families take 3 hours to process, and 8 take less than 30 minutes, it is likely these need to be assigned to different value streams. If some of the products are very large and require a team of people to work on them, whereas others are smaller and can be handled by one person, then it is likely they need to be assigned to separate value streams.

For example, imagine a company with three factories making similar, machined metal products. These three factories are close to each other and Factory A made all the high-volume products, Factory B made the slow-moving products, and Factory C handled all the nonstandard orders. When they drew the production flow matrix they found that there was no difference between the high-volume and low-volume products, and that they went through similar production processes. The nonstandard products also went through similar production processes, but they had a configuration process prior to moving into production.

What differentiated the processes were the materials (aluminum, steel, and stainless steel) and the required method of production (machined castings, machined bar-stock, machined tubing). These different kinds of products also addressed different segments of the market. The value stream maps for these new product families crossed from one plant to another, then back again. The need was to bring the products with similar production processes into the same physical plant and to minimize the flow within the value streams.

Size of the Value Stream

Do not create value streams for product families that represent a very small amount of the plant's output—less than 10 percent perhaps. Do not create value streams for products that represent too large an amount of the plant's output—greater than 60 percent. Be open to having two or three primary value streams and a value stream for the rest. It is fine to start off with the value streams that are clear and address the other products later, after you have more experience with lean value stream management.

Draw the Current State Value Stream Maps

Once you have a reasonably clear idea of which products fit into which value streams, draw a value stream map for each. Identify the customer demand, calculate the value stream takt time, sketch out the flow, identify the associated inventory, identify the major suppliers, show the cycle times and other information in the data boxes, and create a time-line.

Look at the value stream map as broadly as possible. Think through the processes that occur up front, and the processes that occur after the product is shipped. Include finished goods warehouses or distribution operations, post-sales services, and any engineering or design processes that are a part of fulfilling the customers' orders.

You may not, at this stage, have all the required information to draw the value stream maps fully, but this does not matter. At this stage, the purpose of the map is to understand the material and information flow through each of the value streams and use the maps to communicate your value stream ideas to the other people involved.

Machines and Monuments

Think through which machines and equipment are needed to support the value streams you have in mind. In most cases, it is quite straightforward to identify which machines are required, although many people find it difficult to imagine moving these machines and dismantling the production departments. Try to suspend disbelief during this stage—assume anything is possible.

It is not uncommon to find certain machines or processes that are used by many of the products. These are called monuments in lean parlance. The classic monuments are heat-treat ovens, wave-soldering machines, large automated machining centers, or paint spray or coating equipment. Monuments typically have long changeovers, large batches, are expensive to buy and run, and are specialized pieces of equipment.

As far as possible, you need to minimize the monuments in your process. The ideal value stream does not have any monuments because they are obstacles to the flow of material, they require high inventory levels, and they undermine the lean goal of making one part at a time only on demand, known as single-piece-flow. Sometimes it is possible to find other machines that can be used in one of the value streams. Sometimes a monument department has more than one machine and these similar machines can be moved from the department and assigned to specific value streams. Occasionally, the monuments can be eliminated from the process by purchasing different equipment that fits more appropriately into the value streams.

If the monuments cannot be minimized—and this is often the case—then you will need to employ lean manufacturing methods to minimize the problems they cause. This will require:

- A supermarket of buffer inventory to overcome the disruption of flow caused by the monument.

- A pull system for the replenishment of the buffer, so that the monument is working to customer requirements, even if there are larger batch sizes.

- Quick change-over projects to reduce the production batch sizes for the monument.

Identify the People in the Value Stream

Make a list of the people who will be assigned to each value stream. Usually the operators and supervisors can be readily assigned to a particular value stream. The problems come with the support people. People in some departments (production planning or inventory control, for example) can be assigned to the value streams. Others may have skills that are required by all three value streams. It may be impractical to assign people from other departments to any specific value stream.

The purpose of this list is to identify how easy or difficult it will be to create a value stream team. From experience, when you begin to make these lists, the problem often becomes less complex than it seems at first sight.

Make sure you include the broader value stream. If you can, include sales people, marketing, customer service, order entry, engineering, purchasing, maintenance, material handling, and others into the value stream team.

The perfect value stream includes all the people involved in creating value for the customers, but, there are often difficulties. A typical example is an Order Entry process that is customer-focused. If the customers buy products from all of the value streams, it is impractical to have the order entry people working in a specific value stream. They need to be customer-focused, not product-focused. It would be foolish to expect the customers to call different people in the company according to which products they wanted to order. Under these circumstances, it makes no sense to include an order entry worker in the value stream teams.

Another problem might be that there do not seem to be enough people with the right skills to have one team for each value stream, or one person who could contribute to every value stream. This is where cross-training becomes important; but cross-training takes a lot of time. Ask if the function

Table 7.3: Format for Aligning People with Value Streams

	Value stream 1	Value stream 2	Value stream 3
Manager			
Operators			
Supervisors			
Materials handlers			
Production control			
Inventory control			
Maintenance			
Production engineers			
Design engineers			
Configuration			
Quality assurance			
Purchasing			
Cost accounting			
Tool crib			
Customer service			
Order entry			
Information systems			
Marketing			
Sales			
Transportation			
FG warehouse			

(not the specific person) fits into the value stream. If the answer is yes then, in the long term, these tasks will be cross-trained and performed by full-time team members. In the short term a few of the people will need to work in more than one value stream.

Do We Need To Change Our Organization Chart?

All lean companies manage by value stream. All lean companies focus their continuous improvement efforts through the value streams. All lean companies assign value stream managers. But, not all lean companies reorganize by value streams.

Many of the most successful lean companies establish their organization chart around the value streams, with little reference to functional departments. Others retain their functional structure and create the value stream management through a matrix-management approach. There is no right or wrong approach. Either method can be used successfully to achieve the lean objectives of value stream management, customer-focused teams, and continuous improvement to increase value, eliminate waste, and increase earnings.

Figure 7.5 shows the decision matrix used by one company to address these issues. There was reluctance within the organization to make changes to the departmental organizational structure. The management team defined the criteria they had established for a structure to support their lean journey. These criteria are shown in the first column of the decision matrix. Across the top of the matrix they listed various possible organization structures. The management team then assigned scores for each criterion—9 for the structure that most supported the criteria, 5 for the next, and 1 for the next. The outcome was a clear decision in favor of a value stream organization with

Objectives	Importance	Departmental organization	Departmental, matrixed to value stream, traditional costs & measures	Departmental, matrixed to value stream, value stream costs & measures	Value stream organization, matrixed to department managers, value stream costing	Value stream organization with specialist "coaches"	Value stream organization
A team of people working together to increase customer value	5			1	3	5	
Identify waste and improve the flow through the value stream	5			1	3	5	
Continuous improvement to grow business and increase profitability	5				1	3	5
Simple, meaningful, low-waste, and understandable costing	3				1	3	5
Performance measurements focused on continuous improvement	5				1	3	5
Provide specialist knowledge in each area of the value stream	3	5		3	1		
Clear accountability for achieving the goals of the lean company	5						
Ease of implementation	1	5		3	1		
		20	0	22	47	89	65

Figure 7.5: One Company's Decision Matrix for Value Stream Organization

specialist coaches providing functional expertise. The management team successfully implemented this approach.

DEVELOP A PLAN

When you complete these steps, your team should have a clear picture of the value streams. It may be that only the primary value streams have been defined; that is fine. You have enough to start the process. The last step is to develop a plan for moving from the current management methods to lean value stream management. This will entail implementing value stream performance measures and eliminating the existing department organizational structure. Value stream performance measures and other tools for managing value streams are discussed in Chapters 8, 9, and 10.

SUMMARY

Lean organizations manage their business by the value streams. The value streams are where the value is created and the money is made. The value streams are also where the waste and delays can be identified and eliminated. Continuous improvement teams are established by value stream because it is important to make improvements from an understanding of the value and the flow. We need a team of people within each value stream whose sole focus is to grow the value stream, increase customer value, eliminate waste, and, as a result, make more money.

As lean manufacturing matures within the company, it becomes increasingly necessary to manage the value streams. Performance measurements are reported by value stream. Value stream managers are appointed. The managers have profit and loss responsibility for the value stream. Growth and improvement strategies revolve around the value stream. The value stream focus greatly clarifies the management of the organization.

The change to value stream management is another part of the maturity path. There is no need to make management changes when the lean improvements are restricted to pilot cells. However, when lean manufacturing and other lean initiatives are widespread in the plant, we begin to manage by value stream. This does not require dismantling the company's departments—there can be a matrix approach where people work in the value stream, but still report to a functional manager. Over time, however, it usually becomes clear that reorganizing the company around the value streams is the best way to run a lean operation.

CHAPTER 8

Value Stream Performance Measurements

The performance measurements required for lean production cells were described previously in Chapter 3. This chapter addresses the performance measurements required for the value stream as a whole. The cell-level performance measurements are typically reported by the hour and by the day. Value stream performance measurements are typically reported weekly and show how the value stream is achieving its performance goals.

WHAT IS THE PURPOSE OF VALUE STREAM PERFORMANCE MEASUREMENTS?

The purpose of cell performance measurements is to assist the cell team to serve the customers today. The purpose of value stream performance measurements is to initiate continuous improvement in the value stream.

Continuous improvement and the pursuit of perfection are both vital to lean thinking. All lean companies put methods in place to motivate the ongoing improvement of the company's processes. This continuous improvement is best approached through the value streams. The value stream manager and the value stream team are accountable for improving the performance of the value stream. The waste within the value stream processes shows clearly on the value stream maps. The value stream team is required to increase value for customers, to eliminate waste within the value stream, and to increase the amount of money the value stream earns.

The selection of performance measurements for a value stream should focus on improvement. The measurements must show the value stream's ability to effectively produce value for the customer. The measurement must motivate the value stream team to improve the performance of the entire value stream. There is little purpose in improving isolated areas of the value stream if those improvements do not create an overall improvement to the value stream. The value stream performance measurements focus the attention of the value stream team and the value stream manager on what needs to be improved.

While the value stream performance measurements are not necessarily intended to be a comprehensive assessment of the value stream, they are intended to drive the value stream team to make changes in the value stream by monitoring the key indicators of lean effectiveness relative to expectations. These changes must lead to increased value, reduced waste, improved flow, and higher profitability. The value stream performance measurements are selected to motivate the right kind of change and improvement.

VALUE STREAM CONTINUOUS IMPROVEMENT TEAMS

Lean value streams contain continuous improvement teams. There may be one continuous improvement team (CI team) for the value stream, or there may be more than one. These teams are set up with the express purpose of improving performance measurements for the value stream. The value stream CI teams study the value stream performance measurements each week and initiate projects to make the performance measurements move in the right direction each week.

TYPES OF CONTINUOUS IMPROVEMENT

Cell teams are required to make continuous improvement within their cells. These improvements are generally restricted to the cell and are motivated by the need to improve cell performance measurements. These improvements may be designed to solve problems that come up in production or to increase the overall effectiveness of the cell.

Value stream CI teams work together on projects designed to improve the effectiveness and flow of the entire value stream. These projects are cross-functional and are generally within the authority of the value stream team. The improvements are locally led and the CI team is a permanent improvement team. This typically results in a large number of smaller changes that, together, make a major improvement.

Other improvement projects are initiated by senior management or by the lean team outside of the value streams. These are typically major breakthrough improvements, often utilizing *kaizen*-blitz methods, and completed by a temporary team for the purpose. The term, "*kaizen*-blitz," although in common use in the lean manufacturing community, is somewhat of a contradiction in terms in that the word "*kaizen*" in Japanese refers to continuous incremental improvement and "blitz" refers to an intensive, focused project. So, a *kaizen*-blitz is an intense project, usually less than one week, that is intended to achieve the goals of a longer, *kaizen*, program in a much shorter time period. A lean coordinator or other professional facilitator usually leads the team performing the *kaizen*-blitz.

The value stream CI teams are cross-functional. Most of the people in the CI teams work in that value stream, although it is common for outside specialists also to be team-members. In some cases, suppliers and even customers may have representatives on the value stream CI team. Accounting and finance people are often CI team members.

The CI teams meet weekly to review the latest performance measurements, to update team members on the progress of the team's improvement projects, and to initiate new improvement projects. All the projects are designed to improve the value stream performance measurements. The continuous improvement projects the value stream CI teams perform are usually short term (less the two or three months). They address specific issues within the value stream, they are within the authority of the value stream team, and there are many of them. While each individual project may have modest improvement objectives, the sum of all these projects creates significant ongoing improvement to the value stream.

The value stream performance measurements are designed to guide the value stream CI teams in their continuous improvement efforts.

VALUE STREAM MEASUREMENTS AND PROCESS CONTROL

Value stream performance measurements are a primary control mechanism within the company. They not only drive the continuous improvement process, they also to ensure that out-of-control situations are resolved. Once a week, a team of experts from the CI teams closely review the performance measurement results and initiate action plans to solve problems and improve the processes.

This is a control mechanism—the actual outcomes are compared to the desired results and action is taken to bring the results into line with the expectations of the processes. If significant problems arise that are beyond the authority or capabilities of the CI team, then these problems are escalated to senior managers. The company's accounting and finance people are very concerned about the level of control within the business processes. The value stream performance measurements and the continuous improvement processes are keys to monitoring and maintaining control.

HOW DO VALUE STREAM MEASUREMENTS DIFFER FROM TRADITIONAL METRICS?

Some of the measurements used for lean value streams are similar to those used in traditional manufacturing organizations. The difference is how the measurements are used. Most traditional manufacturers measure by the entire production plant (rather than for value streams), and the results are usually reported monthly (rather than weekly). Most traditional manufacturers use the measurements to assess the capability and skill of the plant management team. The same measurements are used across all the plants, so that the plant managers can be compared and competition can be developed between the plants.

Lean value stream performance measurements are designed, to initiate continuous improvement, not to judge the managers' effectiveness. The measurements are usually reported weekly because this frequency fits the schedule of the value stream CI teams. Weekly reporting is also important for process control. Monthly reporting is usually too late to solve problems and bring the processes back under control.

The measurements are never used to create undesirable competition between the value streams. It is important for the value stream managers and their teams to work cooperatively and together. This cannot be achieved if the value stream managers are compared and judged.

Lean value stream measurements are used to create continuous improvements and as a primary control mechanism of the business. They drive change, not merely report outcomes. The actual numbers reported for each measurement are of less importance than the rate and direction of the change. The CI team is responsible for the rapid and continuous improvement of all the value stream measurements. The actual result achieved varies from one value stream to another, but all value streams must show steady, step-by-step improvement of the measurement results.

The Starter Set

There is no right set of measurements for a lean value stream, but over the past 10 years of working with many lean value streams, we have developed the following starter set:

- Performance measurements that reflect lean thinking

- Measures that can be presented visually

- Measures that are tried and tested within lean manufacturing companies

These measurements are not perfect and they do not fit every situation, but they are a good starting point for most lean pilots.

The complete starter set is shown in Figure 8.1. In this chapter, we will address the value stream measurements only. The other starter set measurements are described in Chapter 3 and Chapter 19.

The value stream measurements contained in the BMA, Inc. starter set contains just six measures. It is important to have few measurements. To focus people's attention and motivate continuous lean improvement, we must select a few, well-chosen measures. The measurements also provide a balance of information, are easy to understand and use, and reflect lean issues.

Strategic Issues	Strategic Measures	Value Stream Measures	Cell/Process Measures
Increase cash flow Increase sales and market share Continuous improvement culture	Sales growth EBITDA Inventory days On-time delivery Customer satisfaction Sales per employee	Sales per person On-time delivery Dock-to-dock time First time through Average cost per unit AR days outstanding	Day-by-the-hour production WIP-to-SWIP First time through Operation equipment effectiveness

Figure 8.1: Lean Performance Measurements Starter Set

BOX SCORES

The box score provides a summary of the value stream performance. A box score is typically updated weekly with the latest operational and financial information.

Performance measurements and value stream profitability are updated every week. Value stream capacity is updated only when a major change is made to the value stream and new value stream maps and cost analyses are completed.

There are several uses for the box score.[1] Here we use it to present the weekly performance information used by the value stream manager and his/her team to monitor the operation and create improvement.

SALES PER PERSON

Sales per person measures the value created by the value stream—the productivity of the value stream. It is important that the productivity of the value stream increases steadily over time.[2] When productivity increases, the value stream can make and sell more products with the same resources, and, therefore, the value stream increases its value.

How Do I Measure Sales per Person?

To measure sales per person you need to know the sales and the number of people involved. The sales are the sales value of the products manufactured in the value stream. It is necessary to identify the sales orders or products associ-

---

1. Chapter 10, "Using the Box Score" and Chapter 18, "The Lean Accounting Diagnostic," provide more detailed explanation of the box score.

2. Jacobs Brakes, a division of Danaher Corporation has a very effective lean manufacturing process. The sales per person at "Jake Brakes" is measured in terms of units per person. Jake Brakes have shown a consistent increase in units per person of 2 percent per month for more than 10 years. The graph is almost a straight line, despite recessions and business downturns. This is an excellent application of continuous value stream improvement.

ated with the value stream. This usually requires setting a flag or field within the sales processing systems and coding the sales order to identify which value stream the order-lines belong to. Sales so coded are then reported by value stream. The number of people refers to everyone who works in the value stream. These will all be people assigned permanently to that value stream. If part-time or temporary people are employed within the value stream, these may be included as equivalent full-time heads. As mentioned in previous chapters, in the early stages of value stream management it may be necessary to allocate a person to more than one value stream[3] and to use equivalent heads. However, you should only do this for a short period of time, because it can easily distort the results. As soon as possible you should use cross training to eliminate the need for people being assigned to more than one value stream.

What Should Be the Target?

As with all lean performance measurements, we are less interested in the actual result and more interested in the rate of change. Radically, lean organizations establish goals of 20 percent or 25 percent improvement per year. This is the equivalent of 1.5 percent to 2 percent per month. Other companies establish less ambitious levels of achievement.

It is best to set targets as general, long-term goals. The people within the value stream need to set their own local and short-term targets. The lean principle of empowerment and accountability comes into play here. The people on the lean team will have the authority to determine their own approach to the achievement of the long-term goals.

ALTERNATIVE MEASUREMENTS

For some companies units per person is a better measurement than sales per person, because it is easier for people to understand. For units per person to work well, the products must be very similar. If the value stream has an entirely homogenous product family, then units per person is excellent. If the value stream manufactures a wide range of products with different prices, processes, and materials, then sales per person is more helpful.

In highly machine-driven operations, it can be useful to measure sales per machine hour. Machine hours must be either the total machine hours available, or the machine hours for the company's normal working hours. Do not use machine run-time, because this distorts the result. First, it requires tracking of machine hours—a wasteful action—and it shows improvement even if the sales go down and the manufacturing time decreases.

Temporary or part-time people employed in the value stream can be included as equivalent heads, or you can report them by sales per labor hour, where the labor hour is the number of hours for everyone in the value stream.

---

3. See Chapter 7, "Managing by Value Stream" and Chapter 9, "Value Stream Costing."

Companies with heavy seasonality find sales per person to be difficult because they may be building to temporary seasonal inventory. Seasonality shows great fluctuations in the sales per person according to the season. These companies often use units manufactured per person. This must be used carefully as there is no productivity in making a product; only in selling a product. In a highly seasonal environment, however, it can be necessary to build inventory during one part of the year and sell from finished goods during the high season.

Some organizations prefer to measure earnings per person rather than sales, so they can focus on the profitability of the value stream.

On-Time Shipment

On-time shipment is a measure of the percentage of orders shipped to customers on time and measures the level of control within the value stream. If the value stream is under control, on-time shipments are high. If the on-time shipment is low, then the value stream is not performing and the processes are out of control.

Measuring the level of control is very important to finance people in a lean organization. As Lean Accounting progresses, the traditional, transaction-based control systems are eliminated in favor of lean operational control. The finance people use the performance measurement to ensure that processes are under control. On-time shipment is a good general measure of the degree of control within the processes.

How Do I Measure On-Time Shipment?

On-time shipment is measured as the percentage of customer orders that are shipped on the date they are due for shipment. There are several different methods of calculating this. Some operations track the number of units shipped in comparison to the number of units required. Others track the number of order lines shipped complete; and others track the number of full orders shipped on time. Some companies track the shipment date against the date the products were promised to the customer; others measure from the shipment date requested by the customer. In most cases, an order shipped earlier than the shipment date would be regarded as not on time.

The most stringent measurement is full orders shipped against the customer-requested date. The least demanding measurement is the number of units shipped on time in comparison to the promise date. It is not important which measurement method is used, providing it is suitable for the products and the customers, and provided the value stream team focuses their work on improving the results. If you start using a less demanding measurement, then, when the percentage reaches the high 90s, you can introduce a more stringent method. This way you will continue to improve and perfect the process.

If the company has a major customer who reports its on-time receipts, then it makes sense to use the same method of measurement in the customer reports.

Alternative Measurements

The measurement of on-time shipments usually requires a computer system to track the due date and the shipment date. Most lean organizations prefer to use manual and visual methods of performance measurement. A good manual measure counts the number of orders (or order lines or units) that each day should have been shipped, but were not. This tracks just the delinquent orders, which can be reported visually on a performance measurement board. Sometimes the delinquent orders are divided into those that are one day late, two days late, etc. This measurement can be displayed with other box-score measures, or, alternatively, shown on the visual board used to schedule the customer orders. This way the delinquent orders can be readily seen and there is no need for additional reporting.

If the data is available, it can be better to measure on-time deliveries, rather than on-time shipments. Companies that have a method of real-time reporting of receipts from their customers can use this kind of reporting. Measuring on-time delivery is better than on-time shipment, because shipping the product does not add value for the customer; only receiving the product does.

Dock–to–Dock Time

Dock-to-dock measures the flow of materials through the value stream. It is the time it takes for a component or raw material to go from the receiving dock, through production, and to shipment from the shipping dock. It is the speed of conversion of raw material into a finished product within this value stream.

Lean manufacturing is very concerned about flow; in this case, the flow of materials. The third principle of lean thinking focuses on flow.[4] There are three kinds of flow: material, information, and cash. Lean organizations place great emphasis on increasing the speed of flow. Dock-to-dock is the measurement we use to motivate the improvement of material flow. As the dock-to-dock days (or hours) come down, the rate of material flow increases, and the level of inventory in the value stream decreases.

How Do I Measure Dock–to–Dock Time?

Dock-to-dock is calculated by counting the total inventory within the value stream and dividing by the average rate of products shipped. The inventory includes raw materials, work-in-process, and finished goods. The rate of shipments is the average number of end units shipped per hour. The result is the inventory within the value stream expressed in hours (or days).

$$\frac{\text{Dock-to-dock}}{\text{Hours}} = \frac{\text{(Raw Material + WIP + Finished Goods Inventory)}}{1} \Big/ \frac{\text{Products Shipped this Week /}}{\text{Hours in the Week}}$$

For example, a value stream has the following inventory:

---

4. See Womack, James and Jones, Daniel, *Lean Thinking*, pp. 50–66, John Wiley & Sons, 1996.

Inventory	Shipments	Dock–to–Dock
Raw materials: 46 units Work-in-process: 72 units Finished goods: 6 units	Units shipped this week 1203 Hours this week = 80 Shipment per hour = 15.04	124 units / 15.04 Ships per hr = 8.24 hours
TOTAL 124 units		

How Do I Gather the Data?

Companies with a simple product and few component parts can just count the number of items in inventory. The number of units shipped per week is readily available from the shipping and sales information. The dock-to-dock time is then calculated manually.

Companies with more complex products, but a good kanban pull system throughout the value stream, can count the kanbans for the primary flow of the product and multiply by the kanban quantity to obtain the total inventory quantity.

Most organizations need to use representative parts. The problem is that most production processes have hundreds of parts, raw materials, components, WIP sub-assemblies, and finished products. To count these manually each week is arduous and wasteful. The solution is to count representative parts.

A representative part is a component purchased from a supplier that is used in every stage of manufacture, and is present in the finished products. The representative part must be a mainstream component of the product because we use it to represent the entire material flow of the product. A typical representative part in a machine shop is a purchased casting. The casting is received from the supplier and a certain amount of component inventory is maintained, either adjacent to the first cell or in a stockroom. The casting is machined through the production process and assembled into a finished product. The WIP inventory that contains the casting is readily identifiable. The finished product contains the casting and to count the quantity of castings in finished goods, count the number of finished goods. Once each week, a materials handler (or other value stream team member) counts the number of representative parts in the value stream. This number is then used to calculate the dock-to-dock hours. In electronics manufacture, a printed circuit board is often used as a representative part.

One of our customers manufactures guitars and the dock-to-dock is calculated by counting the number of guitar necks throughout the process. These exist as blanks in the wood shop, as machined necks in the wood parts finishing cells, and as a neck in the various stages of manufacture. The company fabricates thousands of different parts; but every guitar has a neck in one stage of production or another. Raw material (wood) is not included in the dock-to-dock calculation, because this is purchased opportunistically and requires many years of curing and preparation.

Another customer has an injection molding and assembly operation. The principle material flow centers around the plastic used in the injection molding process. The plastic is counted by weight. The raw materials are stored in drums, or gaylords, by weight. This material is replenished daily by supplier kanban and the level of inventory is quite consistent. The work-in-process (WIP) inventory weight is gathered by counting the kanbans in production. There are generally only a handful of WIP kanbans at any one time, and the plastic weight of the product represented by the kanban is printed on the card. Similarly, any finished goods inventory is managed using kanban pull cards with the plastic weight printed on the card. The materials person counts the kanbans, calculates the total weight and dock-to-dock using a report that shows the plastic weight of shipped products. The product weight information is easily obtained from the product bills of materials, which express the plastic content in terms of grams.

If it is not possible to identify representative parts, then it may be necessary to use inventory figures from the company's perpetual inventory system. This is undesirable because it violates the lean practice of manual and visual measurement. Also, our objective is to eliminate the perpetual inventory system over time. However, it is often a necessary compromise when there are no clearly identifiable representative parts.

How is Dock-to-Dock Reported?

The dock-to-dock time is generally reported weekly along with the other value stream performance measurements. The results can be displayed graphically as a run chart, block chart, or other visual method. Alternatively, the dock-to-dock can be shown on the box score as a primary value stream measurements.

Alternative Measurements

Some companies just track the total inventory within the value stream in pieces, weight, or money. Others use the classic stock-turns ratio. Some choose to focus on the primary materials while others choose to include all of the inventory. If the total inventory is included, changes in flow may be obscured by massively overstocked or obsolete materials. The purpose of this measurement is to focus on the flow of materials. We are not trying to measure the entire inventory at this time. The entire inventory will be shown on the Balance Sheet and is often included in the plant-level performance measurements.

Other lean organizations do not focus just on the material flow. They create a composite measurement that includes material flow, with order processing flow, and cash flow. The purpose of this kind of measurement is to draw attention to the fact that the flow of information and the flow of cash are equally important to the flow of materials.

FIRST TIME THROUGH

The First Time Through (FTT) measures the percentage of products manufactured in the value stream without any rework, repair, retesting, recalibration, or scrap. While some see this as a measurement of production quality, it is better thought of as a measurement of process capability. To increase the value stream's FTT, you should address all the processes within the value stream and eliminate the variability within the processes. The successful introduction of standardized work is a key to good FTT results. FTT also can be considered as a measurement of the degree of standardization within the company's work methods. How well is the standardized work working?

How Do I Measure First Time Through?

You will remember that FTT is also a measurement contained in the starter set for the production cells in Chapter 3. The FTT for the value stream is calculated by multiplying together all of the FTTs for the cells within the value stream.

These may be production cells, but they can also be no-production cells like order entry, invoicing, product configuration, etc. Anytime a process is performed there is always an opportunity for error—FTT is used to help systematically eliminate these errors by identifying them and allowing the CI teams to find the root cause and devise a permanent solution to the problem.

In the following example, the value stream contains six steps. Each step has a cell-level measurement of FTT. The Value Stream FTT is calculated by multiplying the six cell-level FTT measures to calculate their combined effects.

Value Stream FTT						
Order Entry	Fabrication	Sub-Assembly	Final Assembly	Shipping	Invoicing	TOTAL VALUE STREAM
92%	88%	95%	100%	90%	85%	58.84%

A Word of Warning

First Time Through at the value stream level can be discouraging. If there are many steps in the value stream, and the FTT for each step is recorded, the individual FTTs may be quite good—more than 90 percent, for example—but when all the steps are multiplied together, a series of high results can very quickly become disappointingly low. It is not unusual for the value stream FTT to be 20 percent or less. Some companies have had value stream FTTs of zero for many weeks when one cell or another had a serious quality or process problem.

The purpose of measuring the value stream FTT is to highlight the level of control within the process to the CI team and the value stream manager. These are the people who can work systematically to standardize the work and eliminate variability.

Alternative Measurement

Some companies use PPM (parts rejected per million) as their principle measurement of process quality. This may measure the internal PPM—the parts rejected throughout the production process—or it may measure the parts rejected by the customer. Other companies use scrap rates or production yield measurements.

These measurements are successful in many organizations and readily understandable to the people. They do not, however, encompass as much as FTT. FTT tracks rejects, scrap, *and* rework. It is the tracking of detailed rework that helps to bring improvement to the standardized work.

AVERAGE COST PER UNIT

An argument can be made for not reporting product costs to the value stream manager and his or her team. Our experience is that most value stream managers find the average cost per item to be an important indicator of the overall improvement of the value stream processes.

How Do I Measure the Average Cost per Unit?

The average unit cost is calculated by gathering all the costs of the value stream for the week and dividing by the quantity of units shipped to customers that week. Some value streams use the average of the total value stream costs (including material costs); others use the average conversion cost per unit. (The conversion cost is the total value stream cost less the material costs.) If the products are very similar and have similar material costs, then the average of the total cost is suitable. If the products have divergent material costs, but similar production processes, then the average conversion cost is more useful. For example, a value stream manufacturing similar products from both aluminum and titanium will have very different material costs from one product to the next, but the conversion processes are similar. The average conversion cost makes a good value stream measurement.

The total value stream cost is calculated using the Value Stream Costing methods described in Chapter 9. The costs include all the costs of the value stream, including the material costs, the machine costs, the labor costs including the production operators and all the people supporting the operation, facilities costs, and other costs such as supplies and tooling. As the company begins to be managed by value stream, it becomes easy to collect all the costs as direct costs to the value stream. There is no distinction between production labor costs and other support costs. The diagram in Figure 8.2 shows this direct, summary collection of costs.

Once the total value stream cost for the week is available, we can calculate the average cost. The average cost is the total cost divided by the number of products shipped to customers. The number of products shipped can be readily determined from the sales and invoicing systems. An example is shown in Figure 8.3.

How Valid is the Average Cost?

The average product cost is meaningful and useful if all the products in the value stream are similar. The average cost is also meaningful if the products

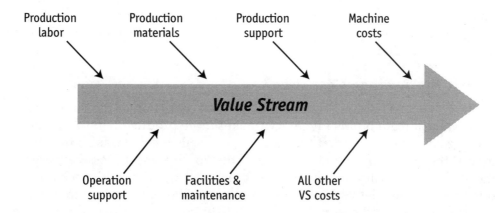

All labor, materials, machines, support services, and facilities directly within the value stream. Little or no allocation.

Figure 8.2: Value Stream Summary Direct Costs

Employee cost	$ 34,130
Machine cost	$ 3,230
Outside processing	$ 3,441
Other costs	$ 6,713
Materials costs	$ 60,125
Value stream cost	$107,639
Conversion cost	$ 47,514
Units shipped	3,000
Average product cost	$ 35.88
Average conversion cost	$ 15.84

Figure 8.3: Calculating the Average Cost for the Value Stream

in the value stream are dissimilar, but the mix of production is reasonably consistent each week. Sometimes the average cost is shown as a moving average over a longer period so that the trend is not obscured by weekly mix changes.

Many lean companies use level scheduling methods to even out the flow of production through the value stream. When this is used, a consistent production mix is forced upon the value stream flow and the average product cost becomes valid.

If the value stream has a heterogeneous mix of products and/or the products are custom-designed and manufactured in small quantities, then it can be necessary to normalize the average cost to take into account the product mix. The features and characteristics described in Chapter 11 to calculate product costs are used for this normalization. Normalization of the average cost should be avoided, as it brings complexity and an element of subjectivity into the calculation.

How is the Average Cost Used?

The average cost per unit highlights the overall direction of the value stream. If the value stream builds inventory (makes more product than sales), the average cost will increase. If the value stream sells more products than it makes, the average cost will go down. If the volume of business increases, the average cost will go down. If there are problems with bottleneck operations and on-time deliveries, the average cost will go up. As lean improvements take place and cost reduction initiatives come to fruition, the average cost reduces.

Average cost is a summary of the changes taking place in the value stream and the market/customers being served. The value stream cost information shows the real, actual direct costs of the value stream. The sales quantity is real, or the actual number sold that week. The average cost reflects the real changes taking place, for better or worse.

Many lean manufacturing initiatives do not have an immediate financial impact, but the improvements accrue over time. These improvements manifest themselves in the average cost of the product over time. For example, as the value stream introduces visual management methods, 5S, and pull systems short-term financial improvements are unlikely, but the people in the value stream will work more effectively, owing to easy availability of information. Another example is a company that redesigned its products to reduce the number of raw materials, components, and sub-assemblies, while increasing the variety of finished products. This was a substantial effort with no short-term, tangible effects on the bottom line. However, the changes were reflected in the gradual and steady reduction in average product cost.

As a summary measurement, the average cost leads the value stream team to research root causes and initiate many different kinds of projects to bring the cost down. The best way to reduce cost is to increase sales without increasing resources; this is the lean way.

The average cost is used when calculating product costs using features and characteristics. This is described in Chapter 11. The average value stream cost is also used as a part of the target costing process described in Chapter 17. In some circumstances, the average cost can also be used for inventory valuation, but the primary use of the average cost is to point the value stream team towards ongoing improvement.

Alternative Measurements

Some value streams measure the average total cost of the product. Others use the conversion cost. Some prefer to break the cost down to the costs of various steps of the value stream; for example, procurement cost, conversion cost, distribution cost, etc.

ACCOUNTS RECEIVABLE DAYS OUTSTANDING

This measurement of the speed in which cash is received from the customers is widely used. Lean manufacturers are concerned about flow, and this includes cash flow. Accounts receivable is an important element of cash flow.

Many lean organizations are more focused on cash flow than on profitability, because they recognize that as material and information flow increase, cash flow improves. The element of cash flow over which the company has the least direct control is the accounts receivable time.

How Do I Measure AR Days Outstanding?

This measurement is well known. It divides the accounts receivable (AR) balance by the average daily sales amount:

AR days outstanding = AR balance / (Monthly sales / # days in the month)

SUPPORTING MEASUREMENTS

The primary value stream performance measurements in the BMA, Inc. starter set are:

- Sales per person
- On-time delivery
- Dock-to-dock hours
- First time through (FTT)
- Average product cost
- Accounts receivable days outstanding

In addition to these performance measurements, most companies like to track some other information. These supporting measures do not track the value stream performance, but they do provide useful information about the value stream's progress with lean transformation.

Safety Cross

The safety cross shows the days in the month and indicates if the day was accident-free, had a near-accident, a reported accident, or a lost-time accident. If this information is tracked at the cell level, then the value stream safety cross will be the sum of the cell information.

Cross–Training

Figure 8.4 shows the level of cross-training among the value stream people. The chart lists the people in the value stream together with the tasks and methods the people must be trained in. Colored shapes are used to show who is cross-trained in which tasks. The shape of the mark indicates if the person is just trained, or certified, or they are trainers themselves.

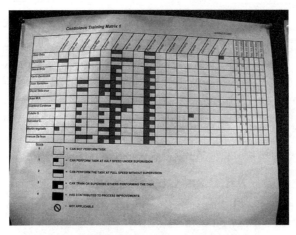

Figure 8.4: Value Stream Cross-Training Chart

Improvement Project Participation

Some companies find it helpful to keep track of how many people within the organization are actively working on improvement projects. When participation in improvement projects is voluntary within the company, then this measurement gives an indication of the degree of commitment and enthusiasm within the work force. Even when participation is required, it is still useful to keep track of how many people are actively working on improvements, as this shows how quickly the principles of continuous improvement are taking hold within the organization.

PRESENTING THE INFORMATION

The value stream performance measurements should be presented visually. Most of the measurements are manually created by the value stream team members and should be prominently displayed on a performance measurement board. The performance measurement board is often posted in the team room, where the continuous improvement team(s) works. In some organizations, they are displayed in the cafeteria where team-members and others can sit together and work on the issues.

These measurements are working documents. They are not used for marketing purposes or for reporting to senior managers or corporate organizations. There is no need to make the information look good—it must be readily available, timely, and clear.[5]

The performance measurement board will also have information about the improvement projects the CI team is currently working on. This informa-

---

5. Organizations occasionally become troubled about displaying this information visually. They are concerned that a customer or corporate executive visiting the plant might see the information and use it against the plant. If this is so, then they will have to develop a method of covering the information when visitors are in the building.

tion shows who is doing the work, the status of the project, the data being used, and the story of the project.

Examples of visual performance measurement boards are given in Figures 8.5 and 8.6.

Figure 8.5: Performance Measurements in a Continuous Improvement Team Room

Figure 8.6: Performance Measurement Board on the Shop Floor

MAKING THE VALUE STREAM PERFORMANCE MEASUREMENTS WORK

The value stream performance measurements are used primarily to motivate continuous improvement. To achieve this, formal method for the continuous improvement process must be in place. In most organizations, this happens through CI teams.

Listed below are some methods that successful lean companies use to make their value stream measures work:

1. The no-blame environment discussed in Chapter 3 is extended to the value stream. The measurements are not used to assess whether the value stream is doing well or not; they are used to initiate lean (and other) improvement projects designed to move all the value stream performance measurements in the right direction every week. The value stream performance measurements are the property of the value stream team. They create them, usually manually; they use them; and they are responsible for the outcome of the measurements.

   In line with the fifth principle of lean thinking—the pursuit of perfection—the value stream team is charged with making systematic, ongoing, relentless process improvement. The performance measurements (together with the weekly value stream profit and loss statement and target costs[6]) guide the team members in their pursuit of perfection.

2. It is unhelpful to compare one value stream with another. The measurements for two or more value streams may be the same, but it is counter-productive to develop undesirable comparisons between them. It is important for the value stream managers and the value stream teams to work together and, through cross-training, help each other out when high demands or problems arise. We want to share improvement opportunities and methods across the value streams so that good work in one value stream can be readily incorporated into the others.

3. The continuous improvement teams should use a standard, formal improvement method. There are many good methods. The starting point of most of the processes is the need to identify effectively the problem that must be solved, or the opportunity that must be developed. This is done using the value stream performance measurements, the target cost voice-of-the-customer information, and the value stream profit and loss statement.

4. The performance measurements must be directly related to the company's business strategy. The starter set measurements are based upon a typical business strategy for a company pursuing lean manufacturing and lean thinking. However, company strategies vary and they change. The measurement systems must fully support the business strategy.

   It is not necessary to set the performance measurement the same for all the value streams. There are often considerable differences within the company's various value streams. Consistency of measurement can be helpful, but not at the expense of the usefulness and usability of the measurement set.

   The performance measurement linkage chart, shown in Chapter 21, is designed to ensure the company's performance measurements support and enhance the company's business strategy.

---

6. See Chapter 16.

SUMMARY

This chapter presented the BMA, Inc. starter set for value stream performance measurements. We do not claim that this is the last word on value stream performance measurements, but this starter set has been tried and tested in a number of lean organizations.

Here is a summary of the starter set measurements:

Value Stream Performance Measurement	What does it Measure?	Lean Principle
Sales per person	Productivity of the value stream expressed in terms of sales amount achieved per person. Sales amount divided by the number of people in the value stream.	Increase value created with the same, or less, resources.
On-time shipment	The ability of the value stream to ship products to customers on the day (or time) required by the customer. Percentage of sales order lines shipped on the right day.	Bring all the processes within the value stream under control.
Dock-to-dock time	The amount of inventory throughout the value stream expressed in days or hours of requirement. Total amount of inventory of within the value stream divided by the rate of shipment of products.	Increase the rate of material flow through the value stream.
First Time Through (FTT)	The ability of the value stream to make the product and perform the service perfectly every time. The product of the FTTs calculated at each step in the value stream process.	Make to standardized work every time throughout the value stream processes.
Average product cost	Total value stream cost divided by the number of products shipped to customers.	Continuously reduce the amount of resources required to make and sell the products.
Accounts receivable days outstanding	The amount of money owed by customers expressed in days of shipments. Total amount of money owed by customers for products shipped from the value stream divided by the average shipment sales value.	Increase the rate of cash flow through the value stream.

CHAPTER 9

Value Stream Costing

Value stream costing is introduced when a company's lean manufacturing methods begin to mature. It reduces waste because it eliminates most of the transactions associated with cost accounting. Value stream costing provides relevant and timely information to the value stream team-members. Value stream costing is simple; everybody can understand where the financial information comes from and what it means. Value stream costing does not require wasteful tracking of information, because the financial data is gathered and reported in summary form for each value stream, not for each production job or product. Unlike standard costing, we do not try to report the so-called actual cost of each production job. The value stream costs are reported each week using up-to-date cost information.

We no longer need to report or backflush the labor and overhead costs. You will remember from Chapter 5 that backflushing is used to relieve inventory and to cost production work orders without the need to track labor, materials, machine, and overhead resources manually against the work orders as they pass through production. Backflushing is achieved by multiplying the number of items produced by the standard cost of the resources required to produce them, once the items are complete, rather than tracking them as they are applied. This reduces the number of transactions required to maintain the standard cost data. In the early stages of lean manufacturing most companies introduce backflushing of production jobs, to keep the inventory records up-to-date and to apply cost to the production job. These costs include material, labor, and overhead costs. If the standard costs are accurate, backflushing provides a reasonable approximation of the cost of the products made. However, as companies progress with lean manufacturing, they replace the work orders with kanban and other pull systems to authorize and control production. At this point, product-oriented costing using standard costing can be replaced by a process-oriented method called value stream costing. When value stream costing is introduced, we can stop backflushing the labor and overhead costs. They are no longer needed because costs are not collected by production job; they are collected for the value stream as a whole. Thus, very few transactions are required to support value stream costing. (This topic is also covered in Chapters 5 and 12).

Value stream costing provides better information than traditional standard costing. The value stream cost information contains the real cost of the value stream. The information is not distorted and complicated by the allocation of overheads. The average cost information from the weekly value stream costing provides one of the primary value stream performance measurements and is used to drive improvement in the value stream.

Value stream cost information can be readily and reliably used for day-to-day decision-making. This information is related to such issues as the profitability of an order or contract, make/buy decisions, product rationalization, etc.

Value stream costing can be easily understood by anybody. One of the problems with traditional standard costing is that few people in the company really understand the costs and how they are calculated. Overhead absorption, while driving people's behavior, is rarely understood. There is no mystery or complexity about value stream costing. It is simple to understand, and therefore useful to people throughout the value stream and the company.

WHAT IS WRONG WITH TRADITIONAL STANDARD COSTING?

One way to answer this question is simply to say there is nothing wrong with traditional standard costing. It was designed to support the mass-production methods used so successfully by American (and other) manufacturers throughout the 20th century. Standard costing works quite well within that context. The problem arises when an organization wants to move to lean manufacturing and away from mass production. The assumptions behind traditional standard costing support mass production. These same assumptions are harmful when applied to lean manufacturing.

One assumption made regarding standard costing is that all overheads need to be assigned to the product and that these overheads relate (in most cases) to the amount of labor required to make the product. This leads to the distortion of product costs. Some products appear to cost more than they really do and other products appear to cost less. These costs are misleading and cause wrong decisions to be made relating to pricing, profitability, make/buy, and so forth.

Standard costing motivates non-lean behavior in operations. The key measurements used with a standard costing system include the personal efficiency of production workers, the utilization of machines and equipment, and the amount of overhead absorbed by production each month. It does not take long for production managers, supervisors, and operators to recognize that the best way to show good results on these key measurements is to use large batch quantities and build inventory. This is the opposite of lean manufacturing. Standard costing actively motivates non-lean behaviors.

Standard costing requires an expensive and wasteful data collection system. Traditional companies use standard costing as their primary method of maintaining control of production costs. To achieve this they must track the actual costs at each stage in production. This leads to the development of complicated shop-floor data collection systems and the generation of huge quantities of wasteful and confusing transactions. This, in turn, leads to the implementation of wasteful and confusing computer systems.

This kind of data collection system is the opposite of lean thinking. Every transaction is wasteful. These transactions then lead to reports and meetings that are equally wasteful. The information is hidden inside the computer, instead of providing dynamic visual management, and is often reported too late to be useful. The reports rarely lead to the kind of ongoing continuous improvement required by lean-thinking organizations.

Standard costing does not provide the information required to support and motivate lean manufacturing. The costs are provided by product and work centers; there is no understanding of the value stream or the flow of the process.

Waste is concealed within the standard cost. Instead of revealing waste, accounting systems hide it within overhead allocations and it is very difficult to unravel. An emphasis on reducing the standard cost often leads to changes being made in the process that do not reduce the true cost of the product, and often increase it.

The genesis of these problems lies in the assumptions of standard costing, which are derived from the assumptions of traditional batch and queue mass production. The following are just a few of these assumptions:

- There is one ideal cost for any product.
- Overhead costs are directly related to the amount of labor required to make the product.
- Maximum profitability comes from the maximum utilization of production resources.
- All excess capacity is bad.
- High levels of customer service are provided by high levels of inventory.
- Production costs are controlled by the detailed tracking of actual costs.
- Cost optimization is achieved by optimizing each individual part of the production process.

Lean manufacturing and lean thinking violate these assumptions. The cost of the product varies according to the product volume and the production mix. Overhead costs are related to the value stream as a whole and not to production labor time. Maximum profitability comes from creating the maximum flow of product through the value stream at the pull of the customer. The cost of any particular product depends primarily on how quickly it flows through the value stream, particularly at the bottleneck operations within the value stream. We are much more interested in the rate of flow through the value stream than we are with the utilization of resources, the efficiency of each individual, or overhead allocations.

A lean organization needs a cost accounting process that:

- Focuses on the value stream
- Is simple and easy to use

- Provides usable value stream performance measurements
- Eliminates the need for transactions and overhead calculations
- Is clearly understandable to anyone

Value stream costing fulfils these needs.

How Does Value Stream Costing Work?

Value stream cost is typically calculated weekly and takes account of all the costs in the value stream. It makes no distinction between direct costs and indirect costs; all the costs within the value stream are considered direct. Costs outside of the value stream are not included in our value stream costing.

Figure 9.1 shows the costs that make up the total value stream cost. These include all labor costs, traditionally direct costs, and traditionally indirect costs. Employees working in the value stream are included, irrespective of whether they make the product, move materials, design the product, maintain machines, plan production, make sales, or do the accounting.

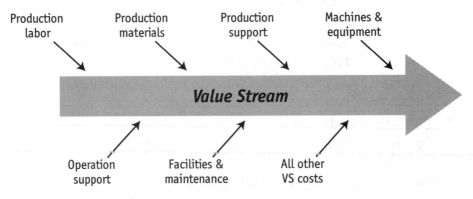

All labor, machine, materials, support services, and facilities directly within the value stream. Little or no allocation.

Figure 9.1: Costs included in Value Stream Costing

The production material costs are generally calculated from how much material has been purchased for the value stream during the week. Every time material is brought into the plant, its cost is assigned to the value stream. The total value stream material cost is the sum of everything purchased during the week. For this material cost to be valid, raw materials and work-in-process inventories must be low, and under good control. If the inventories are low, the materials brought in during the week will be used quickly and will accurately reflect the material cost of the product manufactured during the week.

Support costs, like spare parts and soft tooling, often are purchased for the value stream using a purchase credit card assigned to the value stream, so the costs are directly posted to the value stream cost/profit center. The costs of consumables, supplies, and other day-to-day expenses are similarly assigned to the value stream.

The only allocation used regularly within value stream costing is a square footage (or square meters) cost for the facility. The reason for this is to motivate the value stream team-members to reduce the amount of space used by the value stream.

The facilities cost assigned to the value stream will be the cost per foot multiplied by the amount of square feet used by the value stream. The cost per square foot is obtained by dividing the total facilities cost (the sum of the rental payment/depreciation cost for the manufacturing building, the amount spent for utilities, building maintenance, guard and security service, etc.) by the total square feet encompassed by the manufacturing plant. The square footage occupied by the value stream includes the production area, stockroom area, and the office space area used by the people working in the value stream. There is no attempt to fully absorb the facilities costs; only the square footage used by the value stream is included.

Occasionally, the utilities costs are significant and vary considerably between value streams. In such a case, each value stream is metered and the utilities costs are applied as direct value stream costs.

The value stream costs for ECI are shown in Figure 9.2.

	Material cost	Outside cost	Employee cost	Machine cost	Other cost	TOTAL COST
Customer service	–	–	$12,108	–	–	$12,108
Purchasing	–	–	16,145	–	–	16,145
SMT	358,512	–	17,080	16,956	20,000	412,548
Hand load/wave post	25,608	–	23,485	2,016	–	51,109
Test and rework	–	–	17,080	3,528	–	20,608
Assemble and burn-in	128,040	–	10,675	–	–	138,715
Shipping	–	–	2,669	–	–	2,669
Quality assurance	–	–	8,073	–	–	8,073
Manufacturing engineering	–	–	8,073	–	–	8,073
Maintenance	–	–	8,073	–	–	8,073
Accounting	–	–	8,073	–	–	8,073
Information systems	–	–	4,036	–	–	4,036
Design engineering	–	7,760	4,036	–	–	11,796
	$512,160	$7,760	$139,606	$22,500	$20,000	$702,026

Figure 9.2: Value Stream Costs for ECI

The total value stream cost for the week amounted to $702,026. During the week in question, the company shipped 2,134 units of product. The average cost of the product is $328.97.

What is Value Stream Costing Used For?

The results of this simple approach to cost accounting are used to create a value stream P&L and a value stream performance measurement table. The P&L includes the revenue from sales of the value stream during the period less the materials and conversion costs expended during the same period. Figure 9.3 shows the P&L for the ECI value stream.

Electronic Components, Inc. Controller Products Value Stream	
Revenue	$1,280,400
Material costs	$512,160
Conversion costs	$184,380
Value stream profit	$583,860
ROS	45.60%
Inventory	$593,008

Figure 9.3: P&L for the ECI Value Stream

This information is shown in the Box Score in Figure 9.4.

The purpose of the box score is to provide the Value Stream Manager and team with a succinct view of the value stream's performance. The value stream performance measurements are shown in the upper section. A simplified value stream P&L is shown in the lower section, and the current capacity usage is shown in the center section.

The box score is usually reported weekly and shows several weeks of prior history as well as the results for this week. The right-hand column is often used to show the goals the value stream team has set for each of the measurements. These goals do not come from wishful thinking, or by establishing stretch objectives. They come from the plans the team has in place for ongoing lean improvements. The value stream team (or the continuous improvement teams within the value stream) has a specific plan for kaizen events and continuous improvement projects to reach these objectives.

The box score format also is used to document the expected benefits of major lean improvements. This topic has been discussed at some length in Chapter 4. It is discussed in even greater depth in Chapter 21. There is more information about the box score in Chapter 10.

The average cost is sometimes calculated using just the conversion costs, rather than the total cost. This happens when the material costs vary significantly from one product to the next, but the conversion process is

	Last week 4-Oct	This week 11-Oct	Planned future state 31-Dec
Units per person	36.16	42.05	51.39
On-time shipment	98.00%	94.00%	98.00%
Dock-to-dock days	23.58	20.50	16.50
First time through	46%	42%	50%
Average product cost	$388.46	$348.66	$316.91
AR days	34.5	37.0	35.0
Productive	9.3%	10.8%	11.9%
Non-productive	63.7%	54.8%	49.3%
Available capacity	27.0%	34.4%	38.8%
Revenue	$1,101,144	$1,280,400	$1,408,440
Material cost	$462,480	$512,160	$535,207
Conversion cost	$250,435	$231,884	$208,696
Value stream gross profit	$388,228	$536,356	$664,537

Figure 9.4: Box Score for ECI

more consistent. The average conversion cost for ECI is $88.97 ($189,866 / 2134).

Occasionally the average cost is calculated for an attribute of the product rather than for the full product. For example, we have a client that machines hydraulic connectors that are used in the mechanisms contained in commercial aircraft wings and tail assemblies. These connectors help make the wing and tails move up, down, and sideways. They are configured as straight, Y-shaped, and X-shaped, and therefore have 2, 3, or 4 ends. Their manufacture is quite simple. Castings are purchased and then machined to suit the demand of the customer. The mix of products varies considerably from one week to the next. The average cost is reported per end rather than per unit, because this is the primary driver of the product cost.

WHY IS VALUE STREAM COSTING SIMPLE?

Value stream costing is simple because we do not collect the detailed actual costs by production job or product. Costs are collected for the total value stream and are summarized over the weekly period. Labor costs are not collected using any kind of tracking or backflushing of labor hours earned, or consumed in production making products. They are simply the sum of the wages and direct benefits paid to the people working in the value stream. This is derived from the payroll system.

Material costs also are collected in summary over the week. Once the company's inventory is low and under control, the material costs of the value stream will be the cost of the materials purchased for that value stream. All purchases are assigned to the cost center for that value stream. The same is true for supplies, tooling, and other costs. They are applied simply to the value stream cost center, or they are derived from the Accounts Payable process.

A further aspect of the simplicity of value stream costing is the reduction in cost centers. It is no longer necessary to have a huge number of departmental cost centers broken down into all kinds of cost elements. Instead, costs are collected for each value stream and each value stream has very few cost centers.

The information on the value stream Income Statement is real. It comprises what actually happened that week (or month). The revenue is the real amount of invoices processed for products manufactured in that value stream. The labor costs are what actually was spent on labor. Similarly for the material costs and other costs.

The elimination of overhead allocations means that the information provided is not complicated by the unnecessary application of costs outside the control of the value stream managers. This makes the cost and profit information real and understandable to the people working in the value stream and their managers.

How Can We Implement Value Stream Costing?

For value stream costing to work effectively, the following must be in place:

- Reporting needs to be by value stream, not by departments.
- The people in the company must be assigned to value streams with little or no overlap.
- There should be few (or no) shared services departments and few monuments.
- Production processes must be reasonably under control and low variability.
- There must be thorough tracking of "out-of-control" situations and of exceptions like scrap, rework, etc.
- Inventory must be reasonably under control, relatively low, and consistent.

In the early stages of value stream management, these criteria may not all be in place. There is usually a transition period when the costs are reported by value stream, but the information is derived from the old-style methods.

For example, the company may be organized in departments, and the people within the value streams are matrixed into the value stream, while still reporting organizationally to a department. The cost information is reported by department. When this occurs the labor costs are calculated for the value stream based upon the number of people working in the value stream. Often companies use an average cost per head for different categories of people, rather than go to the complexity of tracking each specific person's costs.

If a company is in the early stages of value stream management and some people are still working in more than one value stream, it is common for the labor costs to be calculated using equivalent heads. This is based upon a simple estimate of the amount of time spent in each value stream. We do not track the time—we use well-thought-out percentage splits. This is only temporary and will not continue for very long. It is important to create a real team of people working in the value stream and focus on creating value.

Monuments are dealt with in a similar way. We allocate the cost of the monuments using a simple percentage for each value stream using the monument. Over time the monuments will be eliminated, but this can take a long time.

To make value stream costing work, the value stream processes must be reasonably under control. Performance measurements are a key to understanding if these processes are under control. Performance measurements must be in place and working at the cells, non-production processes, and for the value streams. These will show that the processes are under control and indicate quickly when and where the processes are going wrong. This is why the cell level measures are reported by the hour and by the day. We can quickly correct out-of-control situations.

Similarly, to expense inventory as it is purchased, there must be low and consistent raw material and work-in-process inventory. If the inventory is still high, then we must track the inventory used by the value stream until the inventory is brought under control. This will require wasteful inventory transactions, but these are required until the inventory is brought under control.

Introducing value stream costing has a maturity path, just like any other aspect of Lean Accounting. It is introduced once the company moves into the management of value streams. In the early stages of lean manufacturing, when a company is working just on local production cells, there is no need to change the costing system. However, once the move has been made to working by value streams, then value stream costing becomes the best way to collect the costs and report the value stream profitability.

How Do We Handle Costs Outside the Value Stream?

In Chapter 7, on value stream management, we discussed that there are some people in the plant or organization who do not work in the value streams. These are people who do tasks unrelated to the value streams (financial accounting, for example) or their work crosses all value streams (ISO9000 or ISO14000 support, for example). The costs and expenses associated with these non-value stream tasks are *not* allocated to the value streams. They are treated as sustaining costs of the business. They are budgeted and controlled, but they are not allocated.

There is no need for full absorption costing. The purpose of the value stream costing is to provide relevant, accurate, and understandable cost information to the people managing the value streams. To absorb into the value stream any costs that occur outside the value stream does not provide anything helpful for managing or improving the value stream processes.

The non-value stream costs are inevitably small because most of the work of the organization will be associated with value streams. These costs will be reported on the plant or company P&L as sustaining costs (or a similar description) and people within these areas will be responsible for the elimination of these costs and improvement of the processes.

How Do We Know the Cost of a Product?

If costs are collected and reported by value stream and the average product cost is calculated, then we do not know the cost of individual products. The question to ask is: 'why is the product cost needed?'

Standard costs are typically used for the following reasons:

- Pricing decisions
- Profit margins on product lines and customer orders
- Performance measurement of the factory (using efficiency measures, utilization measurement, cost variance, and absorption)
- Process improvement through analysis of the product costs and the variances
- Make/buy decisions
- Product and customer rationalization
- Inventory valuation

When using value stream costing, it is not necessary to know the cost of specific products to make decisions on these issues. Pricing decisions for lean organizations are never made with reference to the cost of the product. Lean organizations focus on the value created for the customer or the market. It is value to the customer that determines the price. Customer value has no relationship to product cost.

Stating that prices are market-driven only begs another question: "Are we making a profit on this product if we sell at this price?" Once again, it is unhelpful to determine profitability by referencing the product cost. The right approach is to look at the potential order and work out the effect on the value stream profitability. Figure 9.5 is an example.

Standard costs are certainly not needed for the performance measurement of cells, value streams, or the plant itself. The performance measurements used by lean companies are described in Chapters 3 and 8. These are primarily non-financial performance measurements and make no reference to standard

	Current profitability 180 units	Profitability with new order 198 units	New order 18 units	
Revenue	$110,700	$121,320	$10,620	
Material cost	$44,280	$48,708	$4,428	
Conversion cost	$29,485	$29,485		
Value stream profit	$36,935	$43,127	$6,192	Contribution of the Order
Margin	33.36%	35.55%		

Figure 9.5: Example of Order Profitability using Value Stream Costing

costs or any kind of variances. The value stream performance measurements are the primary method of motivating continuous improvement throughout the value stream.

A decision relating to make/buy is again addressed with reference to the profitability of the value stream as a whole, not the individual product. Using a standard cost to determine the make/buy status of an item is dangerous. The standard cost will almost certainly lead to the wrong decision. If the value stream is capable of and has the capacity for making an item, then there is no (financial) reason for making the item outside. The cost of making it in-house is virtually nothing because the cost of the machines, the people, and the facility is already being paid for.

Alternatively, if there is no capacity within the value stream, then the cost of making the product in-house will be the cost of obtaining the additional resources to make the product. These resources may be simply additional overtime cost, or they may amount to capital investment to increase productive capacity.

The same story applies to such decisions as product or customer rationalization. It is pointless to look at an individual product and its cost. We must look at the effect of the change on the value stream profitability. If product family XYZ is removed from the value stream, how does this change the overall profitability of the value stream? Similarly, the effect of removing customer 123 is assessed at the value stream level, not the individual products or customer level.

Introducing new products into the value stream requires a similar analysis of value stream profitability. If there is capacity available within the value stream, then the introduction of the new product will increase value stream profitability by the contribution of the product. The contribution is the revenue minus the direct external costs. The direct external costs are usually just the materials and components required to make the product, but sometimes include such things as outside processing, or other services required outside the company. Labor or machine costs are not included in the contribution.

If the value stream does not have enough available capacity to make the additional products, then the value stream profitability is calculated taking into account the additional people and machines required to provide the necessary additional capacity. These calculations can be done for various levels of sales for the new product, so that the profitability can be assessed for various production volumes. These assessments often include the marketing forecasts of future sales quantities and prices.

Standard costs are not required for valuing inventory, providing the inventory levels are low and under control. When lean manufacturing is introduced into a value stream the level of inventory falls substantially. If the inventory level is low then the valuation of the inventory is far less important than when inventory is high. If, for example, a value stream has three months of customer demand of inventory, then it is very important to value this inventory in a detailed way, like the use of standard costs. If the inventory is less than five days of customer demand, then the materiality of the inventory value to the calculation of the company's profits and financial position is low.

When inventory is low and under control, there are several methods of valuing inventory. These run from the use of average costs, the use of direct material costs, but adjusted for the labor and overhead required to bring the valuation up to full absorption, through to a simple calculation based upon the number of days of inventory and the estimation of a day's cost-of-sales amount.

Lean manufacturing creates low and consistent inventory. This, in turn, enables a very simple approach to inventory valuation. A standard cost is not required for inventory valuation. Indeed, a perpetual inventory quantity for each item is no longer required either.

VALUE STREAM AND PLANT PROFIT AND LOSS STATEMENTS

Lean companies provide P&L information to the value stream managers. The Value Stream Manager is accountable for increasing the value created by the value stream, removing waste, and increasing profits for his/her value stream. A typical value stream P&L is shown in Figure 9.6. This information is gathered—usually weekly—from the value stream costing. If necessary, the P&L can show an additional breakdown of the information, but it is always best to keep these reports as simple as possible.

As you can see, the report does not take into account the changes in inventory level when calculating the value stream profit. The reason for this is that we want to provide the right motivation for the value stream team. If the value stream reduces inventory by selling more than it makes, the box score will show a higher profit and a lower average unit cost. Conversely, if inventory is increased, this will show bad results in the box score.

The P&L for the plant or division of the company is made up of all the value streams within the division. The example in Figure 9.7 shows a division with three value streams: the Controllers value stream, the Vertical Products

Electronic Components, Inc. Controller Products Value Stream	
Revenue	$1,280,400
Material costs	$512,160
Conversion costs	$184,380
Value stream profit	$583,860
ROS	45.60%
Inventory	$593,008

Figure 9.6: Value Stream P&L Report

value stream, and a New Products Development value stream. The fourth column shows the administrative and business sustaining costs that are outside the value stream.

Electronic Components, Inc.

	Value Streams				
	Controller products	Vertical positioners	New product development	Admin. & overhead	Division P&L
Revenue	$1,280,400	$2,048,640	$0		$3,329,040
Material costs	$512,160	$614,592	$12,766		$1,139,518
Conversion costs	$184,380	$313,445	$678,574		$1,176,399
Value stream profit	$583,860	$1,120,603	($665,808)		$1,038,655
Value stream ROS	45.60%	54.70%			
Employee costs				$44,355	$44,355
Expenses				$27,943	$27,943
Prior period inventory					$1,788,549
Current inventory					$1,252,432
Inventory change					−$536,117
Division gross profit					$438,287
Division ROS					13%

Figure 9.7: Division P&L Report

The division P&L information shown in column 5 is summed across from the previous columns. The division level P&L requires adjustments to take into account the change in inventory over the period, in order to state the

Divisional Gross Profit correctly for external reporting. Other adjustments may also be necessary to bring the Divisional P&L into line with the accounting requirements for external reporting.

SUMMARY

As a company matures with lean manufacturing, it moves from applying lean thinking only to individual production cells, to viewing the flow through the entire value stream. When a company moves to value stream management, the simple methods of value stream costing become much more useful than traditional standard or detailed actual costing.

Value stream costing is simple, because the cost information is collected in summary form across the whole value stream and is collected weekly (or monthly). The value stream costs contain almost no cost allocations because all the value stream costs are directly applied. Value stream costing provides better information because the information is the real, direct cost of the value stream. Value stream costs are easy to understand because the cost collection and calculations are simple; anyone can understand them.

Value stream costing provides excellent performance measurements and provides a P&L statement for each value stream. These value stream P&Ls are combined to provide a plant-wide or company-wide P&L statement.

Standard costs can be eliminated in favor of value stream costs because there is no longer a need to use standard costs for such decisions as order profitability, make/buy decisions, or inventory valuation. These decisions are made with reference to the overall profitability of the value stream.

CHAPTER 10

Using the Box Score

Throughout this book we present value stream information in a box score. This concept appeals to our clients, because it presents, in a concise way, lean targets, as well as the key information that lets everyone know whether the value stream is on track towards these targets. Presentation of goals and targets in the same format allows all levels of the lean organization to understand the effectiveness of lean and what needs to be done to create improvement.

Within lean companies, virtually everyone in the value stream uses the box score, giving every person a common view and language for talking about lean performance:

- Value stream managers use the box score to plan and evaluate lean improvements.

- The value stream continuous improvement team uses the box score to design improvement programs and *kaizen* events that will have the greatest impact on financial and operating results.

- Plant and division managers use the box score to understand value stream improvement plans and to evaluate performance.

- Other executives use the box scores as the basis for simulating the potential impacts of product-market and capital investment plans.

The box score has multiple purposes, including:

- Weekly reporting of value stream performance.

- Showing the planned effects of lean improvements.

- Planning strategic changes such as capital investments and product and/or customer rationalization.

As shown in Table 10.1, the box score has three major sections—measuring operational performance, capacity usage, and financial performance.

The measurements should be familiar, inasmuch as they have already been discussed in this book.

- The operational measures are the value stream performance measurements discussed in Chapter 8.

- The capacity information was the subject of Chapter 4.

- The financial information is the value stream costing, the subject of Chapter 9.

Table 10.1: Example of a Box Score

		Last week 4-Oct	This week 11-Oct	Next week 18-Oct	23-Oct	Planned future state 31-Dec
Operational	Units per person	36.16	42.05			51.39
	On-time shipment	98.00%	94.00%			98.00%
	Dock-to-dock days	23.58	20.50			16.50
	First time through	46%	42%			50%
	Average product cost	$388.46	$348.66			$316.91
	AR days	34.5	37.0			35.0
Capacity	Productive	10.8%	10.8%			24.7%
	Non-productive	54.8%	54.8%			23.4%
	Available capacity	34.4%	34.4%			51.9%
Financial	Revenue	$1,101,144	$1,280,400			$1,408,440
	Material cost	$462,480	$512,160			$535,207
	Conversion cost	$250,435	$231,884			$208,696
	Value stream gross profit	$388,228	$536,356			$664,537

There is a great deal of latitude as to what should be included in operational and financial measures. As a rule of thumb, companies generally select those measures they intend to use in evaluating the effectiveness of their value streams.

Let us look at some examples of the box score in its most common uses.

REPORTING VALUE STREAM PERFORMANCE

A popular way to use the box score is for the weekly measurement and tracking of value stream performance, an example of which is provided in Table 10.2.

The primary purpose of the weekly box score report is to focus the attention of the value stream team on the areas that can benefit from continuous improvement efforts. The improvement in value stream results can be tracked weekly as an indicator of the effectiveness of the continuous improvement efforts.

The report shows the three dimensions of value stream performance to assess:

- How the value stream is performing operationally
- How the value stream is performing financially
- How the value stream resources are being used

Changes in capacity usage are the bridge between operational and financial change. As resource capacity is used effectively, financial results improve. Lean improvements create newly available capacity as waste is eliminated from the value stream and capacity, in the form of people's time, machine time, and other resources, become available.

The box score is usually posted in an area that has maximum visibility, such as the value stream performance board, the continuous improvement team's meeting room, the cafeteria, or a main passageway. Such prominent visibility promotes the culture of continuous improvement and teamwork by maintaining focus on progress toward expected value stream results. It clearly displays the value stream team's lean achievements in a way that elicits positive feedback from colleagues in other value streams and pride among fellow value stream teammates. These are all desirable behavioral outcomes of the lean performance measurement framework, and of the lean program itself.

SHOWING THE EFFECTS OF LEAN IMPROVEMENTS

This application was described in Chapter 4. In that chapter, it was shown that lean improvements frequently have a dramatic impact on operational results, but minimal impact on financial results. The box score is a useful way of showing this effect, as depicted in Table 10.3.

The inclusion of the resource capacity analysis shows the shift in the use of capacity from Non-productive to Available, as a result of the lean improvements—Table 10.4.

Table 10.2: Example of a Box Score Used to Track Weekly Value Stream Performance

	Last week 4-Oct	This week 11-Oct	Next week 18-Oct	23-Oct	Planned future state 31-Dec
Operational measurements					
Units per person	36.16	42.05			51.39
On-time shipment	98.00%	94.00%			98.00%
Dock-to-dock days	23.58	20.50			16.50
First time through	46%	42%			50%
Average product cost	$388.46	$348.66			$316.91
Air days	34.0	34.0			35.0
Productive	10%	8%			24.7%
Non-productive	54%	8%			23.4%
Available capacity	34.4%	34.4%			51.9%
Revenue	$1,101,144	$1,280,400			$1,408,440
Material cost	$462,480	$512,160			$535,207
Conversion cost	$250,435	$231,884			$208,696
Value stream gross profit	$388,228	$536,356			$664,537
Financial results					

Capacity usage

Show performance history for as many weeks as possible

Show planned future state based on the value stream strategic plan

Operational

Capacity

Financial

Table 10.3: The Effect of Lean Improvements—Future State

		Current State	Future State	
Operational	Sales per person	$131,429	$131,429	Improved operational results
	On-time delivery	82%	96%	
	Dock-to-dock time—days	23.60	4.50	
	First time through	90%	90%	
	Average cost per unit	$4.94	$4.94	
	AR days outstanding	30	30	
Financial	Annual revenue	$1,840,000	$1,840,000	No improvement in profits
	Annual material cost	$772,800	$772,800	
	Annual conversion cost	$317,752	$317,752	
	Value stream profit	$749,448	$749,448	
	Value stream cash flow	$749,448	$1,813,672	

Table 10.4: The Effect of Lean Improvements on the Use of Capacity—Future State

		Current State	Future State	
Operational	Sales per person	$131,429	$131,429	
	On-time delivery	82%	96%	
	Dock-to-dock time—days	23.60	4.50	
	First time through	90%	90%	
	Average cost per unit	$4.94	$4.94	
	AR days outstanding	30	30	
Capacity	Productive capacity	25%	22%	The lean improvements have freed up capacity.
	Non-productive capacity	30%	8%	
	Available capacity	45%	70%	
Financial	Annual revenue	$1,840,000	$1,840,000	The revenue and costs are still the same.
	Annual material cost	$772,800	$772,800	
	Annual conversion cost	$317,752	$317,752	
	Value stream profit	$749,448	$749,448	
	Value stream cash flow	$749,448	$1,813,672	

The box score here can show the planned effects of the uses of capacity freed up by the lean improvements—Table 10.5.

Table 10.5: The Box Score Used to Show the Effects of the Use of Freed-Up Capacity

		Current State	Future State	Long Term Future
Operational	Sales per person	$131,429	$131,429	$235,936
	On-time delivery	82%	96%	96%
	Dock-to-dock time—days	23.60	4.50	4.50
	First time through	90%	90%	90%
	Average cost per unit	$4.94	$4.94	$4.73
	AR days outstanding	30	30	30
Capacity	Productive capacity	25%	22%	29%
	Non-productive capacity	30%	8%	11%
	Available capacity	45%	70%	60%
Financial	Annual revenue	$1,840,000	$1,840,000	$3,303,100
	Annual material cost	$772,800	$772,800	$986,832
	Annual conversion cost	$317,752	$317,752	$317,752
	Value stream profit	$749,448	$749,448	$1,998,516
	Value stream cash flow	$749,448	$1,813,672	$3,062,740

The company introduced new products, rented space to a sub-contractor, and grew the business using the capacity and cash freed up by lean.

SHOWING THE EFFECTS OF STRATEGIES AND PLANS

Perhaps one of the most important features of the box score is its usefulness for evaluating a broad range of management decisions. Two examples from recent client assignments demonstrate this point.

Table 10.6 shows the use of the box score in product rationalization decisions.

Another application involved adding more machines and people to the value stream in order to launch a new product family— Table 10.7.

Table 10.6: Using the Box Score in Product Rationalization

		Current Value Stream	Remove "Low Margin" Products	Introduce New Products
		Jan-03	Jun-03	Sep-03
Operational	Units per person	466	395	505
	On-time shipment	92	99	99
	Dock-to-dock days	15	7	9
	First time through	65	75	75
	Average product cost	$112.75	$120.94	$109.23
	AR days	42	35	35
Capacity	Productive	24%	18%	28%
	Non-productive	63%	35%	42%
	Available capacity	13%	47%	30%
Financial	Revenue monthly	$10,667	$9,866	$12,800
	Material cost	$3,758	$3,185	$4,073
	Conversion cost	$2,547	$2,547	$2,547
	Value stream gross profit	$4,362	$4,124	$6,180

SUMMARY

This chapter has described a value stream reporting tool that provides a common language for all personnel associated with lean in a company. The box score has proven itself to be very versatile in reporting on value stream operations, the planned impacts of lean improvements and the effects of strategic changes to the business. Lean companies find that its comprehensive scope provides a unifying framework for evaluating the effectiveness of lean from multiple perspectives.

Table 10.7: Using the Box Score to Evaluate New Product Introduction

		Current	6 Months	1 Year	18 Months	2 Years	30 Months	3 Years
	Additional monthly quantity	0	1	5	10	15	20	30
Operational	Units per person	1.52	1.54	1.63	1.80	1.90	2.16	2.59
	On-time shipment	100%	100%	100%	100%	100%	100%	100%
	Dock-to-dock days	6.00	6.00	6.00	5.00	5.00	4.50	4.50
	First time through	80%	80%	85%	85%	85%	85%	85%
	Average product cost	$3,481	$3,480	$3,278	$2,985	$2,821	$2,497	$2,092
	AR days	42	42	42	42	37	37	37
Capacity	Productive	29%	33%	38%	34%	36%	41%	50%
	Non-productive	54%	52%	55%	35%	33%	33%	33%
	Available capacity	17%	15%	7%	31%	31%	26%	17%
Financial	Revenue	$466,670	$472,670	$502,568	$562,461	$630,170	$714,132	$834,172
	Material costs	$172,085	$175,385	$178,685	$181,935	$184,686	$187,101	$189,160
	Conversion costs	$119,584	$119,584	$119,584	$142,584	$142,584	$152,593	$158,084
	Value stream gross profit	$175,001	$177,701	$204,299	$237,942	$302,900	$374,438	$486,928
	Value stream ROS	37.50%	37.60%	40.65%	42.30%	48.07%	52.43%	58.37%

	Current	6 Months	1 Year	18 Months	2 Years	30 Months	3 Years
Additional people				5		2	1
Additional machines				3		2	1
Material cost per unit		$3,300	$3,330	$3,250	$2,750	$2,325	$2,150

CHAPTER 11

Calculating Product Costs—Features and Characteristics

In Chapter 9, we showed you how to calculate the average value stream cost, and how to make management decisions using that cost. This approach looks at the impact of management choices related to order pricing, make/buy, and other product profitability decisions. These are based on the impact these choices would have on the value stream cash flow profit before and after the action contemplated by the decision. This decision method, based on overall value stream profit impact, departs from traditional methods based on individual product profitability, as it takes into consideration the impact of real value stream costs on the profitability of any business choice. Traditional methods focused on product based on the assumptions of standard costing. These assumptions, particularly the methods of allocating overheads, provide misleading and inaccurate costs, leading to bad business decisions. For most business decisions, focusing on the cost of an individual manufactured product is misleading and unhelpful. These decisions are best made by taking account of the profitability of the value stream as a whole, not the individual order or transaction.

However, there are times when it is important to know something about the cost of an individual product. For example, transferring products from one division or location to another requires a transfer price. Exporting usually requires the product cost to be on the export documents.

Going beyond merely reporting the cost of a product, the following kinds of questions need to be addressed:

- What are the product features that create cost?
- How much do product features add to the cost of the product?
- How do these features relate to product design decisions?
- How do these features relate to the value that customers place on our products?
- What features do we need to modify or improve in order to create greater value for customers?

It is unlikely that a company will need to develop answers to these questions daily, or even monthly. The issues underlying these kinds of questions are strategic and will likely be addressed on an annual basis. Nevertheless, to answer these strategic questions, we need more detailed information than can be provided by the average cost of all products made by the value stream. We need an understanding of what causes cost in a value stream.

Some companies address these questions using the standard costing system. This method has inherent problems that have been described in detail in Chapter 9. Other companies have developed activity-based costing systems to compensate for the problems of allocating overhead to products that use overhead activities differently. For example, a product that requires extra engineering would include an engineering activity, whereas those that did not use engineering would not. While this method may be useful in some contexts, it requires that information be collected and maintained on all products made by a company, what activities they use, and how much of each activity is used—a methodology that requires a great deal of transaction data and systems support. Because one of the objectives of lean accounting is to eliminate transactions, we advocate a method that gets to the same result without the need to generate additional transactions.

We use features and characteristics costing to calculate product costs when they are needed. Features and characteristics costing recognizes that value streams are designed based on the common processes used to make similar products. It is necessary only, therefore, to define how an individual product departs from the norm, and then to understand how significantly that differs from the average.

In this chapter we discuss how to calculate product costs in value streams in which some products incur more work than others. We will discuss how to define the features and characteristics that cause cost and how to use the features and characteristics information to modify the average value stream costs.

WHAT DRIVES COST IN A LEAN VALUE STREAM?

A lean value stream differs markedly from traditional manufacturing, as it is a defined set of processes through which similar products flow. In traditional manufacturing each product has its own unique routing. In lean, the products that have similar production flows are grouped together into a value stream. This grouping greatly simplifies the costing process, because instead of costing out each individual product through multiple routings, we now have to worry only about the cost of the value stream as a whole.

The primary driver of product cost through the value stream is the rate of flow of the individual product. A product manufactured at ten units per hour, for example, has twice the conversion cost of product running at twenty per hour through the value stream. Generally the rate of flow through the value stream is determined by the rate of flow of the product through the bottleneck operation within the value stream flow.

As described in Chapter 9, the average product cost is equal to the total cost of the value stream divided by the number of units shipped during the period. The number of units that can be shipped is limited to the number that can be processed through the bottleneck operation. Figure 11.1 provides an example.

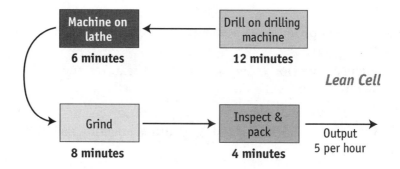

The cost of a product is dependent upon the cycle time through the bottleneck operation.

Figure 11.1: Cycle Times in the Value Stream

By looking at the individual process cycle times we can see that the bottleneck process is the drilling operation, which takes twelve minutes to make a product. Thus, by dividing that cycle time into sixty, we see that the cell can make five products an hour (sixty minutes divided by twelve minutes per product). In general, the maximum number of units (Y) that can be processed by a cell (or value stream) during a given period of time (X), given that the bottleneck operation can produce at a rate of Z units per period of time (X), can be calculated using the formula: $Y=X/Z$. It does not matter that other operations take less time to perform. The cell, or value stream, can only work as fast as the slowest (or bottleneck) operation.

Now, if all products took exactly twelve minutes to go through the bottleneck, then the average time of twelve would be correct for each and every product. However, in most cases, products in a value stream do not have the same cycle times through the bottleneck operation. Depending on their features, products consume more or less of the bottleneck operation's time than the average. In the example, there may be some products that consume as few as nine minutes and some as many as fifteen minutes. A primary goal of features and characteristics costing is to understand how product features use the bottleneck resource differently.

How to Use Features and Characteristics

The lean accounting team at ECI wanted to use features and characteristics costing to determine product cost. They believed that the average value stream cost did not accurately reflect the fact that some of the components required more effort to manufacture than others. There are seven steps to developing features and characteristics products costs:

1. Calculate the average product cost for the value stream.

2. Analyze available capacity.

3. Identify the primary bottleneck and pacemaker within the value stream.

4. Identify how product features and characteristics affect use of the bottleneck.

5. Calculate conversion costs using product features and characteristics' effects.

6. Calculate material costs.

7. Identify other significant product features affecting use of the bottleneck resource.

Each of the steps in the methodology is described below.

Step 1: Calculate The Average Product Family Cost for the Value Stream

In Chapter 9 we discussed how to calculate value stream average costs. The average cost is equal to the Total Value Stream Cost divided by the Number of Units Shipped of the products included in the value stream for the period under study. We need to emphasize that you should be careful to use the quantities for the units shipped and not units produced. Using units produced will encourage making for stock, which is definitely not what we want to encourage with our lean accounting methods.

A further emphasis is that the costs for the period should be equivalent to the total cash outflows plus depreciation of machinery for the period.

- Materials—total cost for materials used in production during the period

- Labor—cash paid for employees working in the value stream during the period

- Supplies and tooling—cash outflows during the period

- Facilities—cash outflows for leased space and utilities used by the value stream

- Machines—depreciation cost from the company's books and records

How Average Cost Drives a Lean Approach to Inventory

We must digress to discuss an important technicality concerning the calculation of average cost per unit. It is important because it marks a difference between traditional accounting for financial statement preparation and lean accounting using value stream costing. Our use of total cost of materials used in production and cash paid for labor and other costs in the numerator and units shipped in the denominator has the effect of increasing the unit cost of items shipped under conditions in which units produced exceed units sold. Under traditional accounting, the value of this difference would show as an increase in inventory and would have the effect of decreasing the unit cost. That is why traditional accounting works as a disincentive to reducing inventories; it encourages building inventory to keep unit cost and total cost down. We want an accounting method that promotes the proper lean values: to increase cost when too much is made (amounts produced exceed amounts shipped) and to decrease cost when inventories are drawn down (amounts produced are less than amounts shipped).

Using value stream costing in our previous example, in which production exceeds units shipped, the impact of the value stream cash flow on the difference between units produced and units shipped is equivalent to the difference between units produced and units sold, multiplied by the unit cost of materials used in production. The cost per unit shipped will increase. On the other hand, if the number of units sold exceeds units produced, this method will reduce the cash flow cost, thereby reducing the unit cost of the product. In general, the effect on value stream cash flow (Y) created by the difference between production volumes (X) and sales volumes (Z), given the value stream cost per unit shipped (C), can be expressed as an equation: $Y = (X-Z)^* C$. For example, if in a given month, the volumes produced by the value stream were 200, the volumes shipped were 100, and the unit cost was $50, the impact on total cash flow cost increases by $5,000: $(200-100)^* \$50$, and cost per unit sold increases. The 100-unit excess of production oversold units would have the effect of increasing inventory by 100 units. If the situation is reversed and units sold exceed units produced by 100, cash flow cost decreases by $5,000. Under traditional accounting, the effect would be to increase costs by $5,000, a very negative effect for lean.

Using value stream costing creates incentives to reduce inventory (an excess in units shipped over units produced) as that will increase cash flow profitability. On the other hand, an increase in inventory will be equivalent to the excess of items produced over those shipped, and will reduce cash flow profitability.

In the same manner as materials, this method includes the total cost of labor and overhead as conversion costs for the period in value stream cost. As all current costs are charged to cost of sales and not to inventory, the differences in units produced and shipped affect profitability in the proper way, as is the case with material costs. The amount of conversion costs included is the sum of total cash outflows plus accruals (for depreciation) for the period. As the costs are largely fixed, and the cost per unit is derived by dividing the amounts paid and accrued for the period by the units shipped, unit conversion costs can be decreased either by reducing the cash paid during the period for labor and other conversion costs, or by increasing the volume of sales.

Therefore, when unused capacity increases, whether through production for inventory or from declines in shipments, the cost per unit of the products produced increases. Decreases in unused capacity produce decreases in cost per unit. Table 11.1 shows the calculation of the total costs for the period for components value stream of ECI.

Table 11.1: Calculation of Total Value Stream Cost

	Material cost	Outside cost	Employee cost	Machine cost	Other cost	TOTAL COST
Customer service	–	–	12,108	–	–	12,108
Purchasing	–	–	16,145	–	–	16,145
SMT	358,512	–	17,080	16,956	20,000	412,548
Hand load/wave post	25,608	–	23,485	2,016	–	51,109
Test and rework	–	–	17,080	3,528	–	20,608
Assemble and burn-in	128,040	–	10,675	–	–	138,715
Shipping	–	–	2,669	–	–	2,669
Quality assurance	–	–	8,073	–	–	8,073
Manufacturing engineering	–	–	8,073	–	–	8,073
Maintenance	–	–	8,073	–	–	8,073
Accounting	–	–	8,073	–	–	8,073
Information systems	–	–	4,036	–	–	4,036
Design engineering	–	7,760	4,036	–	–	11,796
	$512,160	$7,760	$139,606	$22,500	$20,000	$702,026

Note that in addition to the production processes, they included the shipping, customer service, maintenance, engineering and management resources that were dedicated to the components value stream. In defining its value streams, ECI eliminated allocations from its costing process, and assigned resources that worked primarily on components to the components value stream. In addition, they calculated the costs of the facility, primarily lease cost and utilities, to the value stream on a square-footage basis. The actual cost of tools used for machine maintenance is charged to the value stream.

The invoiced cost of Outside Cost for the orders produced was charged to the value stream, as were the costs of the materials used for items produced, including scrap.

Labor costs were obtained from the payroll records for the actual amounts paid to employees and temporaries during the month, including straight time and overtime during the period. The amounts included their wages and employee benefits. The cost of machinery was the depreciation expense as recorded in the company's books.

The total cost of operating the value stream was calculated as $702,026, and the average cost of units shipped was $328.97 ($702,026 divided by 2,134 units shipped).

Step 2: Analyze Available Capacity

As discussed above, in an environment in which cost per unit is determined to a great extent by the throughput of the value stream, the limitation on throughput determines the maximum volumes and minimum cost per unit of products produced by the value stream. Therefore, for a value stream or cell, the volume that can be shipped is totally determined by the volume that can flow through the bottleneck cell, that is, the cell with the least unused capacity, and that volume determines the average cost.

In Chapter 4, we discussed how to analyze capacity in a value stream by using the information in the value stream maps and the company's general ledger. The resulting analysis shows productive, nonproductive, and available capacity for the current and future states of lean. Table 11.2 shows the analysis of productive, nonproductive, and available capacity by process for both employees and machines for components value stream.

Step 3: Identify the Primary Bottleneck and Pacemaker within the Value Stream

The bottleneck (or constraint) cell is the one that has the least available capacity. This is the cell that sets the pace for the value stream and has to be scheduled and optimized. It would appear, from the analysis in Table 11.2, that Loop 2: Hand Load/Wave/Post has the least capacity with less than 4 percent available employees, implying that in order to produce to demand for the period the company had to get additional resources, either by working overtime or borrowing from another work center. As the cell was able to borrow resources from the Test and Rework cell, the Hand Load/Wave Post cell did not operate as a bottleneck. What we want to determine is the work center that is the most limiting to the volume that the value stream can produce. In this case, the machines in Loop 1: SMT served as the bottleneck, having 2 percent available capacity, which could not be obtained from any other cell. We call this the bottleneck cell, and it is knowing how individual products use this cell that allows us to vary the cost of the product. So the capacity of the machines in the SMT cell operates as the bottleneck to increasing the volume produced and, hence, the average cost per unit of the value stream. From the point of view of cost reduction, increasing the capacity of the SMT cell becomes paramount. Figure 11.2 shows the available capacity graphically.

The SMT (Surface Mount Technology) work center automates the processes of mounting components on a printed circuit board. The average completed product contained $1\frac{1}{2}$ boards. The SMT cell has a total cycle time of 224 seconds per end, the cell cycle time is 392 (224 times $1\frac{3}{4}$) seconds per end. The average set-up time per unit is 44.99 seconds. So the total time per unit is 436.9 seconds. When the total cell cycle time is compared to the takt time required by the customers the cycle time represents 91 percent of takt time. The boards can be made within takt, but there is not much additional capacity to provide flexibility or cope with production problems. This cell is

Table 11.2: Analysis of Capacity by Process for ECI

		Totals	Customer service	Configuration	Purchasing	SMT	Hand load/wave post	Test & rework	Assemble & burn-in	Shipping	Quality assurance	Manufacturing engineering	Maintenance	Accounting	Human resources	Information systems	Design engineering	Test engineering
EEMPLOYEES	Cost	$139,606	$12,709	$0	$16,145	$17,080	$23,485	$17,080	$10,675	$2,669	$8,073	$8,073	$8,073	$8,073	$0	$4,036	$4,036	$0
	Productive	16%	5%	0%	8%	0%	52%	0%	28%	24%	0%	8%	0%	0%	0%	0%	0%	0%
	Non-productive	41%	13%	0%	1%	41%	53%	57%	67%	47%	31%	30%	2%	51%	0%	51%	8%	40%
	Other	0%	0%	0%	0%	0%	0%	0%	0%	0%	0%	0%	0%	0%	0%	0%	0%	0%
	Available capacity	43%	81%	0%	91%	59%	-4%	43%	5%	29%	69%	62%	98%	49%	0%	50%	92%	60%
MACHINES	Cost	$22,500	$-	$-	$-	$16,956	$2,016	$3,528	$-	$-	$-	$-	$-	$-	$-	$-	$-	$-
	Productive	29%	0%	05	0%	25%	67%	0%	0%	0%	0%	0%	0%	0%	0%	0%	0%	0%
	Non-productive	55%	0%	0%	0%	73%	3%	59%	0%	0%	0%	0%	0%	0%	0%	0%	0%	0%
	Other	0%	0%	0%	0%	0%	0%	0%	0%	0%	0%	0%	0%	0%	0%	0%	0%	0%
	Available capacity	16%	0%	0%	0%	2%	31%	31%	0%	0%	0%	0%	0%	0%	0%	0%	0%	0%
	Average conversion cost	$75.96	$5.67	$-	$7.57	$15.95	$11.95	$9.66	$5.00	$1.25	$3.78	$3.78	$3.78	$3.78	$-	$1.89	$1.89	$-

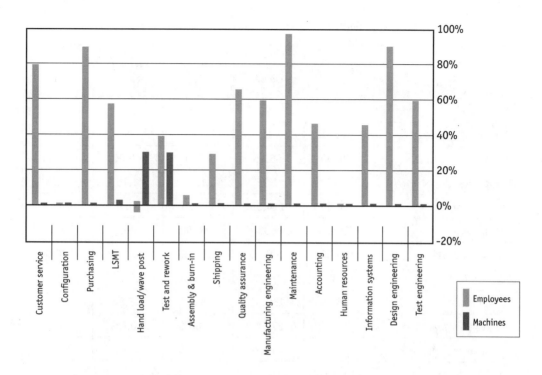

Figure 11.2: Graphical depiction of available capacity in the Components Value Stream

the bottleneck of the value stream. This information is summarized for all cells in the Table 11.3

As the bottleneck resources are the machines in the SMT cell, the use of these resources largely determines the cost of a particular unit.

Step 4: Identify How Product Features and Characteristics Affect Use of the Bottleneck

Next, the ECI team defined the primary features that determined the rate of flow through the machines in the SMT cell. These features also determine the flow through the value stream. It is, therefore, important in determining product cost to understand just how the product features consume the resources of the bottleneck resource. The team did not have much difficulty in identifying two product characteristics affecting the cycle time through the bottleneck:

- **The number of components to be affixed to a board.** This was determined visually by counting the number of glue dots placed on the underside of the board at each spot a component was to be affixed in the SMT process. These were grouped into three broad categories:
  - Average number—120 seconds cycle time (200-700 dots)
  - High number—165 seconds cycle time (over 700 dots)
  - Low number—60 seconds cycle time (less than 200 dots)

Table 11.3: Bottleneck Table for the Components Value Stream

	SMT	Hand load/ wave post	Test and rework	Assemble & burn-in	Shipping
Cycle time	224	720	360	360	360
Number of resources	1	11	8	8	8
Resource cycle time	224.00	65.45	45.00	45.00	45.00
Number per unit	1.75	1.75	1.75	1.75	1.75
Cell cycle time	392.00	114.55	78.75	78.75	78.75
Set-up time	1680	600	750	750	750
Number of batches	100.00	100.00	100.00	100.00	100.00
Set-up/unit	44.99	16.07	20.08	20.08	20.08
Total unit time	436.99	130.61	98.83	98.83	98.83
% of value stream takt	91.0%	27.2%	20.6%	20.6%	20.6%
Available capacity	1.7%	-4.4%	42.9%	4.5%	28.9%

- **The number of components not dedicated to the SMT machine.** The greater the number of such components, the greater the setup time. These were grouped by the ratio of such components to the total, as follows:
  - Medium ratio—5–10 components out of 300
  - High ratio—greater than 10 components out of 300
  - Low ratio—less than 5 components out of 300

In your company it may not be obvious how the product features use the bottleneck resource. However, lean companies have had success in getting at this by assembling operators and process engineers who are familiar with the value stream in question, by using the detailed production data, and by obtaining informed estimates of the difficulty of the products in terms of effort at the bottleneck resource, relative to the other products, or relative to an average product. The goal is to define the product features that increase the cycle time at the bottleneck resource. If the detailed information is not readily available, it may be necessary to conduct a time study in the cell. But most lean companies have these details because they are required for designing and improving the cells.

Step 5: Calculate Conversion Costs Using Product Features and Characteristics' Effects

Having determined that the product characteristics that affected the use of the bottleneck were the number of dots on the underside of the board and the number of non-dedicated components per board, the team then set out to determine the average conversion cost of a finished unit, which constituted 1.75 boards. Table 11.4 displays the conversion cost of a finished unit under all possible combinations of numbers of dots and non-dedicated components as they had been categorized in the previous step.

Table 11.4: Calculation of Conversion Cost per Unit for the Components Value Stream

- Total value stream cost = $702,026
- Conversion costs = $189,866
- Average conversion cost = $88.97/unit (1.75 boards)

		Number of dots		
		<200	200-700	>700
# non-dedicated components	<5	$32.97	$74.17	$90.70
	5-10	$39.56	$88.97	$108.81
	>20	$52.14	$117.27	$143.42

Note that for the average component having 200–700 dots and 5–10 non-dedicated components per board, the cost per unit is equal to the total conversion costs for the period ($189,866) divided by the number of finished units made during the period (2,134), or $88.97. This can be seen in the central cell of the table. Figure 11.3 displays the calculations of costs under other conditions:

- Varying the number of dots, leaving the number of non-dedicated components constant:
  - at over 700, cost equals $108.81
  - at less than 200, cost equals $39.56

- Varying the number of non-dedicated components, leaving the number of dots constant:
  - at over 10, cost equals $117.27
  - at less than 5, cost equals $74.17

It can be seen from Table 11.4 that there is a wide range of cost between the least costly to make (less than 200 dots and less than 5 non-dedicated components), and the most costly to make (over 700 dots and over 10 non-dedicated components). As we are dealing with the constraint resource, the SMT machine, the product mix run on the machine determines the quantity run in the value stream and the cost per unit of product. Therefore, the total cost of operating the value stream is fixed at $189,866. The volume run determines what the cost per unit is.

- **Number of Dots**

  If # dots >700, cycle time = 165 seconds

  Number of product made if 165 second cycle time = 1745

  Conversion cost = Total Cost / 1745 = $108.81

  Cycle time for <200 = 60 seconds

  Conversion Cost = $39.56

- **Number of Non-Dedicated Components**

  If non-dedicated components > 10; set-up = 50 minutes

  Number of products made with 50 minute set-up = 1619

  Cost of product = $117.27

  If non-dedicated components < 5; set-up = 0 minutes

  Cost of product = $74.17

Figure 11.3: Calculations of Conversion Costs Using Features and Characteristics

Step 6: Calculate the Material Costs

Material costs can be developed in one of two ways:

1. Actual cost for each item from the bill of materials and the latest invoice cost.

2. Create a sample matrix relating material cost to a relevant factor, for example, board size in the ECI case.

We have found that many companies prefer to use the former method when they first implement features and characteristics costing, and may shift to a simpler technique after they have become more comfortable with using the technique. Either way, the company will not need to calculate standard costs to calculate the costs of material.

Step 7: Identify Other Significant Product Features Affecting Use of the Bottleneck Resource

Occasionally companies will identify other product features that affect the cost of the product. In the case of the Controllers value stream, there were custom products that were customized in a separate cell. The costs developed in Table 11.3 were modified based upon the impact on the bottleneck in the custom cell:

- High impact: add $50
- Medium impact: add $21
- Low impact: add $9

Any custom material costs should also be added.

USES OF FEATURES AND CHARACTERISTICS COSTING

Lean companies find that after they eliminate the need for standard costs to measure performance and price inventory, they find that features and characteristics costing is much simpler and easier than retaining the standard costing system.. The question then, is whether they need to maintain and operate an expensive system merely to calculate product costs, particularly when product costs are no longer used for decision-making. Many companies are finding that they do not want to do this if there is an alternative. Features and characteristics costing is this alternative.

Another important reason for using this method of costing products is that it links costing methodology more closely to value in the marketplace, that is, to the product features that customers find valuable, as well as those that they do not. By associating both cost and value with features and characteristics, the tool helps the company to develop product designs that improve value in the high-value areas, as well as reduce cost in the lower value areas. Finally, the simple table of the relationship of product cost to product features and characteristics shows an understanding of how product features relate to product cost and why production capacity is useful to sales personnel in negotiating product price.

SUMMARY

This chapter has described how features and characteristics costing can work to tailor the average value stream cost to the features and characteristics of the product manufactured in the value stream. The primary determinant of product cost is the use of the bottleneck resource in the value stream by products having features and characteristics that cause more or less time on the bottleneck than average. By understanding how features use the bottleneck, costs can be developed to provide for higher cost for those product groups that consume more of the bottleneck resource, and less cost for those items that consume less of the resource.

CHAPTER 12

Eliminating More Wasteful Transactions

In Chapter 5 we introduced the importance of eliminating processes and transactions that had been established to support a batch manufacturing process, once lean manufacturing controls are in place. The chapter described the framework for evaluating what can be eliminated and listed some changes that can be made when a company is first embarking on the lean journey, implementing pilot cells, and experimenting with the lean thinking process.

In this chapter we look at what can be eliminated at the next major stage of the lean accounting maturity path, with the focus on management of the value streams. As we discussed in Chapter 7, a value stream includes everything we do to create value for the customer. In practice, it is defined by the products that undergo similar manufacturing. We measure the effectiveness of the value stream in achieving flow, pull, perfection, and value creation with value stream performance measurements, then use that information to drive continuous improvement. The move to managing value streams end-to-end is a major milestone in the transformation to lean, and it enables significant changes in the accounting and control processes. Table 12.1 shows what has changed in this stage from the first.

As can be seen in this figure, the lean value stream is now the dominant characteristic. Within the value streams, cellular manufacturing is widespread. That means that cells are linked end-to-end in the value stream to enable a flow of production. There is extensive use of visual systems, and for our purposes, the most prominent one is an effective pull system that controls production flow. At this stage, work orders are no longer needed to initiate and control production, and, therefore, the whole MRP shopfloor planning and scheduling system is no longer helpful. Continuing to use it in the face of this visual control system impedes lean progress. Processes are under control; there is minimal variability of the production rates, flows, quality, and demand throughout the value stream. Work-in-process and finished goods

Table 12.1: Maturity Path Stages of Lean Manufacturing

Lean Manufacturing	Lean Manufacturing Attributes	Lean Accounting
Pilot Lean Production Cells	• Successful lean cells in place • Extensive training in lean principles • Flow, pull, kanban • Quick changeover and SMED • Standardized work • Quality at source and self-inspection	**Getting Started with Lean Accounting**
Lean Manufacturing Widespread	• Cellular manufacturing is widespread across the plant with standardized work and single-piece flow • Extensive use of visual systems • Continuous improvement teams trained and established • Initial supplier certification program and kanban pull from some suppliers • Manufacturing managed by value stream • Processes under control; typically some use of SPC • Work-in-process and finished goods inventory relatively low and consistent	**Managing by Value Streams**
Lean Thinking Applied Throughout Organization and Partners	• Company organized by value streams • Extensive cooperation with customers, suppliers, and partners • Continuous improvement is a way of life • Lean thinking applied throughout the entire organization	**Lean Enterprise**

inventories are under control, and are relatively low and consistent. Finally, we see that there have been efforts to extend lean back in the value stream to include suppliers, some certification and kanban pull of materials and components. At this stage, some major changes and simplifications of the manufacturing control systems can be implemented. We will trace these changes by following the same format that was introduced in Chapter 5.

This chapter is organized into the following sections:

• Labor Tracking
• Material Costs
• Inventory Tracking

LABOR TRACKING

The goal of this stage is to eliminate the use of work orders. Work orders are used in traditional companies for various purposes, including initiating production, tracking production, reporting production completions, reporting scrap, providing technical information to the operators, performance reporting, and collecting cost data. The cost data includes material costs, labor costs, and other direct costs. These direct costs (particularly labor costs) are also used as the drivers to apply overhead costs to the production job. All of this work is wasteful and has no place in most lean manufacturing processes.

In addition to being wasteful, work orders are also the most visible aspect of push manufacturing. An MRP (or similar) system uses work orders to schedule production, and push it through the factory. Lean organizations initiate production by pulling it from the customers' immediate needs, either through customers' orders, a kanban card, or another visual pull method. When a pull system is in place and the processes are under reasonable control, work orders are no longer necessary for tracking and controlling the shop floor. Figure 12.1 shows the uses of the work order in a traditional manufacturing push system.

Figure 12.1: Use of the Work Order in Traditional Manufacturing

As can be seen, the work order is the document that controls every aspect of production in the traditional manufacturing system. It is the document that is used to launch production from the planning and scheduling department. It travels with the batch on the shop floor and collects data concerning time and materials expended on the production job. Labor is charged to the job by operator code via the work order. Upon completion, costs are applied to the materials and labor used through standard costing. These standard costs are then compared with the actual costs charged to the work order to determine whether the job was performed profitably. Upon completion of the job, the work order is closed and the costs and quantities of the product are charged to the finished goods inventory. Meanwhile the company has had visibility of the work order as it moves through the production process, and can respond to inquiries from customers and others regarding its progress. From the point of view of a production process, this may take weeks, even months, to complete, Being able to trace via the work order enables jobs to be expedited, and work-in-process inventory to be estimated in order to create financial statements. However, as noted above, the system requires a great deal of work to keep maintain accurate and up-to-date information in the face of changing schedules and mobile work forces inside the factory, who are required to produce shorter product runs of a wider array of products. It cannot work in a lean environment.

When lean is first introduced, the work order is retained, as was described in Chapter 5, but rather than charging time and materials directly into the job, the costs are backflushed to the job. The labor and material costs are based upon the production data contained within the MRP system's standard bill of materials and production routings. The elimination of the work order awaits the implementation of a pull system and the management of the factory by value streams. A kanban is a signal from a manufacturing operation to the preceding operation to make parts in exactly the quantities needed to complete its operation. So, let us say that the shipping department has a schedule to produce ten orders. It would signal the assembly operation, by means of a kanban card (or other kind of pull signal) to assemble the finished product for the order. The assembly operation would signal the fabrication operations to produce the fabricated components required to assemble the finished products, and the fabrication departments would, in turn, signal raw materials inventory or suppliers using a kanban pull to fill their needs. In such a system, the signal to start production is not a work order from the planning and scheduling department. It is a signal from a pacemaker process, such as shipping, to start the pull of production. In this case, the customer order and kanban signals replace the work order at the center of the production control system. In Figure 12.2, we see how this affects the production control processes in the mature lean system.

The production control process looks very different from the work-order-controlled process. The signal to start production comes from a customer order that pulls production at the pacemaker cell.

All the features of the MRP-based production control process have been turned off. Whereas the work order had been used to track production through the process, the existence of short cycle times in the lean process minimize the need to track the production at all. An important production control is known as takt time, which is a way to ensure that the production cells are producing at the rate needed to satisfy customer demand. Cell performance

Lean Enterprise

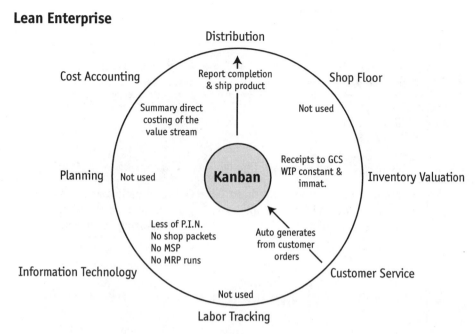

Figure 12.2: Use of the Kanban in the Lean Manufacturer

measurements, such as the Day-by-the-Hour report,[1] are used to keep track of cell production and ensure the cell team focuses on the rate of production achieved in relation to the rate required.

It is no longer necessary to track production labor hours, because variability is controlled at the level of the cell team, using the cell performance measurements. As the focus is on flow and perfection, the measures of efficiency, so important to the traditional system, are no longer required. So, it is not necessary to track the labor hours used in production, because the reasons for tracking no longer exist.

Other purposes of the work order, such as providing work instructions and routings, are now provided by visual means, such as visual work instructions at the cell and kanbans to tell where each item goes next in its production journey through the plant.

Table 12.2 specifies what must be in place in order to eliminate work orders for labor tracking.

Traditional manufacturers use work orders for production control and cost accounting. We have already discussed the conditions under which these documents can be eliminated for the purpose of production control. The introduction of a pull system, supported by lean cell performance measurements, provides the means of confidently shifting production control from the computerized system to a visual pull system. Nevertheless, this, in itself, will not eliminate the need for work orders to support the company's standard costing system. In Chapter 5 we suggested that companies eliminate the use of

---

1. See Chapter 3, Cell Performance Measurements.

Table 12.2: Elimination of Work Orders for Labor Tracking

Number	Actions	What Must Be in Place
1	• Eliminate job step tracking. Track only starts and completions	• Accurate labor routings and bills of materials
2	• Eliminate detailed labor tracking. • Automate the assignment of labor through backflushing using standard labor costs and actual production	• Accurate labor routings and bills of materials
3	• Backflush or prorate the overhead Eliminate detailed tracking and variance reporting	• Cell level performance measures in place in pilot cells and day by the hour reporting in all work areas
4	• Apply labor and overheads as summary direct costs to the value stream. Do not apply these costs to specific products or production jobs.	• Value streams defined • Value stream organization in place or planned • Inventories low and consistent—over 12 turns • Processes under control • Well-fumctioning kanban control • Level production demand
5	• Eliminate work orders or other production tracking documents	• Extensive use of kanbans and visual systems • Standard work • Statistical process control

Discussed in Chapter 5

variance reporting as soon as they implement cell-level performance measures to provide real-time control of the operations, as opposed to the monthly reporting of variances found in most traditional systems. This method provides feedback on performance relative to expectations in real time, that is, in time to identify and correct the root cause of problems that affect performance, as opposed to the monthly reporting often found in variance reports based on standard costs. However, that does not deal with the other uses of cost information derived from work-order information, such as valuing inventory and providing profitability reports. Consequently we find many companies that have entirely shifted their factories to a pull system to manage the flow of production, but they still create work so they can produce financial statements. This pointless exercise often requires a full-time staff and is totally wasteful, but unless the standard costing system can be replaced, the system will demand that these data be input.

The solution to the standard costing dilemma is Value Stream Costing as described in Chapter 9 and Chapter 11. By charging costs directly to the value stream as they are incurred, we are ignoring work-in-process inventories on the balance sheet. This is possible because the well-functioning kanban system maintains inventories of in-process items that are level and low. Consequently the inputs to production in terms of the amounts expended for materials, labor, and supplies will be roughly equal to the transfers from work-in-process to cost of sales. So, a well functioning kanban system and a level flow of production are important to value stream direct costing.

As value stream direct costing charges all costs to the value stream directly, it is important for employees and machines to be assigned to specific value streams. Otherwise, the costs will have to be allocated among several value streams. We have found that some companies have difficulty assigning support employees to value streams when they first introduce lean value streams. As we discussed in Chapter 9, many such employees work in several value streams, and there is the fear that organizing assignments in such a way will increase costs. However, it should be remembered that the implementation of pull systems, and the creation of value streams, changes the structure of the work of the support departments. Let us look at a few of the functions.

- **Production control:** With the introduction of pull system to control the value stream, the focus of control shifts from a production control department to the pull system itself. The flow of customer sales orders will determine the production schedule instead of a schedule calculated from a forecast. The rate of production will be established in the value stream management function, as will the number and size of the kanbans. Therefore, the role formally played by the production control department will be almost entirely subsumed by the value stream.

- **Transportation and Inventory Management:** A well-functioning pull system eliminates the need for the work-in-process warehouse. In-process inventory will be stored in supermarkets between the production cells in totes that are filled with the exact quantities needed by the next step in production. Inventory control is created visually, and assuming the cells are adjacent to each other, a minimum of material movement required. The control of inventory changes to a control of the kanbans, ensuring that the cards are maintained and delivered to the proper cells to trigger production as needed. All these functions have to be performed by people who are dedicated to the cell; they cannot be performed on a part-time basis, because the actions have to be performed immediately when they are needed. They cannot be deferred.

- **Procurement:** Many lean companies locate procurement people in their value streams. The reason that they can do this is that they have few suppliers for each commodity and these suppliers are certified as reliable. Commodity specialists negotiate the blanket purchase orders with these suppliers annually, and individual value streams pull from these suppliers as needed. Commodity specialists who are in a value stream deal with any problems with suppliers to that value stream. The job of the procurement person has changed from centralized processing requisitions and negotiating individual purchases associated with them, to working in the value stream facilitating its relations with suppliers, ensuring the on-time delivery of items pulled from the supplier. Sometimes the commodity specialists do continue work outside the value streams, and their role is supplier relationships and contract negotiation. They are not involved in the daily pulling of requirements from the supplier; people within the value stream do it.

- **Tooling:** With rapid changeover being a requirement for single-piece production, tool design becomes an important skill for every value stream. Because the problems of each piece of machinery are unique, tooling specialists are increasingly being assigned to value streams and cross-trained to do other needed tasks.

- **Manufacturing Engineering:** In a lean value stream, continuous improvement is the responsibility of the value stream itself, based on the trends in value stream performance measures. The management of the continuous improvement teams for the value stream becomes the full-time responsibility of the assigned manufacturing engineer, who evaluates the meaning of the performance measurements, defines problems and root causes, designs programs of work to correct problems, and manages the improvement teams.

It should be clear from the above that many of the support functions that have been shared in traditional manufacturing will be dedicated to the value stream when the lean manufacturing flow has been established through functioning kanbans. This will happen not because management mandates it, but because the value stream is the proper organization unit for the performance of these tasks. Therefore, there will be very little need for allocation once value streams function as they should.

However, in the interim, it may be important to implement value stream direct costing before all the support functions have been assigned to a particular value stream. In such cases, these costs will be allocated to the value streams using a simple percentage until cross-training and other changes are made to enable the people dedicated to a value stream. Often the reason why these allocations are necessary is due to a lean system that is not properly functioning—kanbans that do not operate throughout the value stream; inability to eliminate in-process and raw material inventories, etc. Once these issues have been dealt with, most support functions will reside in the value stream, and allocation of their cost will becomes unnecessary.[2]

MATERIAL COSTS

The discussion of the need for the work order in the preceding section applies equally to material costs. The progression proceeds from the application of material costs directly to the value stream to the elimination of standard costing for materials, as shown in Table 12.3.

---

2. These issues are discussed more fully in Chapter 7, Managing by Value Stream and Chapter 9, Value Stream Costing.

Table 12.3: Eliminating Work Orders for Labor Tracking

Number	Actions	What Must Be in Place
1	• Automate the assignment of materials through backflushing using standard material costs and actual production. • Keep track of scrap and rework.	• Accurate labor routings and bills of materials • Accurate records for scrap and rework
2	• Establish a supplier certification program	• Reduce the numbers of suppliers for each commodity
3	• Introduce blanket purchase orders with suppliers	• Certified suppliers
4	• Use MRP for planning, not for ordering materials	• Certified suppliers • Blanket purchase orders • Kanban inventory control extending to suppliers
5	• Apply material costs directly to the value stream at the time received.	• There is little inventory in the plant and cycle times are so short that material is used as it is received • Certified suppliers that deliver to the line • There is little raw material inventories. • Kanban inventory control with suppliers
6	• Eliminate work orders or other production tracking documents	• Kanban control of inventories
7	• Eliminate standard costing	• Inventories low and consistent • Blanket POs with certified suppliers for most commodities

Discussed in Chapter 5

In Chapter 5 we discussed backflushing, which is the use of materials at standard cost and actual production. This eliminates the need to keep detailed track of the use of materials and is valid so long as the bills of materials are up to date and accurate, and scrap is reported separately.

When value streams have been defined and pull methods control materials,using work orders to track material usage and costs is no longer necessary. An effective pull system ensures that work-in-process inventories are low; so the next step is to charge materials into the value stream at the time they are received. This requires that raw material inventories are low, so they will be used during an accounting cycle, which is normally one week to one month. This also requires suppliers to be reliable. This is usually achieved through a certification process whereby the supplier is certified for on-time delivery, perfect quality, and correct quantities. Many companies, at this point, use kanbans to pull materials from their suppliers. Other companies have relationships in which suppliers manage the inventories, replacing the amounts that have been used in much the same manner as a supplier replenishes supermarket shelves. The reduction in the number of suppliers and their certification is a major undertaking for the lean company. It entails a winnowing process that often can be very painful for the company that has longstanding relationships with many suppliers. Certification requires an education of suppliers to the lean company's standards and may often require that the supplier be lean itself. The end goal is to have the supplier deliver to the line with a minimal amount of quality inspection and in the quantities that are required for the next day's production. Hence, certifying some suppliers and letting go of others is a major first step towards eliminating the standard costing system for materials.

Blanket purchase orders that stipulate the terms of the relationship need to be established with the key suppliers to eliminate the need for a separate purchase order to be created for every daily delivery. Blanket purchase orders define the products supplied by the vendor, the prices of the items, and the terms of the relationship. They do not specify any delivery quantities, because the items are pulled when they are required; they are not ordered through the blanket purchase order. Lean companies commonly provide long-term forecasts of their requirements to the suppliers, but these generally have no quantity commitments.

Once the three steps are established—reduction of the numbers of suppliers for each commodity, certification of the key suppliers, and the establishment of blanket purchase orders—the company can have suppliers deliver directly to the production line, and raw material inventories can be drastically reduced.

When there are pull systems at the level described above, work orders can be eliminated. Further, the costs of the materials that have been received can be expensed directly to the value stream as cost of sales at the purchase order cost. There is no need to have standard cost of materials, so long as there are blanket purchase orders that lock in the cost of the commodity purchased. The system can automatically voucher into cost-of-sales the items received at the blanket purchase order cost. Invoices from the suppliers can also be eliminated at this point.

INVENTORY TRACKING

This section deals with the elimination of a perpetual inventory system. Most manufacturing companies keep detailed records of the inventory they purchase, the work-in-process, and the finished products they manufacture. In fact, the MRP production and materials planning processes require accurate inventory records.

In Chapter 5 we discussed the elimination of some of the work associated with these perpetual inventory records through the use of material backflushing. The transactions required to issue materials to a production job are no longer done individually, by hand. They are done automatically by the system when the kit is issued to the shopfloor, or when the product is completed. If the bills of materials are accurate and scrap reporting is effective, then backflushing can adequately maintain the perpetual inventory balances for each item.

As lean manufacturing and purchasing methods are introduced into the value stream, the level of inventory falls dramatically, and such methods as pull systems and kanban bring the levels under excellent visual control. When the inventory is low and under control, it is no longer necessary to track this inventory on the computer systems. We can eliminate the perpetual inventory and the backflushing required to maintain accurate balances because the inventory is under visual control.

Most traditional companies use their perpetual inventory systems and standard costing to value their inventory on the balance sheet. When the inventory is low and under control, this is replaced by simpler methods of inventory valuation. The importance of the inventory value diminishes because it is a much lower amount, and this gives us flexibility in the way we value our inventory. It is common for lean companies to expense materials on receipt and make simple month-end adjustments to bring the inventory value onto the balance sheet. The inventory value can be calculated from the number of days of inventory within the value stream. This measurement—dock-to-dock days—is commonly used as a value stream performance measurement, and the value of the inventory can be readily calculated from the days of raw material, days of WIP, and days of finished goods.

The elimination of the perpetual inventory renders cycle counting unnecessary. Many companies move from full annual physical inventory to regular cycle counting. The purpose of the cycle counting is to maintain inventory record accuracy. As you move to value stream costing, pull systems, and flow through the value streams, the inventory is brought low and under control, the perpetual inventory tracking is eliminated for the majority of items, and cycle counting also can be eliminated.

SUMMARY

This chapter has discussed the elimination of work orders and tracking labor, materials, and inventory in the lean value stream. Generally, the requirements are for value streams to be defined and the company to be moving toward organization by value stream and pull systems controlling production. At that point the company can shift entirely from control of production and costing by using work orders to relying entirely on the pull system. Cost accounting can be greatly simplified by charging costs directly into the value streams.

CHAPTER 13

Sales, Operational, and Financial Planning (SOFP)

Lean manufacturing operations are very well planned. Some people make the mistake of thinking that fast and responsive processes work ad hoc to meet the short-term needs of the customers. Nothing is further from the truth. True flexibility is built on excellent planning.

Another reason some people feel lean operations are unplanned is that they do not see huge planning departments replete with complex information systems. Lean companies do not need complex planning and scheduling systems for detailed production planning because the structure of the value stream has been established to accommodate the planned flow of the work well in advance of the receipt of the orders. When the orders arrive, the scheduling built into the pull system takes over. There is no need for detailed scheduling or planning of the orders because the operations themselves are well planned.

The planning process, usually a monthly ritual, enables the lean value streams to operate in an orderly and flexible way. By the time detailed shop-floor scheduling is required, the value stream has already been planned and organized. A planned approach, a well-designed flow, and a pull system make for a highly flexible and capable production operation.

Does this mean that there are no surprises or crises within lean operations? Of course there are, but problems can be resolved more quickly in a well-planned operation. The monthly operational planning process is essential to effective lean plants.

Purpose of Lean Sales, Operations, and Financial Planning

The purpose of lean planning is to anticipate future customer needs and to establish the capacity to meet these needs and provide the flexibility to cope with the unexpected. Lean organizations plan for the medium term usually looking ahead 9, 12, or 18 months. These plans are used in the short term to determine required production cycle times, to level schedules, and to plan the people and equipment required.

Over the medium term, this planning is used to identify when additional resources are required and to obtain those resources in the best way. Lean organizations generally add resources in incremental steps, rather than buying large pieces of equipment designed to meet long-term (and therefore uncertain) needs.

Underlying lean sales, operations, and financial planning (SOFP) is teamwork. For many years, traditional manufacturers have suffered from a lack of cooperation between the people essential to the organization's success. It is not unusual, for example, to see very little cooperation between sales and marketing and production operations. It is common to witness animosity rather than cooperation. Everyone recognizes that sales and marketing, product engineering, production operations, and others within the organization must work together closely and cooperatively if the company is to be successful; and yet this rarely occurs.

Lean companies recognize the importance of value streams. An order-fulfillment value stream always starts with a sales process, leading to the acceptance of an order, the manufacture of products, shipment and invoicing of the goods, and the collection of cash from the customer. It is essential that every aspect of the value stream be well planned and coordinated for the value stream to flow effectively.

This same level of cooperation is required to sustain ongoing continuous improvement. While improvement projects occur at individual departments and cells within the value stream, the improvement is planned and initiated across the entire value stream. Active planning and cooperation among the people in the value stream are essential for effective operation of the value stream and long-term, sustained lean improvement.

The primary outcome of the SOFP process is an agreed-on game plan for each of the value streams. Everybody within the value streams then sets about the task of successfully executing the plan. The plan is updated every month as circumstances change. The value streams become well-planned, well-coordinated, and flexible lean organizations.

Lean Financial Planning

Traditional budgeting is unhelpful to lean organizations. Here are some of the problems that occur:

- An annual budget process quickly becomes out of date. It is not dynamic enough for a lean company seeking to meet customers' changing needs.

- The budgeting process is highly wasteful. Most companies spend significant time developing budgets. The process requires managers from each department to submit budget information, which is then consolidated across the operation and rolled up to the division, group, and corporate levels. Then a protracted and wasteful review process often results in each department's carefully calculated budgets being summarily reduced and adjusted. This, in turn, leads to the managers playing political games to ensure they receive the budgets they feel are required. They often over-budget in anticipation of budget cuts, etc. The result is a wasteful and unseemly process.

- Budgets are focused on the financial outcomes, not operational inputs. The budgets are almost always expressed in financial terms and do not provide insight into the operational requirements. The budget process begins with operational issues, but the entire process and reporting soon becomes a financial planning exercise that is often divorced from the operational realities.

The SOFP within a lean organization is dynamic, and usually updated every month. The process is fast and effective, providing relevant information with very little wasted time and effort. The planning process is rooted in the operational needs of the business—sales operations, marketing operations, production operations, product development operations, and others. The financial plan is the outcome of the operational plan.

Once operational planning is complete, we have the best available information relating to the expected sales, production, improvements, and new product information, etc. From this and our knowledge of the value stream costs we can quickly develop valid and accurate financial forecasts. This means we have valid balance sheets and P&L reports in advance of the month-end and further into the future. This gives the managers the ability to manage and control the organization proactively It also means that the month-end close, so beloved of managers and accountants alike, becomes much less important and urgent. Valid financial information is known weeks ahead of the month-end.

LEAN SALES, OPERATIONS, AND FINANCIAL PLANNING

The SOFP is a formal process conducted every month within each value stream. The culmination of the SOFP is the executive planning meeting, where all the value stream plans are brought together into a single game plan for the organization.

The primary inputs and outcomes of the SOFP process are shown in Figure 13.1. Sales and marketing people provide forecasts of expected sales

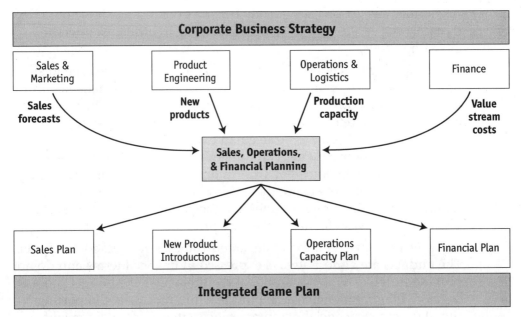

Figure 13.1: Sales, Operations, and Financial Planning

for the next 12 months.[1] The product development people provide information about new products and design changes. The production people bring information about the available capacity throughout the production and logistics segments of the value stream, and the finance people bring the detailed financial information. The outcome of the SOFP process is an integrated game plan for each value stream and for the wider organization. This agreed-on game plan reflects the company's business strategy and provides the sales people, the new product people, the operations people, and the supporting personnel with their marching orders for the short term and the long term.

SOFP is a formal process running to a strict timetable each month. While much of the detailed work is done by middle managers within the value streams, the senior executives of the organization are actively involved in the decision-making and authorization of the plan. A typical SOFP process is shown in Figure 13.2.

SOFP starts when the prior month's sales and production information for the value stream is available. This information is used for demand planning and capacity planning. The outcome of the demand planning is a new set of monthly sales forecasts for the next 12 months. There is one monthly forecast for each product family and that forecast is expressed in units to be sold.

The operations capacity over the next 12 months is then compared to the required demand to identify shortfalls or overcapacity. The operations capacity is established for each month, taking into account the newly forecasted product mix and the bottlenecks (or constraints) within the value stream flow.

---

1. The length of the planning horizon will be discussed later, but for this example, we will assume a 12-month horizon.

Day 1-5	Day 6–10	Day 12	Day 13–15	Day 15
Value Stream Demand Planning	**Value Stream Operations Planning**	**SOFP Planning Meeting**	**Value Stream Financial Planning**	**Executive SOFP Meeting**
INPUT 1 Month-end data. 2 Customer forecasts 3 New product plans OUTPUT 1 VS product family forecasts in units. 2 New SOFP Spreadsheet WHO 1 Sales & marketing 2 New product development team	INPUT 1 Demand forecasts 2 Value stream cost analysis 3 Lean improvement plan 4 Value stream changes OUTPUT 1 VS capacity forecast 2 Updated SOFP sheets WHO 1 Production operations	INPUT 1 SOFP spreadsheet OUTPUT 1 Decisions to balance demand & capacity 2 VS improvement plan 3 New product introduction plan 4 Month-end financials 5 Agenda for Executive SOFP Meeting WHO 1 Value stream mgrs 2 Sales & marketing 3 New product develop 4 VS Finance 5 Other key operations people	INPUT 1 SOFP spreadsheet OUTPUT 1 Updated rolling budgets for next 18 months 2 Major budget issues list 3 Major new expenditure WHO 1 VS Finance 2 Plant or Division controller	INPUT 1 SOFP spreadsheets 2 Exec SOFP Meeting agenda 3 Updated budgets 4 Major budget issues 5 Major new expenditure OUTPUT 1 Operational decisions 2 Authorized business "game plan" 3 Financial decisions WHO 1 President 2 Senior managers 3 Value stream mgrs 4 Sales & marketing 5 New products 6 Other key people

Figure 13.2: Sales, Operations, and Financial Planning Schedule

These assessments include new product introductions and the expected effect of the value stream's lean continuous improvement. The financial outcome of these plans month-by-month can then be calculated.

The value stream planning teams meet together on Day 12 of the month, for example, to review the spreadsheets containing the sales, operations, and financial planning information. The purpose of this meeting is to make decisions to match the operations capacity to the customer demand, and to optimize the profitability of the entire operation. It is during this meeting that the value stream teams work out ways to assist each other in resolving upcoming problems. Most of the planning decisions are made during this meeting. An outcome of this meeting is an agenda for the SOFP Executive Planning meeting as well as recommendations for action. The agenda for the Executive meeting will include a list of decisions that cannot be made at the value stream level and require action from the executive team.

The culmination of the SOFP process is the Executive Planning meeting on (for example) Day 15 of the month. The preparation work within each value stream ensures this meeting is short and action-oriented. The Executive Planning meeting is led by the CEO of the organization, includes all the company's executives, and the value stream managers. Using the information gathered through the SOFP process and an agenda developed by the value stream SOFP teams, the executive team reviews the operational and financial spreadsheets, makes any decisions requiring their input, and authorizes the plan. The outcome of the Executive Planning meeting is an integrated game plan for the organization that everyone has reviewed, agreed on, and understood.

The final step of the SOFP process is to put the plan into action. There are short-term actions and long-term actions. The short-term actions include establishing the value stream takt and cycle times, creating level schedules for the next month, manning levels for each value stream, sales plans, and finalizing projects for new products and continuous improvement. The long-term actions can include such things as capital acquisitions, increasing or decreasing staff, make/buy decisions, marketing strategies, and new product development plans.

The financial reports from SOFP show income statement and Balance Sheet information for each month, and budget information for each value stream and support department. This is powerful information, because it is current and proactive, and based on the company's current action plans.

SOFP Team

Each value stream has an SOFP team. The responsibilities of this team are to work through the SOFP process each month, develop the SOFP spreadsheets, make the planning decisions, identify required decisions that are outside the team's scope of responsibility, and provide the information required to execute the plan.

This is a cross-functional team of people within the value stream including people responsible for production operations, purchasing, sales and marketing, financial control, materials management, new product introduction, and continuous lean improvement. Some of these people may not be organizationally in the value stream; but they need to be brought into the SOFP process.

Larger value streams may specifically appoint a person as the SOFP coordinator. For less complex value streams, in which teams are less formally organized, much of this work can be done by the value stream manager. There are two important issues:

1. The people responsible for executing the plan must also be responsible for the planning process.
2. SOFP must be a formally organized process so it becomes a natural part of value stream management.

VALUE STREAM DEMAND PLANNING

Demand planning is done by the sales and marketing people responsible for the product families within the value stream. A forecast is required for each product family for each month of the planning horizon. The product families used for demand planning are groups of products with similar production characteristics. Value streams are defined as groups of products with similar production flows. Many value streams have only one product family; other value streams have two or three. It is important to define the product families within the value streams and to provide monthly forecasts for each.

For the purposes of SOFP, it is important to have few product families. A product family forecast is the expected monthly demand for all the products within the product family, expressed as the number of units or items. The demand forecast of a product family is always more accurate than the forecast for individual items within the family.

When it comes to sales forecasts, sales and marketing people have difficulty accurately forecasting the demand for individual products. It is much less work and much more accurate to calculate a forecast for the whole family of products. SOFP does not need a sales forecast for each individual item; forecasts are for the product family. The forecast is the number of units expected to sell that month for that product family.

Planning Horizon

There is no correct answer to the question: "How far into the future should our planning horizon extend?" However, a good rule-of-thumb is to extend the planning horizon as far as you need to look if major capital investment were to be required. In other words, if it would take you 9 months to make a significant change in your production output that requires new equipment and a lot of new people, then the planning horizon needs to be no less than 9 months.

The purpose of the SOFP is to anticipate future business needs and create an orderly, cross-functional plan to meet these needs. To achieve this we must look ahead far enough into the future so we have time to make and execute these plans effectively. In most companies, 12 months is a good planning horizon. Others need to look farther ahead. Some can plan over a shorter time frame if their processes are more readily flexible.

The farther into the future you look, the less accurate the forecasts will be. It is common for companies to forecast monthly for the immediate future and use quarterly forecasts for the long term. For example, they may have monthly forecasts for the next six months and quarterly forecasts for another 12 months. The total horizon is 18 months, but the forecasting periods change over the horizon.

Who is Responsible for Calculating the Forecast?

The obvious answer to this question is that the people who know the most about future customer demand should calculate the forecasts. In reality, this is almost always the sales and marketing people. They are the ones within the value stream who have the most contact with the customers, and who are constantly studying the value created for the customers by the company's products and services. They have their fingers on the pulse of the market place and are putting marketing plans in place to maximize sales and profitability. The sales and marketing people are best equipped to create these forecasts.

Another reason the sales and marketing people should be responsible for these forecasts is that they will be accountable for achieving these levels

Product family: **2.3" Accumulators**
Value stream: **Hydraulic Accumulators**

HISTORY

Sales	Apr-04	May-04	June-04	Jul-04	Aug-04	Sep-04	Oct-04	Nov-04	Dec-04	Qtr-1-05	Qtr-2-05	Qtr-3-05
New Forecast	203	265	250	240	240	280	320	360	250	855	935	820
Actual Sales	214	258	261									
Difference: Month	11	–7	11									
Difference: Cum		4	4									

Figure 13.3: SOFP Spreadsheet Showing Demand Forecasts

of sales. One outcome of the SOFP is a sales and marketing plan that is executed by the sales and marketing people. It only makes sense that the people accountable for the outcome must contribute the data upon which the plans are developed.

The demand forecasts must take into account new products being introduced into the value streams. The sales and marketing people must work with the product engineers within the value stream to determine the effect of new products on the demand for other products within the family.

What If Sales Is Not a Part of the Value Stream?

In many organizations it does not make sense to have the sales operations included as a part of the value stream organization. The sales people often need to address the market differently from the product family orientation of the value stream. The sales group may need to be organized by industry, market segment, or geographic region. It is very common for companies to have customers that buy products from more than one value stream. It makes no sense to have different sales people working with those customers for different product families.

The need for effective SOFP is even more important when the sales people and the value streams are organized differently. The communication and planning must be smooth and effective. In some cases, it is possible to have the marketing people organizationally within the value stream, even when the sales organization is set up differently.

When the sales and marketing people are not a part of the value stream, it is important for those people to provide the SOFP process with product family forecasts. Using their knowledge of the market, relationships with customers, and the history of product demand, the sales and marketing people need to provide valid forecasts of expected demand each month for each of the product families. These forecasts are then applied to the value streams that support them.

What Happens If Marketing Product Groups Are Different from Value Stream Product Families?

Occasionally the sales and marketing product groups are set up quite differently from the value stream product families. A company may address several markets with a range of products. Each value stream may provide products to every market.[2] The sales and marketing forecasts would be calculated by market, not by product family.

---

2. For example, take a customer that makes marine guidance equipment for the commercial fishing market, for the recreational boating community, and for OEM boat manufacturers. Three very different markets. The products—radar, navigational, fish-finders, sonar, and supporting software—are manufactured by several process focused value streams. In this case, it makes no sense for marketing to be organized by product families, or for production to be organized by market—the technologies and production processes are quite different and in different cities. The SOFP process is essential to the planning of this kind of organization.

When this occurs it is necessary to translate the marketing forecasts into product family or value stream forecasts. This translation can be done automatically using spreadsheet calculations that make assumptions of consistent product mixes across the marketing product groups. Or, the forecaster can include an additional step in the SOFP process to study these forecasts and make the necessary adjustments. In either case, the sales and marketing people must be confident that the information used for the SOFP process truly reflects the needs of their markets and customers.

Forecasting Methods

The methods for calculating sales forecasts vary significantly. In some industries, customers provide reasonably accurate forward forecasts, and the forecasting process is relatively easy. Some automobile parts manufacturers, for example, have blanket sales orders from their customers based on customers' annual build plan. These annual forecasts are updated each month as the build plans (and other circumstances) change. The introduction of new products is a three-year process based around the design of new models of the finished automobiles. The forecasting process is relatively easy because the demand is quite predictable.

Companies manufacturing design-to-order products or systems have quite a different forecasting problem. The demand for the products is unpredictable and very much dependent on future customers' needs. The history of demand for the company's products is not very helpful in calculating future demand. The forecasts must be based on sales and marketing people's knowledge of other customers' needs and current market conditions.

Companies manufacturing a wide range of standard products that are sold to a large number of customers have a different forecasting problem. Demand history and the use of statistical forecasting methods can be very helpful. These organizations often have to cope with seasonal variability, competitive marketing, and the effect of external factors like the weather, or current fashions, etc.

Forecasting methods vary according to the type of products a company makes, the markets it works in, and where the products are in their life cycle. Newly introduced products are more difficult to forecast than well-established products. In reality, most companies have a mixture of these products. Even make-to-order manufacturers can have a more consistent, higher volume spare-parts distribution business that supports their primary products. A mass production commodity manufacturer may also provide customized products for certain customers or markets. The forecasting methods must be adapted to suit the needs of the product family in question.

There are many books on demand forecasting,[3] and we will not spend time here to describe these methods, but, ultimately, demand forecasting is an art and not a science. The skills and market knowledge of the sales and marketing people are the essential ingredients in the demand forecasting process. Their knowledge of customers' needs and the value created by the company's products and services is the vital intelligence required for effective forecasting.

Is the Forecast Accurate?

The most common complaint about sales forecasts is their accuracy, or rather, their inaccuracy. Forecasts are always inaccurate because they are based upon estimates about the future, and the future is always uncertain. In order to improve the estimation process, it is important to build a continuous improvement process into the SOFP process. When the sales and marketing people create their forecasts for each product family and value stream, they need to provide the assumptions on which those forecasts are built.

In later months, when the actual demand is compared to the forecasted demand, the SOFP team will examine the assumptions and determine the reasons for the inaccuracy of the forecast. From this, the team initiates continuous improvement projects designed to improve the forecast accuracy.

Forecasting inaccuracy is the same as process variability. The solution to forecast inaccuracy is to understand the inherent variability of the process and work to eliminate the causes of variability. The outcome of these continuous improvement efforts, over time, will result in forecasts that are more accurate, and a SOFP team that clearly understands the demand process. This same continuous improvement approach is also used to eliminate the variability of the production capacity forecasts.

VALUE STREAM OPERATIONS PLANNING

The ideal lean value stream manufactures today what the customers require today. Materials and components are pulled into the value stream just-in-time, and there is near perfect flow through each production step, resulting in very low and consistent inventory levels, and 100% on-time delivery. To achieve this, there must be well-designed and balanced production processes, additional capacity to cope with the variability of customer demand, and flawless, self-correcting processes. Most companies on the lean "journey" have not yet achieved this level of capability. They have bottlenecks, imperfectly balanced processes, inventory problems, and volatile processes. The purpose of the operations planning part of SOFP is to identify ahead of time where some of these problems will occur and resolve the issues in advance.

While the sales and marketing people are developing the new product family forecasts, the production operations people develop forecasts of the production capacity of the value stream. This is done through knowledge of

---

3. The following books provide good information about demand forecasting. However, all of these books are written from the point-of-view of traditional push manufacturing. They speak about MRPII, ERP, master production planning, shop-floor control, and capacity planning. None of these methods apply to lean organizations, but the demand planning and forecasting continues to be important. *Sales Forecasting* by Tom Wallace and Bob Stahl (Cincinatti, Ohio, T. F. Wallace & Company, 2002). *Focus Forecasting* by Bernard T. Smith (Pittsburgh, PA, B.T. Smith & Associates, 1997). *Demand Forecasting & Inventory Control* by Colin D. Lewis (Hoboken, NJ, John Wiley & Sons, 1998). *Sales Forecasting Management* by John T. Mentzer (Thousand Oaks, CA, Sage Publications, 1998)

the previously achieved production—the demonstrated capacity—and a detailed understanding of how the capacity is used within the value stream. The demonstrated capacity can be found by studying the day-by-the-hour reports for the previous months. The capacity usage information comes from the *value stream cost analysis*.

In addition to understanding the history and the current capacity usage, the continuous improvement projects and kaizen events will also have an impact on the capacity of the value stream. Almost all lean improvements eliminate waste and create newly available capacity. Often, this newly available capacity will enable the value stream to make more products with the same resources, and increase the throughput of the value stream.

It is important to understand where the bottlenecks are within the value stream, and where there is crosstraining and other flexibility to allow the value stream to cope with changes in customer demand and product mix. The operations people within the value stream adjust the Value Stream Cost Analysis to take into account these changes and improvements.

When the value stream SOFP spreadsheet is available with the newly calculated sales forecasts for the product families, the operations people get to work matching the production output to the customers' demand. If there is plenty of capacity within the value stream, then the job is simply one of assigning the right number of people to the production operations part of the value stream. If there is not enough capacity, the process is more difficult and requires making changes to the production process to meet the customer's needs.

If the production problem is some months into the future, then the value stream team can develop plans to make the required capacity available. This may be done by additional lean improvements, changes in the production process, changes to the manning of the cells, acquisition of additional production equipment, or outsourcing some products. If the shortfall is in the near future, then more pragmatic action may be required. This may include scheduling additional overtime, outsourcing some items, building inventory in advance of requirement, or getting help from another value stream. These are the usual problems of manufacturing. Lean manufacturing methods minimize these problems. SOFP is designed to highlight these problems in advance so that preventive action can be taken.

Short-Term and Long-Term Actions

SOFP instigates both short-term and long-term actions. The short-term actions include:

- Establishing production cycle times to match.
- Creating level scheduling plans.
- Recalculation of kanban quantities.
- Determining manning levels for cells and value streams.
- Initiating sales programs.

Product family: 2.3" Accumulators
Value stream: Hydraulic Accumulators

HISTORY

Sales	Apr-04	May-04	June-04	Jul-04	Aug-04	Sep-04	Oct-04	Nov-04	Dec-04	Qtr-1-05	Qtr-2-05	Qtr-3-05
New Forecast	203	265	250	240	235	280	320	360	250	855	935	820
Actual Sales	214	258	261									
Difference: Month	11	–7	11									
Difference: Cum	11	4	15									

Operations	Apr-04	May-04	June-04	Jul-04	Aug-04	Sep-04	Oct-04	Nov-04	Dec-04	Qtr-1-05	Qtr-2-05	Qtr-3-05
Old Plan	210	250	250	240	240	240	275	275	275	825	825	825
New Plan				230	230	300	330	350	225	856	935	820
NEW vs Old				–10	–10	60	55	75	–50	31	110	–5
Actual	225	225	255									
Difference: Month	15	–25	5									
Difference: Cum	15	–10	–5									
Max. Capacity	275	275	275	300	300	350	350	350	350	1100	1200	1200
Days in Month	20	21	20	22	21	20	23	21	18	67	67	67
Takt Time Mins	45	36	37	42	41	33	33	27	33	36	33	38
Cycle Time Mins	33	35	33	34	32	26	30	28	24	28	26	26
Cycle/Takt ratio	74%	96%	91%	80%	78%	80%	91%	103%	71%	78%	78%	68%

Figure 13.4: SOFP Spreadsheet Showing Production Capacity

- Creating month-end financial results in advance of the month-end
- Finalizing project plans for new product introduction and continuous lean improvement

Long-term actions include:
- Changes in staffing levels to meet expected future demand
- Purchase or redeployment of capital equipment
- Outsourcing decisions
- Developing new market strategies
- Establishing new product development programs
- Budgeting and financial planning
- Establishing long-term continuous improvement plans

Takt Time, Cycle Time, and Level Scheduling

Lean manufacturers work to takt time, which is the frequency of customer demand. If the customers need one product every 5 minutes, then we set up our production processes to manufacture one item every 5 minutes. We match our product cycle time to the customers' takt time. One outcome of the SOFP process is to establish the value stream cycle time. The takt time is available from the demand forecasts. Cycle times are determined by the production process in each cell, the bottleneck operation, and the capability of the process. The cycle time for each value stream operation is established as a part of the SOFP process.

Many lean manufacturers try to balance flexibility with level scheduling. The purpose is to create a level flow of production through the value stream while at the same time meeting customer requirements. This is usually achieved using a *heijunka* method. Heijunka is a visual method for predetermining the production mix to optimize the flow and create a consistency of production. This production consistency in turn creates a consistency in demand for raw materials and components from suppliers. The forecast information, both volume and product mix, is used to establish the heijunka mix as an outcome of the SOFP process.

Substantial changes in demand for the company's products over time will lead to changes in the number of kanbans required for the item and the kanban quantities. These changes are made as a result of the SOFP process. Most lean organizations find that changing kanban quantities has to be systematic, yet conservative. Too many small changes create confusion and break down the control of the operation. However, it is important to change these kanban quantities when substantial demand changes occur.

Identifying Bottlenecks and Value Stream Cost Analysis

In most value streams the operations people are well aware of the bottleneck operations. As you move from job-shop style production into lean value stream production, the bottlenecks that prevent the flow of production become much easier to locate. Bottlenecks can also be identified from the Value Stream Cost Analysis (VSCA).

Value Stream Cost Analysis is used widely in lean accounting. It is used to identify the financial impact of lean improvements, and in target costing to highlight steps in the value stream requiring improvement. VSCA is used to identify the bottlenecks and the flow for features and characteristics costing.

VSCA is a fundamental building block of Lean Accounting, because it addresses the costs in the value stream and how the capacity is used throughout the value stream. This information enables us to manage the costs, the capacity, and the flow through the value stream.

In general terms, bottleneck operations can be identified from the VSCA as the step in the value stream where the available capacity is the smallest. Often, available capacity is negative, denoting overtime used to overcome a lack of capacity within regular work time. As production quantities and product mix change, and continuous improvement is applied to the value stream, the capacity usage and available capacity will change. VSCA is used during the SOFP process to identify when there are significant changes in capacity usage. These capacity usage changes often lead to changes in manpower, machine usage, outsourcing, lean kaizen improvements, and other changes designed to match the production output to the needs of the customers.

Figure 13.5 shows an example of Value Stream Cost Analysis. More details about VSCA can be found in Chapter 21.

Manning Levels

The number of people required to support the production operation is determined from the SOFP process. When a need for additional people is foreseen for future months, the value stream team can work on cross-training, borrowing people from another value stream (if the need is temporary), or obtaining more people to take on the work. The additional people required may be full-time or temporary employees. Many lean organizations that are subject to seasonal or cyclic demand rely on temporary staff to fill periods of high demand. The outcome of the SOFP process is a plan to obtain the right number of permanent or temporary people to fill the need.

New Product Introductions

The introduction of new products can be difficult to plan. The capacity required to support the introduction of a new product, the learning curve of the people in the process, the quality issues and last-minute changes all add up to lost time and capacity. The value stream operations team works with the product engineers during the SOFP process to ensure sufficient capacity is made available to ensure the successful launch of the product. It is sometimes necessary to build inventory to buffer these problems in the short term.

Similarly, the introduction of new products may reduce the demand for other products within the same family. It may be necessary to cut production of the obsolescent products in anticipation of the new products replacing them. These decisions are made in the SOFP process.

EMPLOYEES	Total	Sales and Marketing	Design Engineering	Customer Service	Scheduling	Blending	Mfg. Lube Primaries	Mfg. Lubr Secondaries	Secondaries 4180	Production Engineering	Quality Control	Management and Supervision	Shipping and Invoicing	Maintenance
	$360,400	$2,500	$10,000	$2,100	$5,700	$3,500	$128,000	$104,000	$32,000	$18,000	$3,500	$12,500	$3,500	$32,000
Productive	38%	46%	52%	14%	3%	34%	51%	57%	81%	0%	0%	0%	0%	0%
Non-Productive	28%	20%	23%	14%	91%	28%	25%	22%	7%	75%	100%	65%	62%	69%
Available Capacity	33%	34%	25%	72%	3%	38%	24%	22%	12%	25%	0%	35%	38%	31%

MACHINES	Total	Sales and Marketing	Design Engineering	Customer Service	Scheduling	Blending	Mfg. Lube Primaries	Mfg. Lubr Secondaries	Secondaries 4180	Production Engineering	Quality Control	Management and Supervision	Shipping and Invoicing	Maintenance
	$30,000	$-	$-	$-	$-	$-	$17,000	$10,000	$3,000	$-	$-	$-	$-	$-
Productive	54%						51%	57%	81%					
Non-Productive	3%						2%	9%	2%					
Available Capacity	43%						46%	34%	17%					

Figure 13.5: Value Stream Cost Analysis

Capacity Assumptions and Continuous Improvement

As with sales forecasts, it is important to document the assumptions contained within the capacity forecasts. These assumptions are used later on, when the actual production information becomes available. If the actual results vary considerably from the plan, then the assumptions of the plan must have been faulty. This information is used to improve the forecasting of future capacity. Continuous improvement applies to every aspect of a lean operation, including the planning process. SOFP is a continuous improvement method as well as a planning process.

Sales Plans

One of the most significant and difficult changes experienced by a company pursuing the lean journey is learning to sell products differently. There are many aspects of this and we will touch on one or two of them. Traditional companies usually provide incentives to their sales people based upon the volume of sales they bring to the company. These companies have pricing policies that reward customers for buying large quantities of products. These approaches are entirely in line with the assumptions and principles of mass production. These approaches can be harmful to a lean operation.

A lean operation works best when there is a level production load—a so-called linearity of demand. The way that sales people are compensated needs to change to match these needs. A customer that places a very large order for delivery all at once creates a significant problem for a lean operation. New approaches to pricing and order taking are required.

When the new sales forecasts are known and the capacity analysis completed, it is usual that the output of the value stream is limited by a production bottleneck. However, there may be many products within the value stream that do not pass through the bottleneck, or have other production routes. An increase in the sales of these non-bottleneck products increases revenues without increasing conversion costs. As a result, the production people and sales people work together closely to maximize the throughput of the value stream by developing sales plans to push these non-bottleneck products. The sales and marketing people will develop price and service incentives to increase the demand for these products.

Similarly, the sales and marketing people work together with the production people to develop plans for creating linear demand from the customers. The sales people also work with the customers to develop processes more conducive to lean production. These include pull systems, vendor-managed inventory, smaller daily orders, rather than large weekly or monthly orders, forward forecasts of requirements, and others. This cooperation between the sales and marketing people and the production people is driven through the SOFP process.

Capital Acquisitions

An important purpose of the SOFP process is to identify the need for changes in capacity over the long term. The sales forecasts identify where there is a need to increase or decrease the production capacity of the value stream, or parts of the value stream. The intent of SOFP is to identify these requirements well in advance, so that capital acquisition or divestment can be completed in an orderly manner.

Capital acquisition in lean companies differs from traditional organizations. The traditional organization typically has a discounted cash flow and return-on-investment model to determine the type of equipment to buy and when to buy it. This inevitably leads to the purchase of large, specialized machines and equipment that will provide the largest return on investment over the long term.

Lean organizations take a different view. The basic assumption is that additional capacity should be added in small increments. The intent is to provide capacity just-in-time, rather than relying on long-term demand expectations to bring the returns. The new machines are often flexible and easy-to-use because, in the event of demand changes, the value stream may well need to use the machine for other purposes. The machines will be operated by cross-trained people rather than white-coated specialists, so it is important (where possible) that the machines be designed for use by well-trained generalists, rather than specialists.

Lean organizations are often very careful with capital investment and use such processes as 3P[4] to ensure that a broad range of thought has been given to the decision to purchase new equipment. Lean organizations take time to examine the many ways of solving the capacity issues, before launching ahead with new investments. They are not shy of capital investment, but they do want to ensure their investment money is spent on appropriate equipment and not building the monuments of the future by purchasing capital equipment that creates large amounts of excess capacity that may never be filled.

Raw Material and Component Planning

Once the production rates for the product families and the value stream have been determined, the planning of materials and components can be completed. Lean organizations do not generally use traditional MRP to plan and schedule materials; they use pull systems to pull the material from the suppliers when they are needed. Pull processes for materials replenishment rests on three foundations:

- Certified suppliers
- Kanban quantities
- Blanket orders with forward forecasts

---

4. 3P is a method developed by Toyota for assessing the best solution when major capital investment is required or other significant plant changes. The 3P method requires a very thorough investigation of multiple solutions to the problem and often includes building and running simulations of the processes to gain a thorough understanding of the range of choices before committing to a particular course of action.

Pull systems only work with reliable suppliers that can deliver the right quantities at the right time and to the right quality. The kanbans are very important because they determine how much inventory is maintained within the process and how often the material is pulled. Kanbans always have standard quantities and a standard number of kanban cards, and these quantities are based upon the expected usage of the material or component. The expected usage comes from the production demand for products and the capability of the production process. These kanban quantities are changed as the demand for the products, and therefore, the demand for the materials, change over time.

In most pull systems, it is helpful to provide the supplier with a forecast of expected usage. This is generally done through a blanket purchase order. The blanket purchase order describes the terms of trade between the supplier and the customer—the price, the lead time, the packaging, etc. The blanket purchase order has no committed buy quantities. The buy quantities are pulled each day (or whatever regular interval is agreed) as there is usage for the material. The customer generally commits to providing the supplier with a forecast of requirements going out as far as possible into the future. The suppliers use this information for their own SOFP.

Once the planned build schedule is available, the material and component forecasts can be calculated and sent to the suppliers. The forecasts are generally calculated using planning bills. A planning bill is a single level bill-of-materials relating the required raw materials and components to the product family. It specifies how much of each raw material and component is required to support the production of each product family. The planning bill comes from knowing the bills of material for all the items within the product family, and an assumption of the product mix within the product family.

The planning bill is usually developed on a spreadsheet or simple database, and is updated as the product designs change and the production mix changes over time. When the value stream manufactures highly complex products with multilevel bills of materials, it can be helpful to use a full-blown MRP system to develop these forecasts of materials and component demand.

Troublesome Components

Most companies have troublesome components or materials. These are items that are difficult to get, or have poor suppliers, or must be purchased from distant suppliers, or require special treatment. These items cannot be pulled using kanbans and require a good deal of manual effort and skill to secure. An outcome of the SOFP process may be adjustments to the purchase orders for these troublesome items.

Finished Goods Inventory and Backlog

Ideally, a lean manufacturer carries no finished goods inventory and offers very short lead-times with little or no backlog. However, many companies on the journey to lean find that there is still a need to hold some inventory, maybe far less than before, to buffer where output and demand do not exactly match. Similarly, lean manufacturers with design-to-order or make-to-order processes also have a need to maintain a certain amount of backlog.

The SOFP spreadsheets show inventory or backlog, and also show the company's plans to reduce these. In the early stages of lean manufacturing, when inventory levels are falling substantially, it can be very important to show these inventory changes and plan for them. It is also important to explain these changes to people throughout the value stream and throughout the company. SOFP is used, often counter-intuitively, as a method of communicating the changes caused by lean manufacturing.

Figure 13.6 shows an SOFP planning spreadsheet with inventory information.

SOFP Financial Reports and Budgets

Once customer demand and production operations information has been added to the SOFP spreadsheets, the financial outcome of these plans can be calculated. An income statement is created for each value stream, together with operational performance measurements, expected capacity usage, and one or two pertinent financial ratios. Once the income statements have been developed for each value stream, these are consolidated into an income statement and Balance Sheet for the entire company. This process is similar to the weekly value stream cost reporting and the month-end financial reporting.

The income statement for each value stream is typically produced by people within the value stream using the familiar box score format. The financial controller typically completes the consolidated reporting, or whoever does the month-end reporting.

In many companies, there are additional value streams that are not typical order fulfillment processes. These may include New Product Development and non-production services like training, installation, or technical support. These value streams will also have an income statement or box score that has been modified to the value streams' needs. The support or sustaining departments that are outside the value streams will also have cost and budget information, but these typically appear on the consolidated reporting only.

Source of the Financial Information

The SOFP spreadsheet and the Value Stream Cost Analysis (VSCA) are the two primary sources of financial information. A typical value stream box score is shown in Figure 13.7. Financial information is calculated by using the sales and production information from the SOFP spreadsheet, and applying the financial information from the VSCA. The VSCA will have been used by the operations team to understand how the changing demand from the customers over the planning horizon affects the bottleneck cells, production flow, and other capacity issues. The shortfalls in capacity are understood and the initial plans for overcoming these problems will have been reviewed. From this information, the financial person (or people) in the value stream will have a good understanding of the financial impact of these issues. The financial plans

Product family: 2.3" Accumulators
Value stream: Hydraulic Accumulators

HISTORY

Sales	Apr-04	May-04	June-04	Jul-04	Aug-04	Sep-04	Oct-04	Nov-04	Dec-04	Qtr-1-05	Qtr-2-05	Qtr-3-05
New Forecast	203	265	250	240	235	280	320	360	250	855	935	820
Actual Sales	214	258	261									
Difference: Month	11	-7	11									
Difference: Cum	11	4	15									
Operations												
Old Plan	210	250	250	240	240	240	275	275	275	825	825	825
New Plan				230	230	300	330	350	225	856	935	820
NEW vs OLD				-10	-10	60	55	75	-50	31	110	-5
Actual	225	225	255									
Difference: Month	15	-25	5									
Difference: Cum	15	-10	-5									
Max. Capacity	275	275	275	300	300	350	350	350	350	1100	1200	1200
Days in Month	20	21	20	22	21	20	23	21	18	67	67	67
Takt Time Mins.	45	36	37	42	41	33	33	27	33	36	33	38
Cycle Time Mins.	33	35	33	34	32	26	30	28	24	28	26	26
Cycle/Takt Ratio	74%	96%	91%	80%	78%	80%	91%	103%	71%	78%	78%	68%
Inventory												
Plan	0	0	0	0	0	0	0	0	0	0	0	0
Actual	58	25	19	9	4	24	34	24	-1	0	0	0
Days	4.60	2.00	1.74	0.84	0.30	1.50	2.17	2.02	(0.02)	0.00	0.00	0.00

Figure 13.6: SOFP Spreadsheet showing Sales, Production, and Finished Goods Inventory

	Apr-04	May-04	June-04	Jul-04	Aug-04	Sep-04	Oct-04	Nov-04	Dec-04	Qtr-1-05	Qtr-2-05	Qtr-3-05
2"–4" VALUE STREAM												
Revenue	4,383	6,520	6,794	5,571	6,110	7,280	8,840	9,880	8,570	25,307	25,039	26,325
Material Cost	2,390	3,493	3,640	3,204	3,204	4,596	4,596	4,596	4,457	13,232	13,023	13,594
Conversion Costs	1,134	1,166	1,175	1,147	1,132	1,220	1,306	1,290	1,281	3,813	3,800	3,836
Value Stream Profit	859	1,861	1,979	1,220	1,775	1,463	2,938	3,993	2,831	8,262	8,216	8,894
ROS	-7%	29%	29%	22%	29%	20%	33%	40%	33%	33%	33%	34%
4"–12" VALUE STREAM												
Revenue	2,918	2,893	2,456	2,400	2,275	2,310	2,450	2,240	1,960	5,145	4,704	4,116
Material Cost	1,459	1,446	1,228	1,200	1,138	1,155	1,225	1,120	980	2,573	2,352	2,058
Conversion Costs	506	512	510	520	520	520	520	520	520	1,560	1,560	1,560
Value Stream Profit	953	934	718	680	618	635	705	600	460	1,013	792	498
ROS	33%	32%	29%	28%	27%	27%	29%	27%	23%	20%	17%	12%

Figure 13.7: Value Stream Box Score

will show when additional people or equipment are required, when products or processes will be outsourced, and other changes over the planning horizon. Similarly, if there is more capacity than demand, plans will be in place to adjust manning, machines, production shifts, etc. The financial impact of these changes is shown on the financial planning spreadsheet.

The capacity usage information for each period will also have been assessed as a part of the operational planning and can be readily added to the box score (Figure 13.8). Forecasts of the operational performance measurements can often be calculated from other information in the SOFP spreadsheet and the VSCA. In some cases, people in the value stream will need to estimate the information. An example of this is the value stream First-Time-Through (FTT) performance measurement. There may be several continuous improvement projects planned that affect the value stream FTT. It can be difficult to assess the precise impact of these projects definitively, but the project leaders make their best estimate and document the assumptions. This is all part of the planning process.

SOFP PLANNING MEETING

The SOFP Planning Meeting usually takes place around Day 12 of each month, and is attended by the value stream managers and key people from each value stream. There may also be people from support (or business sustaining) departments within the company that are not a part of the value streams.

The purpose of the meeting is to:

- Make decisions on how each value stream will work to match the customers' demand and the production capacity.
- Resolve conflicts and resource issues, particularly when there are shared resources (monuments).
- Create recommendations for the game plan to be presented to the SOFP Executive Meeting.
- Identify issues requiring decisions from the executive team.
- Agree on an agenda for the SOFP Executive meeting.

The meeting proceeds by reviewing the SOFP spreadsheets and identifying issues and problems. The sales forecasts and the actual sales figures are reviewed, together with the assumptions underlying the forecasts. Improvement projects may be initiated to increase the accuracy of the forecasts. The expected production capacity, the achieved capacity, and the forecasts of future production capacity are reviewed, together with the assumptions underlying them. Again, projects may be initiated to improve the forecasting of production capacity in the future. There is much discussion of how to resolve problems when the value stream is not able to meet the demand of customers, or where customer demand has significantly fallen short of the

HISTORY		Apr-04	May-04	June-04	Jul-04	Aug-04	Sep-04	Oct-04	Nov-04	Dec-04	Qtr-1-05	Qtr-2-05	Qtr-3-05
Operational	Sales per Person ($K)	$86	$112	$117	$96	$105	$126	$140	$157	$136	$422	$417	$439
	On-Time Shipment	92%	84%	83%	85%	85%	85%	90%	90%	90%	95%	95%	95%
	First Time Through	72	62	68	70%	72%	73%	74%	75%	76%	80%	85%	90%
	Dock-to-Dock Days	30.54	33.15	25.47	22.67	20.96	21.19	18.70	14.18	10.04	7.56	7.53	7.05
	Average Cost	$192.10	$185.77	$184.25	$181.29	$184.48	$207.74	$176.59	$154.91	$179.32	$180.37	$179.92	$177.32
	AR Days	37	37	38	37	37	37	36	36	35	35	35	35
Capacity	Productive	46.8%	54.7%	57.0%	43.0%	47.05	48.0%	53.4%	59.7%	50.3%	47.3%	42.9%	45.1%
	Non-Productive	31.2%	36.5%	38.0%	23.0%	27.4%	28.0%	29.1%	32.6%	27.4%	25.8%	23.45	24.6%
	Available	21.9%	8.8%	5.0%	24.0%	25.6%	24.0%	17.4%	7.7%	22.3%	27.0%	33.8%	30.4%
Financial	Revenue ($K)	4,983	6,520	6,794	5,571	6,110	7,280	8,840	9,880	8,570	25,307	25,039	26,325
	Material Cost ($K)	2,990	3,493	3,640	3,204	3,204	4,596	4,596	4,596	4,457	13,232	13,023	13,594
	Conversion Costs ($K)	1134	1,166	1,175	1147	1,132	1,220	1,306	1,290	1,281	3,813	3,800	3,836
	Profit ($K)	859	1,861	1,979	1,220	1,775	1,463	2,938	3,993	2,831	8,262	8,216	8,894
	Return-on-Sales	17.2%	28.5%	29.1%	21.9%	29.0%	20.1%	33.2%	40.4%	33.0%	32.6%	32.8%	33.8%
	Return-on-Net-Assets	10.2%	21.8%	23.5%	-4.8%	21.6%	17.4%	31.0%	42.5%	30.2%	28.1%	28.0%	30.3%

Figure 13.8: Value Stream Planning Box Score.

available capacity. The purpose of the discussion is to work together to solve these problems.

Sometimes the discussion of the value stream SOFP spreadsheets is divided into two sections—short term and long term. The short-term issues (perhaps the next three or so months) require quick fixes. They need pragmatic resolutions that often require cooperation between the value streams. The long-term issues require more strategic changes, including changes in staffing levels, changes in machine capacity, changes in shift patterns, significant lean improvements, and other substantial changes. The people in the meeting can usually agree on short-term solutions and act on them. The long-term problems, however, usually require a decision to be made by company executives and to be included in the agenda for the SOFP executive meeting.

Optimizing the Sales Plan

The discussion of the long-term plans is not limited to the current sales forecast for those periods and often bring up questions such as:

- What are the optimum sales for each product family?
- How can we maximize the potential of our current capacity?
- How can we create more value for our customers?

To address these questions requires the use of three other lean accounting methods, Target Costing (Chapter 16), Value Stream Cost Analysis (Chapter 21), and Features and Characteristics Costing (Chapter 11).

Value Stream Cost Analysis (VSCA) shows how capacity is used at each step of the value stream—how much is used productively, how much nonproductively, and how much is available. The work on features and characteristics costing shows how much capacity is expended at the bottleneck cells for the variety of products manufactured in each value stream. It is quite common during the features and characteristics costing to find that there are products in the value stream that do not go through the bottleneck operation. Making additional quantities of these products (up to a practical limit) will not increase the cost of the value stream. There may be a need for the sales and marketing people to initiate a sales campaign to increase the sales of these products.

The VSCA can also be used to run what-if analysis. For example, what product mix and volumes would maximize the profitability of the value stream? Perhaps some products can be outsourced to a supplier and free up capacity within the value stream. What level of outsourcing would provide additional capacity to enable us to increase our output and sales of more profitable products and increase the overall profitability of the value stream? Would increasing the production volumes of some products be sufficient to reduce the material costs of that family of products significantly?

These kinds of analyses are excellent eye-openers to what could be achieved under ideal circumstances. They motivate the team to move beyond what is currently expected by the sales forecasts. The SOFP team performs this analysis periodically and develops plans and projects to introduce new marketing approaches and operations improvement to maximize the financial performance of the value stream.

Sometimes the sales plan discussion leads to the initiation of a target costing process. Target costing[5] is used to instigate improvement projects that increase customer value for a product, or family of products, and reduce the product cost, so the company achieves the desired level of profitability. The target costing process is not done as a part of the SOFP process; but it is the SOFP process that identifies the need to perform a target costing exercise.

The purpose of these kinds of processes is to focus the team's attention on the financial potential of the value stream, and to motivate the team-members to innovate and think outside the box. SOFP is not only about meeting the customers' needs as expressed by the sales forecasts, but also it is about introducing changes and improvements to increase value and increase profitability.

Financial Plans and Budgets

Towards the end of the meeting, after the primary decisions have been made, the financial people can update their value stream box scores and create the consolidated financial reports. The purpose of the consolidated reports is to show the financial impact of the changes in each value stream and then roll them up, together with any non-value stream sustaining departments, to create a rolling budget for the plant or company. An example is shown in Figure 13.9. The exact format and roll-up methods vary from one company to the next, but the report is produced using the same methods and assumptions as the value stream costing reports and the associated company-wide, month-end reports.

The consolidated financial reports serve, in the short term, as primary management tools for running the plant. The month-end close information is now much less significant because valid information is known in advance of the month-end. There are few surprises, because each month the expected outcomes for every month over the next 12 months are worked out and reviewed.

In the long term, the consolidated financial reports are used as the budget for the company. The budgets are authorized by the senior management and they are updated every month. This resolves the problems of traditional annual budgeting. The information is current and valid. There is no complex and time-consuming budgeting processes, because the new budgets are the outcome of the monthly planning process. The budget process is not a purely financial process. It develops from the practical operational action plans the plant or the company is currently implementing.

Most companies continue to develop the annual budgets that are required for reporting to their bankers, stockholders, and others. However, the time-consuming and wasteful processes to develop these budgets are eliminated because valid budget information is now available every month. The outcome of the SOFP Planning meeting includes:

---

5. See Chapter 16.

	Apr-04	May-04	June-04	Jul-04	Aug-04	Sep-04	Oct-04	Nov-04	Dec-04	Qtr-1-05	Qtr-2-05	Qtr-3-05
2"–4" VALUE STREAM												
Revenue	4,983	6,520	6,794	5,571	6,110	7,280	8,840	9,880	8,570	25,307	25,039	26,325
Material Costs	2,990	3,493	3,640	3,204	3,204	4,596	4,596	4,596	4,457	13,232	13,023	13,594
Conversion Costs	1,134	1,166	1,175	1,147	1,132	1,220	1,306	1,290	1,281	3,813	3,800	3,836
Value stream Profit	859	1,861	1,979	1,220	1,775	1,463	2,938	3,993	2,831	8,262	8,216	8,894
ROS	17%	29%	29%	22%	29%	20%	33%	40%	33%	33%	33%	34%
4"–12" VALUE STREAM												
Revenue	2,918	2,893	2,456	2,400	2,275	2,310	2,450	2,240	1,960	5,145	4,704	4,116
Material Costs	1,459	1,446	1,228	1,200	1,138	1,155	1,225	1,120	980	2,573	2,352	2,058
Conversion Costs	506	512	510	520	520	520	520	520	520	1,560	1,560	1,560
Value stream Profit	953	934	718	680	618	635	705	600	460	1,013	792	498
ROS	33%	32%	29%	28%	27%	27%	29%	27%	23%	20%	17%	12%
NEW PRODUCTS VS.												
Revenue	0	0	0	0	0	0	0	0	0	0	0	0
Material Costs	15	102	32	35	60	75	50	50	50	200	200	200
Design Costs	35	35	35	35	35	35	35	35	35	105	105	105
Support Costs	15	15	15	15	15	15	18	18	18	54	54	54
Admin. Costs	8	12	8	7.5	7.5	7.5	7.5	7.5	7.5	22.5	22.5	22.5
Total Costs	73	164	90	92.5	117.5	132.5	110.5	110.5	110.5	381.5	381.5	381.5

Figure 13.9: Consolidated Rolling Budget from the SOFP Process

continued on next page

	Apr-04	May-04	June-04	Jul-04	Aug-04	Sep-04	Oct-04	Nov-04	Dec-04	Qtr-1-05	Qtr-2-05	Qtr-3-05
SUSTAINING COSTS												
Executive Managers	21	21	21	21	21	21	21	24	24	72	72	72
HR	5.5	5.5	5.5	5.5	5.5	5.5	5.5	5.5	5.5	16.5	16.5	16.5
Finance	17.5	16.3	18	17	17	17	17	17	17	51	51	51
IT	52.4	74.4	73.1	63.0	66.2	75.8	89.2	95.7	83.2	240.6	235.0	240.5
Facilities	21	21	21	21	34	34	34	34	34	115	115	115
Total	127.1	138.2	138.6	127.5	143.7	153.3	166.7	176.2	163.7	495.1	489.5	495.0
CONSOLIDATED P&L												
Revenue	7,900	9,413	9,251	7,971	8,385	9,590	11,290	12,120	10,530	30,452	29,743	30,441
Material Costs	4,464	5,041	4,900	4,439	4,401	5,826	5,871	5,766	5,487	16,004	15,575	15,852
Conversion Costs	1,640	1,678	1,685	1,667	1,652	1,740	1,826	1,810	1,801	5,373	5,360	5,396
Support Costs	200	302	229	220	261	286	277	287	274	877	871	876
Gross Profit	1,597	2,392	2,437	1,546	2,071	1,738	3,316	4,257	2,967	8,198	7,937	8,316
ROS	20%	25%	26%	21%	25%	18%	29%	35%	28%	27%	27%	27%
Corporate Overhead	790	941	925	797	839	959	1,129	1,212	1,053	3,045	2,974	3,044
Inventory Change	12	(3)	(5)	(3)	(5)	(2)	(2)	0	0	(21)	(18)	(5)
Net Profit	819	1,453	1,516	851	1,237	781	2,189	3,045	1,914	5,174	4,981	5,277
ROS	10.37%	15.44%	16.39%	10.68%	14.76%	8.14%	19.39%	25.12%	18.18%	16.99%	16.75%	17.34%

Figure 13.9: *continued from previous page*

- An updated SOFP spreadsheet for each value stream.
- A recommendation for short-term actions for each value stream.
- New product launch schedule and explanation of how this fits into the plan.
- Lean continuous improvement program over the short-term.
- Financial reports and rolling budget for each value stream and for the company.
- Issues and recommendations requiring decisions from the executive team.
- Agenda for the Executive SOFP meeting.

EXECUTIVE SOFP MEETING

The purpose of the executive SOFP meeting is for the senior managers of the company to review the plans and budgets, to make decisions that are outside the scope of the value stream teams, and to authorize the value stream managers (and others) to execute the plan.

The following actions are typical for an executive SOFP meeting:

- Overall business review.
- Review value stream weekly box scores, particularly the operational performance measurements.
- Review of new product introductions and new sales and marketing initiatives.
- Review each of the value stream SOFP spreadsheets. Accept the recommendations of the value stream team or make changes to them.
- Review the company financial forecasts and budgets.
- Authorize or change any long-term planning decisions.

The key to the executive SOFP meeting is to keep it short. If the meeting runs longer than 90 minutes or two hours, then the SOFP process is not working well. The real work and primary decision-making will have been made over the previous two weeks and in the SOFP planning meeting. The executive SOFP meeting should be a snappy, decision-making meeting.

Who Should Attend the Executive SOFP Meeting?

The chairperson of the meeting is the President, or whoever is the most senior person at the location. The people attending include the company executive team, the value stream managers, senior sales and marketing people, senior new product development people, people representing the support departments, which may include purchasing, HR, finance, and others.

Sometimes the company president resists taking the chair of a planning meeting. This is because, in the past, lower level people, such as production planners, did the planning. The president believes that his/her time is not best spent doing such lowly endeavors. SOFP is not production planning. SOFP is planning and budgeting the entire business operation. If the President does not feel it is important to have a two-hour meeting once a month to discuss what the company is going to sell, what the company is going to make, what new products and marketing programs are being introduced, and how much money the company will make, then the president is mistaken. SOFP is an essential part of the lean enterprise and the president's active participation is essential to the success of SOFP.

Outcome of the Executive SOFP Meeting

The Executive SOFP meeting is primarily a decision-making meeting. The outcome is an agreed-on game-plan for the company and the authorization of the value stream managers, the sales and marketing team, the new product development team, and others to execute the plan. Some of the decisions will be short-term tactical actions to meet customer needs. Others will be long-term strategic decisions. Some of the long-term decisions may not be made there and then in the meeting. One purpose of SOFP is to raise issues well in advance so that appropriate thought and planning can be given to them.

The physical outcomes of the meeting include minutes that document the decisions made. This information (or much of it) is transferred to a visual planning board in the plant or offices so that everyone can see the company's current action plans.

VARIATIONS ON A THEME

In smaller companies, it may not be necessary to have a separate executive SOFP meeting. The executives can take part in the SOFP planning meeting, or the latter part of it. There is no reason to have additional meetings if all the key players are involved in the SOFP planning meeting.

Larger organizations often have an SOFP coordinator whose job is to orchestrate the SOFP process. This is not a full-time job, but for a larger and more complex organization it can be essential to have someone to pull the teams together, ensure the information is available, control the spreadsheets, train the people, create agendas, and post the outcome information.

Larger organizations often use the company intranet to pass the information between the various teams of people. The spreadsheets are posted to the intranet and this is the primary method of communication. This can, of course, be very helpful, but it is important to remember that lean enterprise thrives on visual management. The main SOFP meetings should not be conducted with computer screens, but with visual information. The ideal is to post large copies of the spreadsheets on the walls of the meeting room, so that people can stand in front of them and discuss them. It is handy, of course, to have someone with a computer who can record any changes and do some what-ifs on the fly, but the primary communication should be visual.

Many manufacturing companies also have value streams (or parts of value streams) that are purely service operations. This may include maintenance and repair, training, consulting, or other non-production operations. These processes can be readily included in the SOFP process. The unit of measure will not be items or pieces, it will be (for example) maintenance jobs. Their capacity will be the people's time, rather than machine throughput, but the process is essentially the same and can be included in the SOFP process quite easily.

MAKING IT HAPPEN

It is not easy to implement SOFP successfully. For most companies, it is a new and different process that requires them to make changes in the way they do their jobs. In reality, all companies do some kind of SOFP; the question is how well the process is done. Usually the equivalent of SOFP is done badly. The short-term planning is done separately by the individual departments, who are often suspicious of the other departments. The long-term planning is conducted through annual budgets and ad hoc meetings. It is rare for a traditional company to have short-term and long-term plans that are well understood, widely communicated, and jointly agreed upon.

SOFP also requires people to make plans and commitments they previously have not had to make. This requires people to make forecasts of sales, production, new product introduction, and so forth that are then reviewed each month. Some people are uncomfortable with this kind of commitment and scrutiny.

SOFP requires people to work together cooperatively, across departmental lines. This is, of course, an essential element of a lean enterprise. Working cross-functionally across the value stream is one of the principles of lean thinking. Yet many companies, even successful lean organizations are not able to develop perfect value streams. There is a need to create that value stream cooperation through the SOFP process. Companies in the early stages of lean manufacturing often find it difficult to create this value stream cooperation and some people resist the rigors of the SOFP process.

Having said this, there are tried and tested ways to implement SOFP and, when these are used, there is close to 100 percent success. In addition to planning, tenacity, and commitment, these are some of the keys to success:

- **Senior management initiative.** Senior management must be commitment to the SOFP process. Like all lean enterprise methods, SOFP will not be successful if the President and executive team is not fully committed.

- **Formal methodology.** A formal monthly process and a strict adherence to the SOFP process are required. Some companies try to apply SOFP informally and it does not work. People start to delegate the work and the meetings to others, then they do not attend the meetings and schedule other things for those days. The SOFP process and meetings must be seen as a vital part of the business process, and it must be mandatory for people to participate.

- **Tenacity.** It takes about six months for the SOFP process to begin to work smoothly. The first few months the people are learning the process. The next few months they are cleaning up the data and modifying the reports and procedures. Patience and tenacity are required for the implementation to be successful.

- **Meetings must foster decision-making.** If the meetings turn into lengthy talking shops, the process will fail. The meetings need to be strictly facilitated so that decisions are made and plans put in place. There are other occasions for broader discussion and philosophizing; the SOFP meetings are for making practical business decisions.

- **Standard implementation methodology.** There are standard methods for implementing SOFP and it is wise to use them. These are not complicated or novel, just good business project planning and execution.[6]

- **Plan by Value Stream.** All lean operations work by value stream. In the early stages of lean manufacturing, many companies struggle to establish a value stream organization, either by matrix management or reorganization. In many cases, even over the long term, some aspects of the value stream (sales, for example) are not fully integrated with the primary value streams. The SOFP process must transcend these problems and all the planning must be done by value stream. Especially when the value streams within the organization are not yet well defined, the planning must strictly adhere to value streams.

- **Continuous Improvement.** Most companies are surprised, when implementing SOFP, how little good information and coordination they really have within their operations, sales, new products development, and finance operations. Changing this does not happen quickly. SOFP must be seen as a continuous improvement methodology, as well as a cross-functional planning process. Every step and every meeting must have a CI element. Even the SOFP executive meeting should always have a last agenda point where the team critiques the process to make improvement.

---

6. There are several good books with implementation plans. Unfortunately, these books are steeped in MRP thinking. The content is good, but you will need to *think lean* when reading them. They are also quite short on the financial aspects of planning; they deal with S&OP rather than SOFP. I would recommend the implementation process shown in the book "Sales & Operations Planning" by Tom Wallace (Cincinatti, Ohio, T.F.Wallace & Company, 1999). In addition, the book "Enterprise Sales & Operations Planning" by George E. Palmatier (Boca Raton, FL, J. Ross Publications, 2003) and "Orchestrating Success" by Richard Ling (Hoboken, NJ, John Wiley & Sons, 1995).

SUMMARY

Sales, Operations, and Financial Planning (SOFP) is a vital part of lean manufacturing and the lean enterprise. The flexibility and customer-value focus required for successful lean organizations does not come haphazardly—it comes from careful and coordinated planning across the value streams.

SOFP is a formal monthly planning process designed to coordinate the sales and marketing operations with the production and logistics operations, the new product development processes, and other value-adding or support operations within the company. The planning horizon is typically 9, 12, or 18 months and is designed for both short-term and long-term planning, so that the customers demands can be fully satisfied and the company's strategic and financial objectives met. The SOFP process eliminates the need for the annual budgeting charade and replaces it with monthly rolling budgets.

The outcome of the SOFP process, which is sponsored and led by the company President, is a cross-functional sales, operations, and financial game plan that is then executed by the value stream managers and others in the company. This game plan is updated and refined every month so that the company is responsive to the customers' changing needs and the changes in the market. The financial reports coming from the SOFP process provide valid month-end information and make the month-end close a less significant process.

SOFP is an integrated, action-oriented monthly planning process that brings everyone into a coordinated plan to create great value for the customers, continuously "lean out" and improve the company's processes, and put the company's strategy into action month-by-month. SOFP, in common with most lean initiatives, is difficult to implement, because it requires considerable fundamental change. There are proven methods of implementing SOFP successfully. If you follow the formal implementation methods over a 6 to 12 month period, you will be successful.

CHAPTER 14

Lean Financial Accounting II

In Chapter 6, we established the framework for financial management by value stream. We also looked at high transaction accounting processes, asked some fundamental questions about the reasons for the processes, and asked whether those goals could be attained in ways that are not so labor-intensive, such as:

- **Approvals and sign-offs.** What would be the risk of error if the approval were no longer required?

- **Accounts payable.** How can we eliminate the need for processing supplier invoices? Indeed how can we eliminate the supplier invoices themselves? In this scenario, payment for materials used in production is made automatically on completion of that day's production. Materials required to create the products scheduled for that day are delivered to the production line, by the respective suppliers, prior to the start of the day. At the end of the day, each of the suppliers is paid automatically (either electronically or with a paper check) based on the bills of materials for the products made. From the point of view of the accounting function, this approach eliminates the need for matching receipts, purchase orders and supplier invoices in Accounts Payable. The approach to achieving this goal, advocated in Chapter 6, was accomplished in several steps:
  - *Step 1:* Reduce the number of suppliers by eliminating multiple suppliers of the same commodity. The remaining suppliers are designated key suppliers of that commodity. This step, in itself, has the effect of significantly reducing the numbers of invoices received. This step can be performed during the pilot phase of lean manufacturing implementation.
  - *Step 2:* Draft master purchase agreements with all key suppliers. The master purchase agreement specifies the approximate amount of the commodity that will be required during the coming year, its price, and the terms under which the supplier will be notified of the need for delivery against this master purchase order. This step would

eliminate the need for creating purchase orders each time a delivery is required, thereby reducing the amount of work in the purchasing department. It also allows the master purchase order price to be included in the vendor master file, so that the three-way match of purchase order, receiver, and invoice could be reduced to a two-way match of receiver and invoice. This step can also be completed during the pilot phase.
  – *Step 3:* Certify all key suppliers according to conformance of their quality to standards, thereby ensuring they can be relied on to deliver exactly to specifications, on time, and in the amounts desired. Certification cannot commence until key suppliers have been designated. It is assumed that the certification process was commenced during the pilot phase.

The chart of accounts can be simplified. By eliminating general ledger accounts, which have to be analyzed and reconciled, the month-end close can be streamlined. Much of the streamlining can take place during the lean pilot phase.

This chapter takes up where Chapter 6 left off, which addressed initiatives that can be completed during the early phase of lean. The initiatives in this chapter require that the lean process be further advanced. It assumes that the following lean initiatives are in progress or have been completed:

  • Value streams have been identified and manufacturing is managed by value stream, although there may not yet be a value stream organization.
  • Value stream costing is in place.
  • There is extensive use of visual systems, and pull systems like kanbans. Making to customer orders have replaced work orders for controlling the material flow.
  • Key suppliers have been identified, a certification program is in place, and there is kanban pull from some suppliers.
  • Key customers are encouraged to provide blanket sales orders, greatly simplifying order processing.
  • Invoicing is done from shipping, reducing the work in Accounts Receivable.

FURTHER ADVANCES IN LEAN ACCOUNTING

We deal, in this chapter, with questions associated with managing the finance function in a company that is serious about value stream management.

  • Financial Accounting Processes
  • General Ledger and Month-End Closing
  • Internal Control
  • The Role of the Accountant

Financial Accounting Processes

In this section we follow the progress of the model lean company in reducing transactions processed in Accounts Payable and Accounts Receivable.

Accounts Payable. As noted above, the supplier certification process, begun during the pilot phase, is expected to have progressed during the value stream management phase to the point that meaningful progress can be made toward reducing invoices. During this phase, value stream management is introduced and production lead times have been reduced to less than one day, from receipt of materials to completion and shipment of the product to customers. Suppliers deliver directly to the production line frequently (usually daily), based upon a kanban notification to deliver based on what has been used in production. Under these conditions the accounts payable function can change.

- The three-way match of purchase order, receiver, and invoice can be eliminated, and authorization for payment can be initiated at the point of receiving. The logic behind this change is that, if we have received the materials from a pull-generated order to a certified supplier, we can be satisfied that the quantities and the quality are correct. Kanban quantities are preset and generally delivered in standard containers, which makes it difficult for the supplier to make mistakes. And, because delivery is to the production line, any discrepancy will be immediately apparent.

- In most cases, Accounts Payable reviews the invoice from the supplier by comparing the receipts already authorized with the line items on the invoice. At this stage, therefore, the three-way match has been reduced to a two-way match.

- Also at this stage, it is appropriate to begin discussions with key suppliers concerning payment upon use of the materials and, thereby, eliminating the need for an invoice to generate payment. This can be accomplished on a supplier-by-supplier basis during the value stream management phase.

It should be clear that by the completion of the value stream management phase, when all of the value streams are functioning, that a significant amount of the work of Accounts Payable has been eliminated. Since much of the work of the traditional function involves comparing and reconciling purchase orders, receipts, and invoices, the gradual improvements in supplier controls through certification, elimination of invoices, and implementation of the master purchase agreement (or blanket purchase orders) have eliminated the need for the comparison and reconciliation functions listed above. This is possible because a systematic program replaces the audit/inspection controls over purchasing with controls that enhance the reliability of the system itself to produce desired results.

Accounts Receivable. The objective of the accounts receivable function is to speed the flow of cash receipts from the sales of products and services. The normal functions include creating and submitting an invoice to the customer based upon shipment, posting the accounts receivable and cash transactions, and following up with customers on delinquent receivable balances. We have already started invoicing directly from the shipping transaction during the pilot phase of lean, thereby eliminating the need for the Accounts Receivable department to create an additional transaction for the invoice.

During the value stream management phase, it is appropriate to begin to encourage customers to pay on receipt of the materials, rather than processing invoices from us. We assume here that customers are also engaged in the lean manufacturing process and have the same incentives that were discussed in the section dealing with Accounts Payable.

- They have selected our company as a key supplier of the commodity in question.
- Our company has been selected as a certified supplier.
- We have agreed to deliver daily to the customers' production lines based upon pull signals.

In return for performing these functions, the customer pays on receipt of the materials, or on their use in production. It is clear that, under traditional thinking, there is little incentive to pay early. Most companies wish to withhold payments to suppliers and accelerate the receipt of cash. However, lean thinking views the cash flow model throughout the value stream, not just with respect to any portion of the stream. Cash flow is maximized throughout the value stream when both suppliers and customers pay as soon as possible after delivery of the materials.

As more and more customers begin to pay upon receipt, the volume of invoices that need to be prepared shrinks. Accounts receivable can still be posted on shipment, but no invoice is sent to the customer. Cash received can also be posted automatically to the accounts receivable ledger based on bank notification from the lock box, assuming customers pay to a lock box managed by a financial institution. The saving in time following up with delinquent customers frees Accounts Receivable personnel for other, more value-creating tasks.

General Ledger and Month–End Closing. Chapter 6 outlined the issues related to waste generated by the large number of accounts in the general ledger. Such a system causes delays in closing the books, because each account must be reconciled with the detailed subsidiary ledgers in order to ensure accuracy of the financial statements. In a lean company the problem is further complicated when the company has decided to be managed by value stream. So we will deal with the first issue in the context of the second.

To significantly reduce the complexity in closing the books, two changes are required to the accounting procedures:

1. Eliminate all general ledger accounts below the organizational level of the value stream at the division level, and at an expense level containing greater detail than a summary by resource type.

2. To the extent possible, eliminate all end-of-period accruals and allocations, and move to a cash basis of accounting.

To provide context, consider the traditional company, organized by functional department, as depicted in Chapter 7:

- Customer Service
- Product Configuring
- Production Planning
- Purchasing
- Receiving
- Manufacturing
  - SMT
  - Hand Load/Wave Post
  - Test and Rework
  - Assemble and Burn-In
- Shipping
- Quality Assurance
- Inventory Control
- Manufacturing Engineering
- Tooling
- Maintenance
- Accounting
- Human Resources
- Information Systems
- Design Engineering
- Facilities

In the typical traditional manufacturing company, the resources that each of the departments uses are assigned to them. So each of the departments has separate accounts for its resources:

- People
  - Management salary
  - Management benefits (pension, health care, social security, vacation, etc.)
  - Management payroll taxes
  - Hourly wages
  - Hourly overtime
  - Hourly payroll taxes

- Hourly benefits (health care, sick pay, workmen's compensation, social security, vacation, etc.)
  - Training
  - Temporaries
  - Consultants
  - Administration salaries and benefits, as above
  - Travel and entertainment
- Machines
  - Depreciation
  - Outside costs of repair
- Office Equipment
  - Depreciation
  - Supplies
- Supplies used
- Tooling used
- Tooling depreciation
- Electricity
- Heat
- Light
- Warehouse costs
- Property tax, etc.

The list goes on and on. In the example above, there would be as many as 670 separate accounts for the manufacturing function. In some companies, each department's cost is managed by itself. In others, non-manufacturing costs are allocated to the manufacturing departments. For financial statement purposes, departmental costs are totaled by direct, that is, manufacturing departments, and indirect, or all support departments. The balances in end-of-period raw materials, work-in-process, and finished goods inventories are determined. Cost of goods sold is calculated by adding or subtracting the difference between beginning and ending inventories to (or from) the amount of the direct and indirect departmental costs for the period. If ending inventories are less than beginning-of-year, the difference is added, and if more, the difference is subtracted.

To illustrate:

cost of goods sold = (direct departmental costs + indirect departmental costs) + (beginning inventory – ending inventory).

Finally, accruals are made for items in transit at the end of the year to inventory and/or accounts payable as appropriate. Financial statements are developed and presented on a plant-wide or divisional basis, comparing actual and budget for the components of cost of sales.

The system described above is appropriate for a company that has long lead times, high and fluctuating work-in-process, and finished goods inventory balances. It is much less so for one that has production lead times of less than one week and low and stable inventory balances. As we have seen, this lean company should, more appropriately, be organized and managed by value stream within the plant or division.

The accumulation of cost would proceed by value stream, as shown in Table 14.1

Table 14.1: Accumulation of Costs by Value Stream

	Material cost	Outside cost	Employee cost	Machine cost	Other cost	TOTAL COST
Customer service	–	–	$12,108	–	–	$12,108
Purchasing	–	–	16,145	–	–	16,145
SMT	358,512	–	17,080	16,956	20,000	412,548
Hand load/wave post	25,608	–	23,485	2,016	–	51,109
Test and rework	–	–	17,080	3,528	–	20,608
Assemble and burn-in	128,040	–	10,675	–	–	138,715
Shipping	–	–	2,669	–	–	2,669
Quality assurance	–	–	8,073	–	–	8,073
Mfg engineering	–	–	8,073	–	–	8,073
Maintenance	–	–	8,073	–	–	8,073
Accounting	–	–	8,073	–	–	8,073
Information systems	–	–	4,036	–	–	4,036
Design engineering	–	7,760	4,036	–	–	11,796
	$512,160	$7,760	$139,606	$22,500	$20,000	$702,026

As detailed in Chapters 7 and 9, all people, machinery, outside processing costs, and other costs such as supplies, would be assigned directly to a value stream and the resources would be included in the value stream organization. All other resources would be assigned to an administration and overhead category. Departmental organization would disappear, being replaced by the value stream organization. This means that for the example presented above, instead of having 670 accounts, there would be 190 accounts, just by reducing the number of departments from 21 to 6 (five value streams and one administrative and overhead department). However, we strongly recommend that the 32 detailed accounts be eliminated from the general ledger, and leave the detail for the subsidiary ledgers—one for each value stream. Our preferred scenario would be for five accounts per value stream in the general ledger: Materials, Employee Costs, Outside Processing, Machine Costs, and Other Costs. The number of accounts in the general ledger reduces from the original 670 to 30. Having such a thin general ledger will greatly facilitate the speedy production of financial statements. Detailed information would continue to reside in the books of original entry (cash receipts and disbursements journals, payroll journal, purchases and sales journals) and the detailed ledgers of assets and liabilities.

The income statement by value stream produced for the division/plant would look like the following, Table 14.2:

Table 14.2: Presentation of Divisional/Plant Level Financial Statements by Value Stream

Electronic Components, Inc.					
	Value Streams				
	Controller products	**Vertical positioners**	**New product development**	**Admin. & 6verhead**	**Division P&L**
Revenue	$1,280,400	$2,048,640	$0		$3,329,040
Material costs	$512,160	$614,592	$12,766		$1,139,518
Conversion costs	$184,380	$313,445	$678,574		$1,176,399
Value stream profit	$583,860	$1,120,603	($665,808)		$1,038,655
Value stream ROS	45.60%	54.70%			
Employee costs				$44,355	$44,355
Expenses				$27,943	$27,943
			Prior period inventory		$1,788,549
			Current inventory		$1,252,432
			Inventory change		−$536,117
Division gross profit					$438,287
Division ROS					13%

As can be seen, no distinction is made between direct and indirect costs. All costs that are not for purchased materials are included in a category entitled "Conversion Costs." These are identified by value stream.

Some lean companies prefer to show more detail on their Income Statements and may break the costs down under headings such as Procurement Costs, Manufacturing Costs, Distribution Costs, and Administrative Costs. These groupings can provide better insight into the changing cost structure of the organization as it moves further along the lean enterprise maturity path.

Use a Cash Basis of Accounting for Expenses

The second key to rapidly closing the books is to eliminate end-of-month accrual and adjustments by shifting from an accrual basis to a cash basis of accounting. The practical effect of this will be to expense all overhead costs as a period expense, that is, in the period that the cost was incurred. Traditional accounting assigns labor and overhead to the product being manufactured and carries the cost in inventory until the product is sold, at which point the costs are expensed to match with their respective revenues. This method of accounting is required by Generally Accepted Accounting Principles (GAAP) in order to match revenues and related expenses. The result of this requirement is the complex set of accounting transactions to track the movement of inventory through the plant that we have discussed throughout this book. It also results in the need to confirm the accuracy of inventories at the end of the accounting period in order to create accurate financial statements. Typically, this results in adjustments to the financial statements for the differences found between the values of inventory in the company's warehouses and that on the company's books. Any meaningful reduction in the time to close the books at the end of a period must consider ways to eliminate the complexity of the current inventory accounting system.

Our approach is to eliminate inventory accounting altogether and to create an end-of-period adjustment to account for the changes in the value of the inventory from period to period. This adjustment would be made at the level of the division income statement as shown in Table 14.2. The income statement shown has been calculated on a cash basis of accounting. That means that all costs of production have been charged to expense as incurred and none have been capitalized in inventory. The amounts shown for Material Costs and Conversion Costs are equal to the cash actually expended for the materials and labor used in production during the period, with the possible exception of machine depreciation, which is often included in the conversion costs. The statement shows that, during the period, inventories have declined by $536,117. So, an adjustment has been made in this amount to reduce the cash-basis profit to an accrual-basis profit of $438,287. The amount of the adjustment from cash to accrual was calculated by taking the reduction in units from the beginning to the end of the period in each value stream, multiplying that amount by the average cost per unit manufactured in each of the value streams, then summing up the products across all value streams. This effectively allows the division to maintain its books on a cash basis for management reporting and adjusting to accrual-basis income for financial statements prepared in accordance with GAAP. As noted before, this eliminates transactions whose only purpose is to value inventory for financial statement preparation. The cash basis also has the desirable effect of increasing profitability when inventories are reduced, and decreasing it when inventories increase. This has the opposite effect of accrual-basis statements, but is desirable from a lean-manufacturing perspective. (You may remember from Chapter 4 that one of the amazing features of the financial effects of inventory reduction using traditional accounting is that profits actually decline—exactly the opposite of what is desired.)

These two initiatives, eliminating accounts from the general ledger and using a cash basis of accounting for production expenses, speeds up closing the books for the lean company at the end of the period.

How Often Do We Close?

The final issue is the frequency of closing. In this regard, current practice varies. Some companies close the books to prepare financial statements monthly, and some do so weekly. Closing the books has the undesirable effect of motivating a month-end push to produce and ship orders during the final week of the month in order to meet the financially budgeted numbers. This, in turn, creates havoc with a lean manufacturing program that strives to maintain an even rate of production throughout the month. So the question that must be raised is, "why close the books monthly?" For a company that has level inventories, the cash basis income is equivalent to that calculated on an accrual basis. Lean companies in the value stream management phase of implementation typically have pull systems that ensure level inventories and maintain the production flow. Consequently, financial statements can be prepared monthly without the need to close the books. At the end of the quarter, however, a company that trades its securities publicly, is required to report financial results to the Securities and Exchange Commission, and is justified in closing its books. In this case, we would recommend the adjustment from cash to accrual that we described in the earlier paragraphs.

Companies using the Sales, Operations, and Financial Planning (SOFP) methods described in Chapter 12 have valid month-end information several days prior to the month-end. This is based upon planned information rather than actual results, but once the SOFP process is working well, this planned information is excellent for the control and management of the business. One company's CFO explained, "I would rather know at the beginning of the month that my Return-on-Sales will be 14 percent this month than wait six weeks to discover it was 13.97 percent."

Internal Control

The control environment described in the preceding chapters is very different from that existing in a traditional manufacturing company. Essentially, the major shift in emphasis is from reliance on inspection and reviews of transactions, to building control into the structure of the business's processes.

Figure 14.1, which we presented in Chapter 6, is also presented here to depict this shift. Inspection includes reviews and audits of all kinds and forms

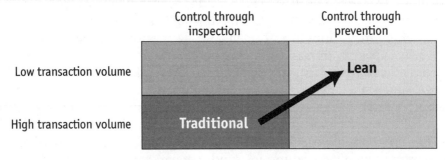

Figure 14.1: Eliminating Waste from the Financial Accounting Processes

the basis of traditional internal accounting control. The problems with this method, as we have seen, are that it is very expensive to maintain, and it is not particularly effective in detecting errors and problems that do occur. Effective control is attained by systems that build mistake-proofing into the system itself. To make this somewhat more concrete, we have contrasted in Figure 14.2 the two different approaches to control in traditional and lean processes: The control process involved with traditional accounting compares the outputs of a process with a standard of some kind. This is what we refer to as "inspection." Examples include the three-way match in accounts payable and the comparison of actual financial results with budget. When errors are found,

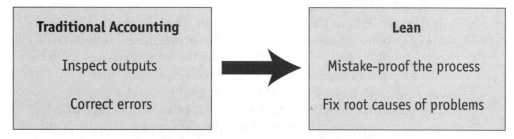

Figure 14.2: Two Models of Control

they are corrected. Normally, nothing is done to determine the systemic problem underlying the cause of the error. So errors continue to happen with a relatively constant frequency, until there is a change in the process that is generating the error. The lean process, on the other hand, seeks to identify process features that make errors more probable, and then to structure the process to minimize that probability. For example, errors and waste are significantly more likely in a production process in which workers cannot find their tools due to messy workspace. The lean approach to this problem, known as the 5S's, is to clean the spaces and have a definite place for every tool, so that they cannot be misplaced. The lean approach seeks to eliminate the causes of the condition observed, whereas the traditional accounting control approach is to increase the level of inspection to catch more errors.

The consequence of the traditional approach in a control process is shown in Figure 14.3.

The process depicted is the monthly financial budget and actual reports that are used to manage how organizations attain anticipated results in traditional companies. Results are measured by organizational units. Deviations from budget show up as variances in the budget/actual report. Normally, all significant variances have to be explained, and any changes desired to fix problems require the preparation of a request to change the system, and management's approval. Once approved, the change is implemented. There are several problems with the approach:

1. The feedback loop is too long from the occurrence of the problem and its correction. Look at the time delays in Figure 14.3. Let us assume that the problem occurs on the 15th of the month and reports are pro-

Figure 14.3: Traditional Control Process

duced on the 15th of the following month. That means that there is a 30-day lag between the occurrence of the problem and detection of its effect. Normally, analysis of what caused the variance takes from two weeks to one month, assuming that anyone can determine what the cause is after 45 days. Preparation of an analysis and a business case to fix the problem may take another 60 days, or more if senior management has to approve an expenditure of funds, and fixing the problem may take another 60 days. So the whole cycle, from occurrence of the problem to its correction, in this example was six months. The typical accounting control cycle portrayed here is too long for a company that aspires to be lean.

2. The basis of the evaluation of performance by organization unit is certain to lead to identification of problems that affect the performance of the unit, but not the system as a whole. For example, if the unit measured is the adherence of the final assembly department to its budget, the cause of the budget overrun may be in another department that is not under the control of the manager of final assembly. Correction of a problem in final assembly will do nothing to improve the overall system performance. For that to happen, a total systems view is required.

3. The financial measurements do not provide sufficient information for the resolution of problems. This is due to financial results being derived from operating results, and therefore not telling us what we need to know to solve the problems. To illustrate the difficulty this creates, let us take a situation in which the monthly financial results show that in one department there was an excess of labor cost incurred during a month over that budgeted. Investigation shows that it was due to overtime worked on the 4th, the 12th, and the 21st of the month. We would like to know why the overtime occurred. But, the financial results in themselves provide no insight into that question. To get at the reason, we must gain an understanding of the operating conditions that were the cause of the overtime. Knowing this, we can begin to eliminate the operating problem that caused the overtime. If we are to manage this problem, we must have information about the cause of the overtime before there is a need to work it. It does not help to see

financial statements at the end of the period telling us that we worked it. In general, we need information that can predict problems and that relate to the factors that cause good performance.

4. And finally, the measurements are taken too infrequently to result in the correction of problems. To foster correction, measures must be taken frequently and workers need to be empowered to fix problems as they occur.

The characteristics of an effective lean control process are depicted in Figure 14.4.

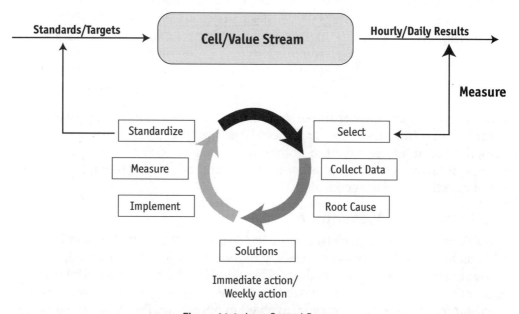

Figure 14.4: Lean Control Process

Such a process is viewed from the perspective of the system (the value stream). It is timely, collecting data hourly at the level of the cell, which is the primary organizational unit in lean. Performance is evaluated based on the effect on system-wide results. The heart of the control system is the improvement process, which uses the performance measurements to identify problems and root causes. To learn more about cell and value stream performance measurement the reader may wish to consult Chapter 3, which dealing with cell-level measures, and Chapter 8, which addresses value stream measures.

Indeed, the heart of the management control process in a lean company is the operations measurement and improvement process. If this is done properly, then the financial results take care of themselves, due to the attention paid to the causes of financial performance.

This shift from focusing control on effects, or outputs, to structural causes of performance is depicted in the examples in Table 14.3.

Most of these examples have been discussed in previous chapters of this book, so a detailed explanation of each example is not required here. The reader may wish to consult Chapters 5 and 11 dealing with the elimination of

Table 14.3: Examples of Traditional Accounting and Lean Controls

System/Issue	Traditional Accounting	Lean
Production/Inventory Accuracy	• Work order • Production tracking • Inventory cycle count	• Kanban • Visual signals • Five-S
Procurement	• Purchase order approval • Three-way match in AP	• Key suppliers • Master POs • Supplier Certification
Quality of Products	• Detailed inspection • Rework or scrap	• Standardized work • Single-piece part flow
Production Cost Control	• Standard cost • Variance reports • Analysis of variance	• Cell/value stream CSFs and measures • Analysis of root causes

transactions to gain greater understanding of the ways that lean operating controls differ from those in a traditional mass production environment. However, the examples are meant to point out the magnitude of the recommended change in focus. A traditional accounting system, relying on the old controls, is not effective for a lean company.

The Role of the Accountant

The role of the accountant must change in a lean company, if that person is to be relevant at all. With control now residing in the operations of the lean cells and value streams, and no longer in the review of transactions and reports by the accounting function, accountants who are concerned about the effectiveness of the control processes must become involved in operations. As we have stated, the key control processes in the lean company need to deal with the following issues:

- Are the cell-level measures effective in assuring that what needs to be done in an hour to meet the customer takt, is being done?
  - Is the day-by-the-hour report maintained?
  - Are results followed up, in terms of cell-level initiatives, to bring the cell's performance into line with takt?
    Are cell level measures linked with critical success factors for achieving value stream goals? Are critical success factors for the cell related to support measures that are monitored on a regular basis?
  - Do cell personnel have adequate direction from management in knowing what action to take in response to poor cell-level performance?
- Are the value stream measures effective in focusing the continuous improvement efforts towards eliminating obstacles to flow?
  - Are the value stream measures linked to critical success factors for achieving plant or division goals?

- Do the value stream measures measure the effectiveness of lean in increasing value to the customer?
- Are value stream measurements used by the continuous improvement team in identifying the causes of less than target performance?
- Are value stream measures used by the lean company in targeting areas for lean initiatives?

- Is there a sales, operations, and financial planning process (SOFP) that regularly matches available capacity with customer demand and develops proactive plans to bring the two into line?
  - Does the lean team regularly evaluate the resource capacity freed up by lean?
  - Are sales, marketing, engineering, finance, and general management actively engaged in the sales and operations planning process at the time that the lean initiative begins?
  - Is financial planning linked to the sales and operations planning?

The accountant should actively address these questions to continuously evaluate the extent to which the key controls underlying these questions are in place and operating as planned. Also, the accountant should be an active player in each of these processes, adding financial and accounting expertise to the skill sets in the operations team.

In fact, the accountant needs to be involved in all aspects of lean accounting—costing, features and characteristics application, and target costing, as well as the control processes. However, he or she needs to be involved at the level of the value stream, not solely at the plant, division, or corporate level. To do the job required, the accountant must be much closer to the operations than currently is the practice.

SUMMARY

This chapter has addressed the changes that can take place in the financial function during the value stream management phase of lean manufacturing implementation. The changes are dramatic and pervasive, ranging from the accounts payable function, the recasting of the chart of accounts, the change in the control model of the company, and a dramatic change in the role of the accountant.

All of these changes create threats to the existing structure of the accounting department, as well as to the jobs of those who are unable or unwilling to adapt to the new demands placed upon them. It is up to the farsighted controller to prepare the organization for the dramatic changes that need to be made.

CHAPTER 15

The Lean Enterprise

WHAT IS A LEAN ENTERPRISE?

Over time, an organization that implements lean becomes a lean enterprise. There is no precise definition of a lean enterprise, but there are at least three characteristics:

- lean methods
- lean culture
- lean relationships

A lean enterprise is not created quickly. It requires fundamental changes to take place within the organization, and between the organization and its business partners. These changes take a great deal of time and careful attention.

When a company first begins to embrace lean manufacturing, it creates lean production cells and gain operational improvements. This is a consequence of using lean methods on the shop floor. As the company improves and lean methods become prevalent across the organization, there is a need to make the rather fundamental changes in the culture of the business. Lean methods do not stand on their own; they were developed out of lean culture. This lean culture needs to be embraced if lean thinking is to flourish.

Companies advancing with lean methods and adopting the culture of lean thinking need to move into new kinds of cooperative and mutually dependent relationships with their suppliers, customers, and business partners. These cultural changes open up the organization to the development of a lean enterprise, which sees the need for lean flow and savings to extend beyond the company's four walls and into the macro value stream comprising customers and suppliers. This comprehensive understanding of how to remove waste and increase value distinguishes a company that is successful with lean manufacturing from a lean enterprise. A lean enterprise applies the thinking, culture, and methods of lean throughout its entire organization and beyond, to the larger value streams of which it is just one part.

PARABLE OF THE LEAN SOWER

Some analogize these aspects of lean thinking with the *Parable of the Sower* (from the *New Testament Bible*, The Gospel of Matthew: Chapter 13). In most companies, the principles and ideas of lean thinking fall on stony ground and no changes take place. Other companies try to apply lean methods, but do not wish to make fundamental changes to the company's culture. As soon as the lean changes emerge, they come into conflict with the business culture and lean changes withers and dies. In other organizations, the seeds of lean thinking gain great acceptance. They are implemented with care and tenacity, and impressive results are obtained. But the lean improvements fail when they become entangled in the relationships with suppliers and customers.

Companies that flourish with lean are those where the seed falls on *good soil*. They change their methods, they change their culture, and they change their relationships with customers, suppliers, and business partners. These companies become powerhouses of excellence, growth, and profitability.

Lean Methods

Most of the literature on lean focuses on lean methods. It is very important that the people within a company use methods that create a lean flow of materials, information, and cash. Methods such as quick changeover, production cells, shop floor supermarkets, kanban, TPM, and single-piece flow are essential to creating lean flow on the shop floor. Methods such as visual management, lean product design, lean order entry, and lean engineering are essential for the effective flow of information quickly, directly, and accurately.[1] The methods of lean accounting, transaction elimination, lean logistics, and lean purchasing, together with very short cycle times, are essential to fast cash flow.

While the methods of lean manufacturing and lean thinking are essential to success, they are not the whole story. There are many organizations that recognize the effectiveness of lean methods and try to implement them, but are unwilling to make the cultural changes required to make those methods

---

1. There are many excellent books on lean manufacturing tools. The following list is a sample of recommended books: *Lean Thinking*, Jim Womack and Dan Jones. Simon & Schuster, NY; 1st edition, 1996; *Learning to See*, John Shook and Mike Rother. The Lean Enterprise Institute, MA; 1999; *Lean Machines*, Richard McCormack. Publishers & Producers; 2002; *Creating Continuous Flow*, Mike Rother and Ed Harris. The Lean Enterprise Institute, MA; 2001; *Implementing World Class Manufacturing*, Larry Rubich and Madelyn Watson. WCM Associates, 1998; *Value Stream Management*, Don Tapping and Tom Shuker. Productivity Press, NY; 2002; *Creating Mixed Model Value Streams*, Kevin Duggan. Productivity Press, NY; 2002; *Quick Changeover*, Productivity Development Team. Productivity Press, NY; 1996; *5S for Operators*, Hiroyuki Hirano and Productivity Development Team. Productivity Press, NY; 1996; *OEE for Operators*, Productivity Development Team. Productivity Press, NY; 1999; *Kaizen for the Shopfloor*, Productivity Development Team. Productivity Press, NY; 2002.

successful. These organizations may see some short-term success, but it is short-lived. They will tell you that they tried lean manufacturing, but it was not suitable for their kind of business. In a way, this is a true statement. Lean methods are not suitable for companies with a traditional, western mass-production business model. Lean methods do not stand alone; they are built on a lean culture.

Lean Culture

Lean thinking turns many of the tenets of traditional manufacturing on their heads. These include such operational issues as batch sizes, efficient use of resources, production scheduling, shopfloor layout, purchasing, and so on. Lean thinking also changes the management of a company. Authority to serve the customers and improve the processes is devolved to people lower down in the organization. Emphasis is placed on increasing customer value, eliminating waste, and improving the flow, rather than merely cost cutting. Improvement is time driven, so that every change makes the processes faster. The lean company is managed by value streams, rather than departments, so the emphasis is on effective flow through to the customer.

There is a focus on the customers' needs that permeates product design, process design, manufacturing, services, and support. Questions of customer value, waste, and flow are always being asked. The responsibility for improving the processes and creating more customer value lies with everyone in the company, and this ongoing lean continuous improvement is recognized as a never-ending endeavor for perfection. These changes go beyond the introduction of lean methods or tools; they change the culture of the business.

Cultural change is not quick. These changes affect the thinking of every manager and worker within the company. They require every one to act differently every day. Culture change requires new ways of measuring success, because the important drivers of success are different.

Cultural change starts when the organization's managers start to act differently. It is not something people just talk about; it is something they do daily, through decision-making and actions. It is only as the people within an organization see their managers walking the talk that they will recognize the change within the company. For example, visual management will only work when the managers are out of their offices and regularly walking through the business processes (production, design, logistics, administrative), observing the flow, and taking action to solve problems and make improvement. In most lean organizations, the managers' offices are removed and they work directly with their people.

The people only see cultural change when the managers of the company stay with the lean program, even when there is pressure to go back to the old ways. These pressures usually come from needing to meet short-term cost and profitability targets, and to provide results against traditional performance measurements that are contrary to lean thinking.

The people will only see cultural change when the managers of the company become involved in the resolution of day-to-day problems without reverting to the usual blame and finger-pointing. Cultural change occurs when the people welcome the involvement of their managers to solve problems, because they know they will receive real, practical help.

The people will see cultural change when their ideas for improvement become the drivers of change within their own processes. They will see it when their ideas do not work out and their managers encourage them to try again with a modified approach, rather than chastising them.

The people will see cultural change when the value to the customers' needs becomes the driver of change and improvement, rather than short-term cost cutting and bottom-line thinking. While successful companies have always striven to provide good value and service to their customers, lean organizations build their entire change programs around increasing the value provided for the customer. It is a fundamental tenet of lean thinking that increased value to the customer leads to increased profitability for the organization.

The methods of lean manufacturing, lean product design, Lean Accounting, and other lean initiatives can only be successful within the context of the culture of lean thinking. Companies attempting lean methods without cultural change throughout the organization, fail to achieve the benefits of lean. They may well see some improvements in the short term, but there will not be the long-term radical improvement that lean thinking has provided for other organizations.

Lean Partnerships

It does not take too long on the lean journey for a company to find that it does not stand alone. The company needs different relationships with its customers, different relationships with its suppliers, and different relationships with other business partners. Lean manufacturing relies on suppliers that can deliver on time, in small quantities, and more frequently, that give perfect quality without inspection, and provide additional value-added services, such as line-side deliveries, in which the supplier delivers goods directly to the production line.

This picture of the perfect supplier is unrecognizable to most western manufacturers, who are familiar with suppliers that are used to large batches, economical order quantities, late deliveries, and questionable quality. They expect to inspect the materials provided by their suppliers because the quality performance is so poor. For a lean organization to be successful, the service provided from its suppliers needs to be radically improved.

The improvement of this supplier performance is approached in one of two ways—either by compulsion or by partnership.

Lean-thinking companies use partnerships. A notable example is U.S. automobile manufacturers, who use the compulsion method. They use their buying-power to gain concessions from the supplier and they punish suppliers who do not meet up with their demands. The result is the suppliers lower their margins, become less profitable, and resent these powerful customers.

There are other examples of companies (also in the automobile industry) that create partnerships with their suppliers. Together, the two companies work out how to improve the processes between their two organizations to most effectively apply lean thinking, improve their effectiveness, and to lower the costs for both organizations. These win-win methods are the most effective over the long term and represent lean partnerships.

It is notable that when a first-tier automotive component supplier has customers with the traditional approach and others with the lean approach, it is often true that the lean partnership companies achieve lower prices and better service, despite the lack of the hard-nosed pressure used by the traditionalists.

Lean-thinking organizations also create partnerships with their customers. The lean company is very focused on creating value for the customer. To achieve this, the lean company must have a close relationship with its customers. The use of such methods as target costing and quality function deployment (QFD) are evidence of a company's need to gain a profound understanding of its customers' needs and translate that into real change and improvement throughout its business processes.

For lean manufacturing to be most successful, the orders received from customers need to be consistent. Many traditional manufacturing methods (including MRPII systems, distribution networks of finished goods inventory, and constant expediting) are in place because the demand from customers is inconsistent and erratic. Indeed, the customers' demand often is inconsistent and erratic, because they too are using similar traditional methods. To resolve these problems, the lean organization will work closely and cooperatively with its customers to establish better methods of handling demand. This cooperation leads to partnership relationships, whereby the two companies work closely to eliminate the waste between their operations. They use such methods as vendor managed inventory (VMI), pull systems, standardized containers, access to each others demand and capacity, frequent joint planning, and so on. These methods go a long way to solving the problems of demand and capacity.

It is common for a traditional company to visit a lean organization and think they simply have easier customers than their own. They do not realize the amount of hard work and good thinking that has gone into creating customer relationships that enable both sides to gain lower costs, improved service, and excellent communications.

The partnership relationships, developed by lean organizations with their customers and suppliers, do not stop at the operational flow of the products. Lean organizations design products and services in partnership with their customers and suppliers. Cooperation in product design creates products that are better designed and serve the end customers better, but also results in processes that are highly effective, create more customer value, and have significantly lower costs. Cooperation and partnership with customer and suppliers is a hallmark of a lean enterprise.

These partnership relationships are often extended beyond direct customers and suppliers. Lean organizations often partner with other companies to provide value for their customers. These partnerships do not need to be complex and legal joint ventures. Companies often entered into them somewhat informally and maintain them only as long as they serve the customer or market they are designed to address. These so-called virtual corporations are an example of the flexibility lean enterprises require in order to serve the needs of their customers and create more and more value.

What Lean Methods Support the Wider Lean Enterprise?

A lean enterprise does, of course, use the classic lean methods for production, product design, logistics, accounting, and administration. The managers within a lean enterprise have also worked very hard to achieve the kinds of cultural change that supports the long-term success of these lean methods. Continuous improvement with a high level of participation is an essential part of the lean culture. The leaders of lean enterprises strive to create the right kind of relationships with their customers, suppliers, and partners.

There are three additional methods used by lean enterprises:

- Lean transaction elimination between partners
- Macromapping
- Target costing

Transaction Elimination

There is much that is wasteful between a customer and a supplier. Such wastefulness includes the need for inspections of products, the paperwork associated with the buy-sell process, and the unnecessary discussions between the two companies to expedite or change requirements. These are all systematically eliminated by lean enterprises. They develop very fast, effective, and direct communication between the companies. They develop enough communication that such things as production planning and inventory scheduling become unnecessary. They develop enough trust that such things as invoices and receiving documents can be eliminated.

Every aspect of the communications between the companies is systematically and carefully examined and, over time, is reduced to the very minimum of work. Traditional organizations and their customers always duplicate work. A purchase order from the customer has been developed by someone in customer organization, calculating needs and creating an order. Meanwhile, someone in the supplier organization has been forecasting that need and preparing for the expected demand. They are both doing the same job, but from different perspectives. The lean enterprise recognizes these wastes and eliminates them.

Many of the transactions required to support traditional organizations are required to ensure the operational and financial integrity of their systems. Before removing these transactions, the lean enterprise ensures they are no longer needed and that the integrity of the processes is maintained. There is no cavalier removal of important business transactions. The need for the transactions is carefully understood and either removed or met in other ways.

The Wider Value Streams

Lean enterprises understand that their value streams extend beyond their own four walls. Companies at earlier stages of lean thinking, extend the boundary of their value streams to their suppliers and their customers. Lean enterprises recognize that their operations are just one part of a wider value stream. The true value stream for their products begins when someone digs something from the ground—iron ore, bauxite, or silicon, for example. The value stream finishes when their products, and the products they are used to create, are destroyed, disposed of, or recycled. They draw macromaps[2] that show the entire flow of the macro value stream and their own place in the wider view.

The macro view of the value streams enables the lean enterprise to work with its suppliers, its customers, and down the line, with its suppliers and customers, to eliminate waste, improve flow, create more value, and improve profitability. This wider view of the value stream is the mark of a company that is moving from being an effective lean manufacturer to being a lean enterprise. The improvement of the macro value stream requires cooperative efforts between the various companies and organizations within the wider value stream.

When working to improve flow with their customers and suppliers, lean enterprises use macromapping, which leads to an understanding of where the waste falls across the bigger picture. For example, many companies make the decision to source some of the products or some of their processes from low-cost countries. They often (wrongly) use a standard cost to make this decision and do not take into account the wider costs and problems caused by having production operating so far away from the customer and the supplier. The macro-map enables them to see and understand the waste created by such an approach. This does not mean that the decision to out-source is necessarily wrong; but it does create additional waste that needs to be understood and eliminated.

Another use of macromapping shows the flow from your operations to your customer. When these are mapped across both the organizations, it is easy to see the amount of waste associated with the sale and shipment of the product. One organization we worked with carefully packed its products for shipment. The customer immediately unpacked them and repacked them into its own containers on receipt of the product at their location. The macromap showed this obvious and immediate waste, enabling the companies to change their processes and eliminate the wasteful unpacking and repacking.

---

2. To gain an understanding of macro-mapping, the reader may wish to consult the very easy-to-read book on the subject, *Seeing the Whole: Mapping the Extended Value Stream*, by Dan Jones and Jim Womack, The Lean Enterprise Institute, Inc., Brookline, MA 02446, USA, 2002.

This is a simple example of how macromapping results in waste reduction and savings. This kind of macromapping can also be used as a sales tactic. By macromapping the process with its customers, a company can understand how it can reduce a lot of waste from the processes and make buying from the company the lowest cost for the customer, even when the price is higher than another supplier. The true cost of the item can be established by taking into account all the processes and their costs. This leads to a very value-focused approach to selling the products—another hallmark of lean enterprises. We will have more to say about this topic in Chapter 17, "Expanding Value Stream Outside Our Four Walls."

Target Costing

Target costing enables lean enterprises to drive their business from customer value. Target costing starts by working closely with the customers and understanding their needs and how your company can create more customer value. From this understanding of how value is created for the customer, the leaders of the lean enterprise drive improvement activities throughout the value streams to create more value, eliminate waste, and increase profitability.

Target costing provides the cross-functional, value stream and enterprise-wide understanding of the value streams, the flow, and the waste, providing a structured methodology for aligning product and process costs with the value they provide from the point of view of the customer (see Chapter 16 for a detailed description of this methodology). The outcome of target costing is a program of changes and improvements that create more value for customers, eliminate waste, and increase profitability. This program may well include sales and marketing projects, product design changes, operational improvements, logistical changes, and other waste reduction initiatives. Target costing is comprehensive, customer-focused, driven through the value streams, and results in improved financial benefit for the company.

It is common for lean enterprises to include their suppliers and partners in the target costing processes. This way, the wider value streams, extending beyond the company's four walls, can be perfected using the methods and thinking of a lean enterprise.

WHY ARE LEAN ENTERPRISES SO HARD ON THEMSELVES?

A characteristic of a lean enterprise is that they are always unhappy with their progress and are always looking for more improvement. Many organizations declare victory too soon. They have some success with lean manufacturing and other lean methods and feel they have made it. They rest on their laurels, start describing the company as a lean organization, and they begin to believe their own marketing.

A lean enterprise is exactly the opposite. They see and understand the improvement they have made. Many are acutely aware of their own history of lean improvement. However, they recognize that for all the improvement they have made, there is much more that needs to be done. This is pursuit of perfection in action. No matter how far they have come, they see there is still further to go. As soon as one problem is solved and celebrated, there are three more problems that identify themselves.

Some people, when visiting lean enterprise, feel that there is a certain amount of false modesty among these organizations. They are wrong. The modesty comes from recognizing that while great strides have been made, there is much farther to go before they even begin to approach perfection. This pursuit of perfection becomes a passion that is not understood by traditional companies, or even by companies earlier on the lean journey. It is this pursuit of perfection that makes a lean enterprise constantly strive for further improvement.

SUMMARY

For a company to be classed as a lean enterprise, it must have moved beyond the implementation of lean methods, and it must have moved beyond merely creating a culture of lean thinking. Each company needs to establish lean enterprise thinking. The characteristics of lean enterprise thinking include:

- Widespread use of lean methods throughout every aspect of the business
- Deeply ingrained lean culture supporting the lean tools and those who use them
- Understanding of the wider value streams leading to close partnership relationships with customers, suppliers, and other business partners
- Passion for perfection leading to a seemingly self-critical approach to ongoing continuous improvement

CHAPTER 16

Target Costing

The purpose of target costing is to drive the enterprise from the value created for the customer. Customer value is the first principle of lean thinking and lean companies require a profound understanding of the value they create for their customers and how this affects the profitability of the value stream. While traditional companies tend to drive their businesses based on costs and margins, lean organizations focus on the value created for the customer and the profitability of the value stream.

Target costing contains a series of cross-functional processes that are designed to achieve these objectives:

- Establish the value created for the customer by the company.
- Determine the maximum cost for the products within the value stream, based upon the value created for the customer and the company's expectations of the value stream profitability.
- Create a practical, cross-functional action plan to increase the value created for the customer and to achieve required value stream profitability.

Companies approaching target costing for the first time often see the process as a series of analyses and steps. However, over time it becomes clear that the most powerful aspect of target costing is the cross-organizational, lean-focused approach to pricing, marketing, design, and operations. Once target costing is working effectively, the company's value streams, from sales and marketing to cash collection and beyond, are focused on creating customer value and achieving profitability. Target costing is a powerful tool for integrating improvement activities across the value streams.

Target costing is not a one-time exercise. The process is repeated and updated throughout the lifetime of the products and the value streams. In this way, everybody's attention remains on customer value and value stream profitability. Action plans are developed for lean improvement across the entire value stream.

HOW DOES TARGET COSTING WORK?

Target costing starts with the customer. We need to understand what creates value for the customers we wish to serve. This value is created not only by the product itself, but also by the services we provide and other value-adding aspects of our business. Once we know the value we are creating for the customer, we can calculate the allowable cost. The allowable cost is the selling price less the profit percentage required for the product. The required profit percentage is assigned as a part of the company's overall business plan. To succeed, we must sell the product at a price that meets the customer's need for value and a margin that meets the company's needs for profitability.

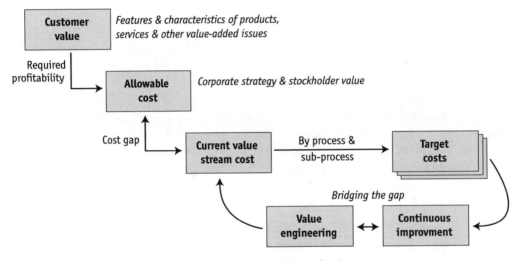

Figure 16.1: Overview of Target Costing

Once the allowable cost is established, we then compare this cost to the current average value stream cost and assess the difference; this is called the cost gap. If the average value stream cost is higher than the allowable cost, then we need to establish lean improvements to bring the actual costs in line with the allowable costs, and the price in line with the value we are creating for the customers.

The outcome of the target costing process is a practical action plan. The action plan often includes changes in the way we market and sell the products, in the material costs of the products, in product design, and in the operations and logistics we use to bring the product to the marketplace. The practical impact of target costing spreads throughout the value stream.

WHERE IS TARGET COSTING USED?

Target costing is used when introducing new value streams, when introducing new products to existing value streams, and for current products in current value streams.

Introducing New Value Streams

New value streams are typically introduced when the company wishes to add new products and/or address new markets. These markets may be geographi-

Principles of Target costing	
Price–Led Costing	How the customer values the company's products, services, and other attributes.
Focused on Customers and Markets	Integration with the sales and marketing people and processes; even when these processes are not organizationally aligned to the value streams.
Focused on Design	Integration with product design. The best way to bring high-value and low-cost products to market is to design them that way. This requires profound integration between sales and marketing, operations, and product design and development.
Cross Functional Improvement Methodology	Company-wide integration for increasing customer value.
	Operations, marketing, product design, customer service, suppliers, and others.
Improvement comes through the Value Stream	Lean organizations focus almost everything around the value streams. It is the understanding of the entire process of value creation for the customer that leads to substantial and integrated improvement.
Contrast Costs to Customer Value	Target costing enables us to understand where and how we create value for the customer, and then contrast this with where and how we dissipate costs. This leads to focused changes to increase value and reduce cost.

cal markets or segments of the marketplace. This is the ideal time to use target costing because the product design and process design can be developed together. We design for customer value, and target cost for highly value-effective processes.

Introducing New Products

The best way to create high-value and low-cost products is to design them that way. Target costing was originally developed (primarily by Toyota) to provide a method for the design and marketing people within the company to gain a true understanding of the customer's needs and requirements. This led to a profound understanding of the value created for the customer by the company's new products. This knowledge within Toyota has had a major impact on the company's ability to prosper within each new market the company has entered.

The ideal starting point for target costing is when new products are being designed, whether for a new or existing value stream. This enables the team to design the products for maximum value and fully take into account the impact of the product design on the flow of the value stream. This can lead to excellent action plans for providing more value to the customers and increasing the profitability of the value stream, not just the new product. The example given later in this chapter shows target costing being used when a new product is being designed for an existing value stream.

Current Products in Current Value Streams

This is how many lean companies use target costing. Target costing is the principle driver of improvement of the value stream. This means the company's lean improvement efforts are focused on customer value and value stream profitability.

Many organizations starting with lean improvements make their improvements somewhat randomly. They address parts of the process that are problematic. This may be the best approach to early lean implementations, but as the company matures with lean thinking, the right approach to lean improvement comes by addressing the entire value stream and focusing on customer value. Target costing achieves this.

WHAT ARE THE STEPS WE TAKE?

The target costing process has twelve steps that are completed in the sequence given in the diagram below, but they can also be iterative. Sometimes the result of one analysis raises questions and suggestions that require revisiting an earlier step. Target costing is a creative process involving a wide range of people within the value stream. The formal structure is important, but it is also important to use the process for deeper thinking and creativity.

The twelve steps of target costing will be discussed briefly, then demonstrated using a real example (Figure 16.2).

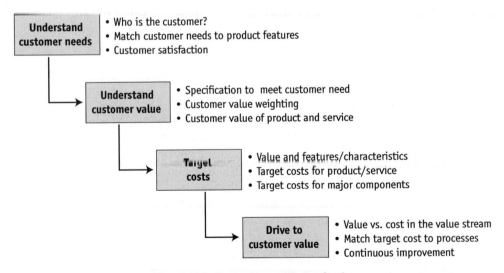

Figure 16.2: Twelve Steps of Target Costing

Step 1: Who is the Customer?

The first three steps of target costing are designed to understand the customer's needs and the extent to which the company fulfills those needs.

The starting point of target costing is the customer and the value created for the customer. We need to define, as closely as possible, the market we are addressing, and who, within the customer organization, is our customer. Often, there is more than one customer within the customer organization. For example, the design engineer, the purchasing agent, and the quality department.

Step 2: Match Customer Needs to Product Functions

The purpose is to understand how our products and services match the customer's needs. Value is only assigned to things we do that meet the true needs of the customer. To achieve this, we list the customer's needs and the priority of these needs. This information must be obtained directly from the customer or market we are working on. There is no substitute for gathering information directly from customers. If we are dealing with a limited number of real customers, then these people can be surveyed using market research methods to gain an understanding of their true needs. If we are dealing with a larger market, then other market research methods can be used, including focus groups, surveys, statistical sampling, and other methods of deriving reliable data. Internal information, such as customer support records and customer complaints, can also provide useful data.

Once the customer's needs are understood and prioritized, the target costing team creates a matrix that shows how we meet those needs. What are the features of our products, the characteristics of our processes, and other issues relating to our organization that fulfill the customer's needs? The needs, and the factors fulfilling those needs, are then correlated so that we can see how much value the various aspects of our product and service created. The outcome of this step is a diagram that shows how our products and processes fulfill customer's needs, and which aspects of the products and processes contribute the most.

Step 3: Customer Satisfaction

The purpose of this step is to gain an understanding of the customer's view of our products and services. How well are we satisfying the customer's needs? Again, good market research and engineering data are required to understand how satisfied the customers are with our products and service. It is helpful also to get information on the customer's satisfaction with competitor's products.

If the target costing is for a new product that has not yet been introduced, then the information gained from customers is based upon descriptions or prototypes of the products.

AFTER STEP 3

After the first three steps have been completed, the team needs to work together to develop and understand the information gained. The questions are:

- How can we create more value for the customer?
- How can we reduce or eliminate features and characteristics of our product and processes that do not provide value to the customer?

The purpose of Steps 1 through 3 is not to draw diagrams, but to create insight and understanding. This is achieved through discussion, brainstorming, and recording these discussions. It is early in the target costing process, but the purpose is to make significant breakthrough improvement. This requires cooperative thinking and discussion.

Here is how the first three steps of target costing worked out for ECI.

Target Costing at ECI, Inc.: Steps 1 through 3

The home automation division manufactures home automation equipment. ECI's home automation systems provide computer control to household appliances and fixtures including heating and airconditioning, security systems, kitchen equipment, and lighting throughout the home. While ECI supplies entire systems, they manufacture only the electronic controllers. Other components of the systems are purchased from other manufacturers. Similarly, other home automation companies purchase ECI's controllers for their systems.

Home automation systems have, until recently, been high-priced luxury items. Increasing popularity and new competition for these products is forcing a need for lower priced components. ECI is about to introduce a new controller designed to address the needs of the low end of the market. The new product, the ZX12 range, has been designed and prototypes have been manufactured.

A target costing team has been established to ensure that these new products can be introduced profitably into the market. ECI is aware that the successful introduction of these products will place the company in a favorable position to lead the new, high volume demand expected over the next few years.

Step 1: Who is the Customer?

ECI identified two kinds of customers—home automation OEMs and home automation installers and integrators (Figure 16.3). The true customer within each of these categories is different. In home automation OEM market, the customer is the person who designs, or the one who purchases the controller. In the system integration market, the true customer is the one who sells or installs the controller in the system. The point here is that an understanding of customer needs requires a clear understanding of who the customer is, that is, the one who uses, installs, specifies, or services the item produced by the value stream. The target costing team sought out these people to gain an understanding of customer needs.

One who uses	Market segments
One who installs	Different uses
One who services	Different kinds of customers
One who specifies	More or less demanding customers
One who pays	
One who has the most influence	

Home automation OEMs	Design engineers
	Purchasing agents
Home automation systems integrators	Sales engineers
	Installers

Figure 16.3: Who is the Customer?

Step 2: Match Customer Needs to Product and Process Features

A matrix (Figure 16.4) is used to show the correlation between the customers' needs and the product and process features. The y-axis shows the customers' needs. This has been gathered directly from the customers using market research and customer interviews. The relative importance of each of the customer needs is shown in column 2.

The product and process features are listed along the top of the matrix. These features include physical specifications for the product, attributes of the process, and intangible value-adding issues, such as the company's reputation.

The team then assigned weightings for the product/process attributes that fulfill the customer's needs. They assigned a score of 5 when a product attribute contributed significantly to fulfilling the customer's need—small size and component density, for example. They assigned a 3 when there was some degree of correlation—ease of installation and rechargeable battery, for example. They assigned a 1 when there was slight correlation—ease-of-use and modular design, for example.

Along the bottom of the matrix is calculated how much value is created by each of the product and process attributes. This appears under the caption *Customer Value Weight*. These are calculated by multiplying the weighting the customer places on the need (for example, small size has a weighting of 5) by

Customer Needs	Importance to customer	Component density	Use of existing high volume components	No tuning required	Proven technology	Rechargeable battery & power supply	ASICS chips	Advance surface mount technology	Lean production	Modular design	Design to standard system	Hot line & technical support
Small size	5	0.86 ●					0.86 ●					
Easy to use	5			0.86 ●	0.52 ▲	0.17 ■				0.17 ■	0.52 ▲	
Reliable	5		0.86 ●	0.17 ■	0.86 ●		0.52 ▲	0.52 ▲	0.52 ▲	0.52 ▲	0.52 ▲	0.52 ▲
Flexibility	4			0.41 ▲						0.69 ●	0.41 ▲	0.41 ▲
Ease of installation	3		0.10 ■	0.52 ●	0.31 ▲					0.31 ▲	0.52 ●	0.52 ●
Rechargeable battery	3					0.52 ●						
Short lead time	4			0.41 ▲				0.14 ■	0.69 ●	0.41 ▲		
Total of importance	29											
Specifications		0.86	0.97	2.38	1.69	0.69	1.38	0.66	1.21	2.10	1.97	1.45
Customer value weight		5.6%	6.3%	15.5%	11.0%	4.5%	9.0%	4.3%	7.9%	13.7%	12.8%	9.4%

Key:
● Value weighting of 5
▲ Value weighting of 3
■ Value weighting of 1

Figure 16.4: Match Customer Needs to Product and Process Features

the correlation (for example, component density scores a 5). The 5 associated with customer needs represents 17 percent of the total customer needs weighting (5/29=0.1724). This is multiplied by the correlation amount of 5, giving 0.86. (5 * .1724 = 0.86). A score of 0.86 represents 5.6 percent of the total amount of value created for the customer.

You can see from the chart that the largest customer value is created by the feature, "No Tuning Required," which provides 15.5 percent of the value to the customer. The customers put great value on the products ease of use and ease of installation. The features, "Modular Design" and "Design to Standard Systems," also provide high levels of value to the customer (13.7 percent and 12.8 percent, respectively).

The target costing team now has a clearer picture of how this new product creates value for the customer.

Step 3: Customer Satisfaction

The marketing experts on the team have already presented prototype products to prospective customers and have gathered information relating to the customer satisfaction with the product as it is currently designed. The results are shown in Figure 16.5.

As you can see, the customers are not fully satisfied with the product. It is too large, it is not easy to use, and it is not easy to install. From the left-hand section of the diagram you can see that there are issues ECI considers

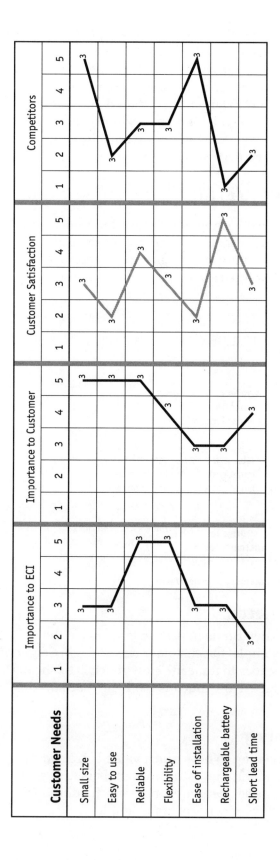

Figure 16.5: Customer Satisfaction Diagram

Ideas for increasing the value to the customer

The first reason our product is larger than the customer needs is that we have built in considerable flexibility through the use of dip-switches to configure the product. These dip-switches change parameters within the software and provide a wide range of compatibilities and features. This flexibility exceeds the flexibility needs of the customers.

The second reason our product is large is that we use a motorized fan to cool the board. We do this for two reasons: first, to enable the use of a larger and more powerful chip; and second, to extend the product's life. If we use a lower-rated chip, remove the cooling motor and the dip-switches, then the customer's size needs can be largely met. This smaller unit will be less flexible, but will still provide the flexibility the customer needs.

important, but these issues do not match to the customer's needs, for example, flexibility. The team's commentary on these issues can be seen below the diagram.

These issues led to a sharp exchange within the target costing team. In the opinion of the people in sales and marketing, the design engineers have over-engineered the product. The product is larger than desired and less easy to use, because the design engineers included a lot more flexibility than the customers need. The design engineers have also built more reliability into the product than the sales experts considered necessary.

Understanding Customer Value

The first three steps (Figure 16.6) of target costing are designed to understand customer needs. The next three steps are designed to specify those needs. We must set hard numbers to the qualitative information gained in steps one, two, and three. The outcome of the next three steps is the determination of the value created by the products and services we are working on.

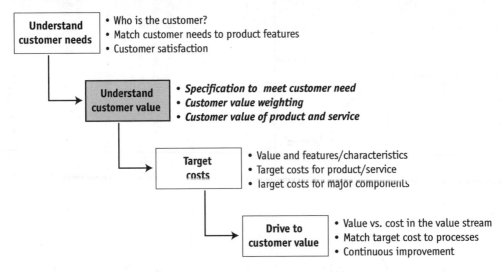

Figure 16.6: Understanding Customer Value

Step 4: Specifying Customers' Needs

In Step 4, we work with customers to determine in precise terms what they mean by each of their needs. If, for example, the customer needs a lightweight product, How many ounces or grams does that mean? How much is too heavy and will reduce the value of the product? How much is too light? Each need is specified as precisely as possible.

Step 5: Customer Value Weighting

It is important to answer questions relating to how much value is created by each of the customer's needs and try to put that into hard numbers. It is also important to understand how elastic these needs are—how much additional value is created by changing the product or service. For example, the customers may put high priority on short lead times and specify a short lead time as five days from order to delivery. The elasticity question is: "How much more value would be created if the lead-time were reduced to two days or one day? Would this increase the value significantly for the customers?"

Assigning value to each customer need starts easily by weighting the current price against the customers' priorities. However, this is simply arithmetic. The team members need to review and discuss these issues thoroughly. The customers are often approached a third time to gain an understanding of the elasticity of the value. From this research, discussion, and planning the team arrives at a good understanding of what really matters to the customer and what changes are required to enhance customer value.

Step 6: Customer Value for the Product and Service

The purpose of this step is to determine where in the value stream customer value is created. We create the customer value, using another matrix chart. The product and process attributes from Step 2 are placed on the y-axis of the matrix, and the steps of the value stream are on the x-axis. The team members then link these to show which value stream steps contribute to the product attributes and processes. From this, we can work out how much value is created by each of the value stream steps.

While this step can be done simply through arithmetic, the purpose is much deeper. The team again spends time discussing how changes can be made to add more value to the product and processes; how to reduce costs; and how to go further than competitors in meeting customers' needs. Often, value is added by removing unneeded features, rather than adding more.

For existing products, these discussions can start with the current price. There may also be on-going negotiations with major customers on future pricing; perhaps price reductions. For new products, there is usually a price that has been established based upon the cost of the product as it is currently designed or specified. These prices need to be examined in the light of the team's understanding of the customers' needs and the changes that can be made to increase value, reduce costs, and overtake the competitors.

The outcome of Step 6 is the team's assessment of the value of the product and services to the customers. Sometimes this is a range of values based on different kinds of customers or different variations of the products. The value may also be shown to change over time. Newly introduced innovative products can have a much higher value early in their life cycle. As time goes by, that value diminishes. The team determines the customer value that will be used to establish the target costs for the product or product family.

EXAMPLE OF TARGET COSTING AT ECI:
STEPS 4 THROUGH 6

As they moved into the customer value phase of target costing, the team at ECI was in crisis. Team-members sharply disagreed about the features that were to be designed into the product. Instead of dealing with these disagree-ments politically, the team members decided to set aside their differences for the moment and move to the next stage of target costing.

Step 4: Specification to Meet Customer Needs

The specification required to meet the customer's needs are shown in Figure 16.7. As you can see, the product is larger and more reliable than the customer specification, but the product does badly on ease-of-use and ease-of-installation. There is not a good match between the customer's needs and the features of the product and services provided by ECI.

The target costing team used this as an opportunity to develop ideas for increasing the customer value and bringing the product into line with the needs expressed by the customer. These ideas are documented on the chart shown in Figure 16.7. Suggestions to reduce the size of the product by chang-ing its design would reduce the product reliability, but would enable the product to meet the customer's need for a smaller size.

The balance between flexibility and ease-of-use is a more difficult prob-lem. The dip-switches inside the product make it flexible, but they increase the size and make it difficult for the customer to use. Dip-switches are tiny electric switches used to configure the product so it can be used for a variety of purposes. To use the dip-switches requires unscrewing the case of the controller, looking up the configuration information in the manual, locating the dipswitches, and making the changes using a plastic tool supplied with the unit. The target costing team knew that they had to make the product smaller and easier to use if they were to increase customer satisfaction; the dip-switch method of configuration makes the product larger and more difficult to use.

The design team was concerned that, if they did not build higher levels of flexibility into the product, the company would lose sales from systems integrators and OEMs who are designing new actuators and other units requiring a wider range of connectivity than can be provided with the cus-tomers' current stated needs. They feel it is short-sighted to not include this additional flexibility, which is provided using the dip-switches.

The compromise suggestion of providing flexibility through software rather than dip switches would solve these problems, but raises a new prob-lem of how to provide a simple interface with the software, without making the product larger and more complex.

The other significant issue is lead-time. The customers define short lead-time as less than five days. The current processes can only meet a 10-day lead-time. The operations experts on the team feel confident that lean manu-facturing improvements can be introduced into the value stream to bring the lead-time down to five days or less.

Step 5: Customer Value Rating

The current price for the product is set at $425. The customers are looking for a maximum price of $350. However, the target costing team is convinced that,

Customer needs	How is this measured?	Customer specification	Current achievement	Comments	Ideas to increase value to the customer
Small size	Physical size	Depth 2.50" Width 1.84" Height 5.25"	Depth 4.10" Width 1.89" Height 5.25"	Is there a trade off of size and functionality?	Size can be reduced by eliminating the cooling motor. This would require different chips and better venting.
Easy to use	Customer perception	Plug and play	Set dip switches	Eliminate use of dip-switch for settings	Eliminating the dip-switches would reduce the size of the product and make it simpler. Flexibility must be provided differently.
Reliable	Mean time between failures	50,000 hours	400,000 hours	If we reduced the currently designed reliability, would we reduce the price and/or size?	Removing the cooling motor would reduce the MTBF—but we would still exceed the customer's needs.
Flexibility	Ability to interface with a wide range of home automation products	Work with any step motor, controller, or home appliance	These criteria are met	Can we achieve the same flexibility and connectivity without the use of dip-switches?	We can achieve the same flexibility and connectivity by using software settings. But how do we change the software settings? There is no screen or keyboard.
Ease of installation	Time to install by an installation engineer	10 minutes with generalist engineer	20 minutes with specialist engineer	The physical installation is quick, but time is required for configuration of the product into the system.	Simplified software switches would reduce the install time and simplify. A generalist technician could do this in 10 minutes.
Rechargeable battery	Battery life and time to recharge	4 hours battery life and 1 hour to recharge	6 hours battery life and 1 hour to recharge	Can the battery be made smaller? Would there be an additional cost? How important is the recharge time to the customer?	Need to experiment with the low-energy chip and eliminating the cooling motor. This will affect battery life.
Short lead time	Days	5 days	10 days	How much value is lost by the longer lead time? When/how can we bring the lead time down to 5 days?	Our lean program will bring the lead time to 5 days or less in approximately 12 months. Would a LT shorter than 5 days add more value?

Figure 16.7: Specify Customer Needs

| Customer needs | Weight | % | $350.00 | $425.00 | $400.00 | Ideas to increase value to the customer |
			Customer Request	Current Price	Value	
Small size	5	17.2%	60.34	73.28	70.00	We believe the value to be $400 when we have reduced the size and simplified the product. We have exceeded the customer's requirements by providing more flexibility and superior ease-of-use.
Easy to use	5	17.2%	60.34	73.28	80.00	If we remove the cooling motor and the dip-switches we can bring the unit down to close to the customer's required size.
Reliable	5	17.2%	60.34	73.28	70.00	If we eliminate dip-switches and introduce configuration using the TV remote—the unit will be much easier to use.
Flexibility	4	13.8%	48.23	58.62	67.50	The lack of a cooling motor, even with a low-energy chip, will reduce the reliability. But the MTBF will still be much higher than the customer request.
Ease of installation	3	10.3%	36.21	43.97	40.00	We can achieve the same level of flexibility without the dip-switches by introducing configuration using the TV remote and an infra-red port.
Rechargeable battery	3	10.3%	36.21	43.97	37.50	Eliminating the dip-switches will make it easier to install. This will achieve the customer's requirement.
Short lead time	4	13.8%	48.28	58.62	35.00	This is subject to testing, but we believe we can achieve the customer's battery life requirement despite the other changes.
	29	100.0%	$350.00	$425.00	$400.00	LT at product launch does not meet the customer's needs of 5 days. But we will quickly move to an enhanced lean flow and bring the LT down.

Figure 16.8: Customer Value Weighting

if the changes they have suggested are implemented, the customer value will be $400 per unit.

As you can see from Figure 16.8, the team has decided to pursue the idea of providing flexibility using software rather than dipswitches and other hardware. Ease of use will be provided by having the software configured to standard applications, but also allowing the equipment to be programmed using a TV remote control device that will be readily available in most homes.

The team is excited about the design changes and the innovative approach to providing both ease of use and flexibility. The sales and marketing people on the team are confident they will be able to market this product at $400.

Step 6: Customer Value for the Products and Services

The target costing team assigned the value of the product to each step in the value stream by completing the matrix shown in Figure 16.9. The bottom row shows the amount of value created by each step in the value stream. You will see that much of the value is created in the support areas of Manufacturing Engineering, Design Engineering, Technical Support, etc.

The team now has knowledge of the value and the cost at each step in the value stream. Figure 16.10 shows this contrast. We will examine this more fully at Step 10.

CALCULATING THE TARGET COSTS

Having established the value of the product in the eyes of the customer, we can move on to the calculation of costs. In principle this is simple. The cost of the product is the value less the required profit.

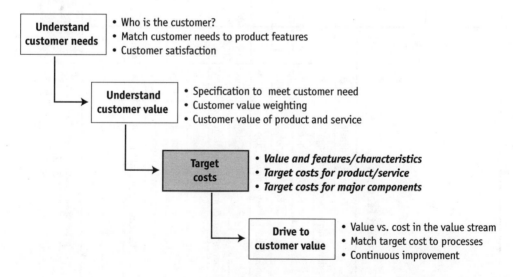

Lean thinking turns almost everything on its head in comparison to traditional thinking. A traditional company calculates costs from the bottom upwards. It blows through a bill of materials and adds up all the materials

Product Features	Customer value rating	Customer service	Purchasing	SMT cell	Hand load & wave cell	Test & rework cell	Assemble & burn-in cell	Shipping	Quality assurance	Manufacturing engineering	Accounting	Information systems	Design engineering	Technical support
Component density	5.6%			5 0.28	3 0.17				1 0.06	3 0.17			5 0.28 ●	
Use of existing high volume components	6.3%		5 0.31	5 0.31						3 0.19			5 0.31 ●	1 0.06
No tuning required	15.5%	◄ 0.24			◄ 0.47	◄ 0.47	3 ◄ 0.47		■ 0.16	◄ 0.47		◄ 0.47	● 0.78	◄ 0.47
Proven technology	11.0%			◄ 0.33			3 ◄ 0.33		■ 0.11	● 0.55			● 0.55	◄ 0.33
Rechargeable battery & power supply	4.5%						5 ● 0.22						● 0.22	
ASICs chips	9.0%		● 0.45		◄ 0.27								● 0.45	
Advance surface mount technology	4.3%			● 0.21			1 ■ 0.04			● 0.21			◄ 0.13	
Lean production	7.9%			● 0.39	● 0.39		5 ● 0.39	■ 0.08		● 0.39		■ 0.08		
Modular design	13.7%		◄ 0.41	◄ 0.41			3 ◄ 0.41		■ 0.14	◄ 0.41			● 0.69	◄ 0.41
Design to standard systems	12.8%		◄ 0.38						◄ 0.38	● 0.64		◄ 0.38	● 0.64	● 0.64
Hot line & technical support	9.4%	◄ 0.28												● 0.47
Customer value apportioned to process		0.52	1.56	1.94	1.30	0.47	1.87	0.08	0.84	3.03		0.93	4.05	2.38
Equivalent percentage		2.7%	8.2%	10.3%	6.8%	2.5%	9.8%	0.4%	4.4%	16.0%	%	4.9%	21.4%	12.6%

Figure 16.9: Customer Value for Products and Services

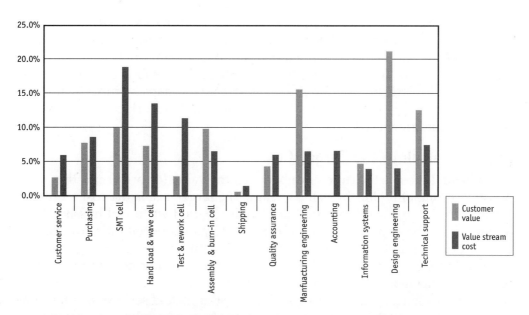

Figure 16.10: Comparing Cost and Value in the Value Stream

costs. It works through the production routing to calculate the labor and machine costs. It applies spurious overhead percentage, and finally arrive at the cost of the product.

In lean thinking we take the value of the product and subtract the amount of profit we need to make. This is a simple, straightforward, and lean-focused approach. The next question, of course, is: Can we make the product at this cost? Steps 7, 8, and 9 address these issues.

Step 7: Value and Features and Characteristics

As we move from Step 6 to Step 7 we move from value to cost. The first six steps are designed to give us insight and understanding into the value created by our products and services for the customers we have identified. As we move into steps 7 through 9, we are concerned with the target costs themselves. How much cost can be expended within the value stream to support this product or product range?

Step 7 is required only when the products will be added to an existing value stream. We need to look at the features and characteristics of the products to see how this product relates to other products within the value stream. We need to understand how adding this new product will affect the average cost of all products made by the value stream, and design it in such a way that adding it will increase value stream profitability. If the new product consumes a great deal of the capacity of a resource that is already a bottleneck, its addition could lower the profitability of the value stream by decreasing the flow of products through the value stream. So, as a first step, we want to examine how the features and characteristics of the new product will affect the value stream's average product cost.

We already have a clear picture of how the features and characteristics of the existing products affect the costs of the value stream. The team needs to assess how the features and characteristics of the new products affect the value stream costs. In some cases, the introduction of the new products change the cost structure within the value stream, perhaps by introducing a different bottleneck in the process. The outcome of this work can be a new average value stream cost.

Step 8: Calculate the Target Cost

The allowable cost is the difference between the value (or price) and the required profitability for the value stream. The target cost is the cost required for the product and services over the planning period we are addressing. Usually these are the same. They are different if the gap between the allowable cost and the current value stream cost is too big. In which case, we will set a target cost for the product that is higher than the allowable cost, but will be achieved in the next (for example) 12 months.

The calculation of the target cost for the product and services is often simple arithmetic, but other times may require the team to work through what is achievable in the time frame. New products usually bring issues related to expected sales volume and still unknown production or distribution issues. These assumptions need to be documented and taken into account.

When target costing new products, it is also common to create target costs not only for the sales and order fulfillment processes, but also for the product development processes. New product development is a separate kind of value stream, although the same approach is used.

Step 9: Target Costs for Major Components

Sometimes the target cost for a product needs to be broken down. If the product is large and complex (like an automobile), then target costs are assigned for different parts of the end product. Typically these segments of the product are manufactured in different value streams and a target cost is needed for each value stream. The automobile may, for example, have target costs for the drive train, the body, the interior, etc.

The target costing team determines how much of the overall target cost is to be assigned to each of the product's major components. Considerable judgment is required at this stage, and there is often unseemly lobbying by the representatives of the value streams involved. The outcome must be the appropriate assignment of cost to each component.

EXAMPLE OF TARGET COSTING: STEPS 7 THROUGH 9 AT ECI

Having established the customer value of the product at $400, the target costing team at ECI moved on to calculate the target costs. This product is not an average product within the value stream and the target cost will need to be adjusted, based on the features and characteristics of the products within the value stream.

Step 7: Linking Customer Value to Features and Characteristics

There are three aspects to the features and characteristics costs for the ECI controller products. They relate to the number of boards used within the product, the number of glue dots required in the bottleneck cell, and the changeover time within the bottleneck cell. The changeover time is itself related to the number of non-dedicated components required on the board. The features and characteristics matrix for the conversion cost is shown in igure 16.11.

# Non-dedicated components		Number of glue dots			
		<200	200–700	>700	Average 1.75 boards per unit
	<5	$32.97	$74.17	$90.70	
	5-10	$39.56	$88.97	$108.81	
	>10	$52.14	$117.27	$143.42	
# Non-dedicated components		Number of glue dots			
		<200	200–700	>700	1 board per unit
	<5	$18.84	$42.38	$51.83	
	5-10	$22.61	$50.84	$62.18	
	>10	$29.79	$67.01	$81.95	
# Non-dedicated components		Number of glue dots			
		<200	200–700	>700	2 boards per unit
	<5	$32.97	$74.17	$90.70	
	5-10	$39.56	$88.97	$108.81	
	>10	$52.14	$117.27	$143.42	

Figure 16.11: Features and Characteristics Cost Matrix

The product we are addressing has only one board, but this board is typical in regard to the bottleneck work center. The current conversion cost of the board is therefore $50.84. The materials cost for the product is $155.00, making a total cost of $205.84.

Step 8: Calculate Target Costs

The target cost calculation is shown in Figure 16.12. The target costing team has decided that the new product should make a profit of 57 percent. The entire value stream has a hurdle rate of 50 percent return on sales (ROS). It is currently achieving only 45.2 percent ROS. In order to increase the value stream's ROS from 45.2 percent, this new product must contribute a larger profitability than 50 percent. The team has agreed upon 57 percent. Therefore, the allowable cost of the new product is $172.00.

Allowable costs = customer value − profit requirement

Customer value $400.00	Home Automation Controller	Current Value Stream	Future State Value Stream
Required profit margin 57.0%			
Allowable cost	$172.00	$328.97	$299.17
Current average cost:			
Conversion	$50.84	$88.97	$81.73
Material costs	$155.00	$240.00	$223.86
Total costs	$205.84	$328.97	$534.81
Cost gap	$33.84	$(0.00)	$33.84
Units sold	500	2,134	2,634
Current value stream cost	$102,921	$702,026	$804,947
Target value stream cost	$86,000	$702,026	$788,026
Cost gap	$16,921	$(0)	$16,921
ROS	48.5%	45.2%	45.6%

Figure 16.12: Calculation of the Target Costs

The current total cost of the new product is $205.84, making a cost gap of $33.84 per unit. The marketing people expect to sell 500 units per month, making a total cost gap of $16,921 for the value stream as whole.

Based on a price of $400 and the current value stream cost of the new product, the profitability comes to 48.5 percent. The current value stream is achieving 45.2 percent. If the new product is added under the current circumstances, the ROS would increase only to 45.6 percent. This does not reach the 50 percent profitability hurdle rate the value stream manager is required to achieve. The team's challenge is to remove the $16,921 per month from the value stream costs.

Step 9: Target Costs for Major Components

The target costing team at ECI did not need to break the costs of the product down to major components, because the entire product is manufactured within a single value stream. They did, however, work out the amount of time required for the redesign of the product and the development of the software. There is no additional cost for this design work because those people are already accounted for within the value stream and they have sufficient time available to perform the necessary design work.

DRIVING TO CUSTOMER VALUE

The final steps of the target costing process are the most important and the most creative. This is where a practical strategy is put into place to bring the value stream costs into line with the target costs. The outcome is a detailed plan containing actions for everyone in the value stream, from sales and marketing, to engineering, and throughout all operations. The combination of these actions is a strategy that will create more value for the customer and make the right level of profit for the company.

These last three steps are iterative processes (Figure 16.13). The current costs are reviewed, plans are made to reduce the costs, the cost information is updated, and the costs are reviewed again. This creative process continues until the cost gap is filled.

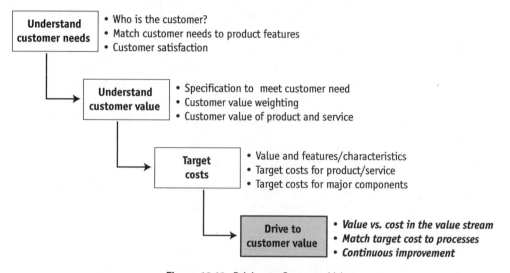

Figure 16.13: Driving to Customer Value

The outworking of this action plan may take many months. It is usual to draw a *future state* value stream map showing the value stream as it will look when these changes are made and the new processes are in place. The target costing process becomes one of the principle drivers of improvement for the entire value stream.

Step 10: Value vs. Cost in the Value Stream

In Step 6, we determined how much value was created by each of the steps within the value stream. We already know how much cost is required for each step. In Step 10, we contrast the costs and the value.

The value stream steps will fall into one of three categories; those that create great value at low cost, those that create little or no value at high cost, and those that create both cost and value. To determine these categories, we divide the percentage of value for each value stream step by the percentage of cost. This cost/value index is then plotted. A value stream step having a high cost/value index (much greater than one) creates great value at low relative cost. Typically, we would want to enhance these steps. A value stream step having a cost/value index of less than one creates more cost than value, so we would want to eliminate this step, or reduce the cost of the step.

Again, the purpose of this process is to give the team another opportunity to study, discuss, and brainstorm the value stream processes. The cost/value index provides further insight into the processes and how value is created for the customer.

Step 11: Matching Target Costs to Processes

Steps 11 and 12 of the target costing process will probably have to be repeated several times before the average value stream cost is aligned with the target cost. These steps are where the team establishes a detailed and practical plan for bringing the value stream costs into line with the target costs.

In Step 11, the team members decide how much of the target cost is to be assigned to each of the steps in the value stream. The current costs of each value stream step is known, the value created by the step is known, and the team must determine how much cost is allowable for that step. There is nothing routine about this process. Working cross-functionally, the target costing team developed an action plan to bring the value stream costs into line with the customer value, and assign where these costs will be used.

Step 12: Action Plan for Continuous Improvement

The outcome of target costing is a detailed action plan for ongoing lean improvement. There are five primary ways to bring value stream costs into line with the target costs:

1. Increase the sales of the value stream. As lean improvement creates more capacity within the value stream, then more products can be made and sold using the same resources. This is the best way to reduce value stream costs, because more value is created with the same resources.

2. Increase revenues by increasing the value created for the customer.

3. Reduce material costs through reduced scrap and rework, through improved supplier processes and cost reductions.

4. Value engineering changes in product design to improve the manufacturability of the products and reduce costs.

5. Reduce the value stream process costs by the elimination of waste and redeployment of freed-up resources.

6. Reduce the cost of administrative processes within the value stream or outside the value stream.

The action plan usually includes elements of all these methods of bringing costs and value into line. Improvement projects are assigned throughout the value stream: marketing initiatives, sales promotions, product design changes, operational process improvements, kaizen events, etc.

EXAMPLE OF TARGET COSTING: STEPS 10 THROUGH 12 AT ECI

The challenge facing the target costing team is to develop a practical action plan to make significant change and improvement to the value stream that removes at least $16,921 per month from the value stream costs. This is what is required to bring the value stream cost into line with the target cost, and support the value required by the customer.

It is important to note that the cost reduction program applies to the value stream, not to the product. While many of the projects and improvements address the specific product the team is working on, other projects improve the value stream as a whole. It is common for target costing teams to exceed their requirement for cost saving because the projects designed to address the costs of a specific product also have a beneficial effect on all the other products manufactured in the value stream.

Step 10: Value vs. Cost in the Value Stream

Figure 16.14 shows the value/cost ratio graph. The entries above a value of 1 contribute more value than cost. Those below 1 contribute more cost than value. From this graph, it is clear that the engineering functions and the technical support aspects of the value stream contribute greatly to customer value. These aspects were not generally recognized throughout the company.

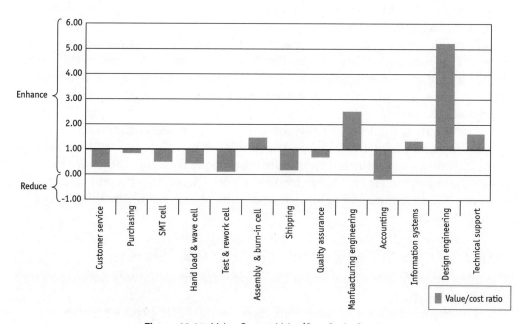

Figure 16.14: Value Stream Value/Cost Ratio Graph

Despite the need to cut costs, the target costing team decided to introduce new programs into the technical support processes and to further increase customer value through improved technical support. These new programs specifically address the needs of customers of the new ZX12 home automation controller. As well as providing additional support for the product, the new technical support programs would also focus on the soon-to-be introduced software configuration features of the new product.

Conversely, the team recognized that the value/cost ratio for many of the production and support operations were less than 1. Improvement projects were initiated to bring these costs down and to enhance the level of service to the customers. These projects are shown in Step 12, below.

Step 11: Match Target Cost to Value Stream Processes

As the target cost team worked together to develop their action plan for increased value and reduced cost, they carefully worked out how the savings would have an impact on the value stream. These results are shown on Figure 16.15.

The top four rows of the matrix show the current state costs of the value stream: the total cost, cost per unit, cost percentage, and the material cost per unit. The next four rows show the target costs per unit and the cost gap between the current state cost and the target cost. The target costs shown are the cost for the entire value stream, including the new ZX12 products being introduced. For example, the total target conversion cost is $70.33. This is the target average cost for all the products in the value stream after new ZX12 products are added to the value stream, and after the improvement projects have all been implemented.

The value stream cost and capacity analysis is shown at the bottom of the matrix. The purpose of this information is to show processes within the value stream where there are high levels of non-productive capacity and available capacity. These are places where there is likely to be potential for improvement and cost savings.

The team studied these analyses and brainstormed solutions to the issues they had uncovered. The result of this work was a series of improvement initiatives that affected many different aspects of the value stream. When these improvements were implemented, the value stream more than achieved the customer value and cost savings objectives of the target-costing project.

Step 12: The Continuous Improvement Program

The table on page 266 summarizes the improvement initiatives developed by the target costing team.

The financial effects of these initiatives on the ZX12 product family are shown in Figure 16.16. The current design and process shows a cost gap of $33.84. The design changes will reduce the materials costs and the conversion costs, because the product will now be smaller, simpler, easier to manufacture,

		Totals	Customer service	Purchasing	SMT cells	Hand load & wave cell	Test & rework cell	Assemble & burn-in cell	Shipping	Quality assurance	Manufacturing engineering	Accounting	Information systems	Design engineering	Technical support
Target costs	Total cost	$215,287	$12,917	$19,160	$39,182	$30,140	$24,758	$14,209	$3,229	$12,271	$12,917	$12,917	$8,611	$8,611	$16,362
	Cost per unit	$81.73	$4.90	$7.27	$14.88	$11.44	$9.40	$5.39	$1.23	$4.66	$4.90	$4.90	$3.27	$3.27	$6.21
	Percentage	100%	6.0%	8.9%	18.2%	14.0%	11.5%	6.6%	1.5%	5.7%	6.0%	6.0%	4.0%	4.0%	7.6%
	Material costs	$223.86	$–		$129.90	$68.00	$10.46	$12.50	$3.00	$–	$–	$–	$–	$–	$–
	Conversion costs	$70.33	$4.75	$4.5	$12.10	$10.30	$9.40	$5.03	$1.23	$2.10	$4.90	$4.00	1.75	3.27	$7.00
	Material cost	$212.67			$123.21	$64.41	$10.10	$11.75	$3.00						
Cost gap	Conversion costs	$11.40	$0.15	$2.77	$2.78	$1.14	$–	$0.36	$–	$2.56	$–	$0.90	$1.52	$–	$(0.79)
	Material costs	$11.19	$–	$–	$6.49	$3.59	$0.36	$0.75	$–	$–	$–	$–	$–	$–	$–
Employee capacity	Productive	42.5	0.0%	0.0%	0.0%	45.0%	0.0%	28.0%	59.0%	0.0%	0.0%	0.0%	0.0%	0.0%	0.0%
	Non-productive	23.2%	28.0%	37.0%	41.0%	51.0%	56.0%	24.0%	0.0%	26.0%	38.0%	51.0%	47.0%	8.0%	56.0%
	Other	0.0%	0.0%	0.0%	0.0%	0.0%	0.0%	0.0%	0.0%	0.0%	0.0%	0.0%	0.0%	0.0%	0.0%
	Available	34.4	72.0%	63.0%	59.0%	4.0%	44.0%	48.0%	41.0%	74.0%	62.0%	49.0%	53.0%	92.0%	44.0%
Machine capacity	Productive	27.0%			25.0%	58.0%	0.0%								
	Non-productive	8.8%			73.0%	3.0%	80.0%								
	Other	0.0%			0.0%	0.0%	0.0%								
	Available	64.1%			2.0%	39.0%	20.0%								

Figure 16.15: Matching Target Costs to Value Stream Processes

Improvement Initiative	Value Stream Process	Benefit
Introduce additional ecommerce into the order entry process, enabling the customer to place orders on-line.	Customer Service Information Systems	Reduced the cost of customer service process, simplified the entire order-entry process, and provided improved visibility to customers.
Redesign the product to eliminate complex hardware configuration and introduce software-based configuration.	Design Engineering Purchasing Production Cells (SMT and Hand Load) Quality Assurance	Increased value to the customer. Reduced materials costs. Simplified production. Improved product quality, reduced scrap, simpler inspection/test.
Work with current suppliers to reduce the cost of incoming materials by applying lean methods, short lead times, and pull systems. Eliminate MRP push purchasing. Standardize containers.	Purchasing	Reduced materials costs, lower inventory, improved service from suppliers, reduced obsolescence and scrap, and simplified processes.
Process improvement within the SMT Cell to reduce waste, level the schedule, and eliminate over-time costs.	SMT Cell	Reduced cost, shorter lead-time, reduced inventory, standardized work, and even capacity usage.
Process improvement in the Assembly cell to reduce waste and level the schedule. Cross-training within the cell team.	Assembly and Burn In	Reduced cost, shorter lead time, reduced inventory, standardized work, even capacity usage, and greater flexibility.
Eliminate transactions (using a maturity path approach) in purchasing, production planning, shopfloor control, shipping, receiving, invoicing, and inventory control.	Purchasing, Production Cells, Shipping, Accounting, and Information Systems.	Reduce cost, free up people's time, eliminate reports, reduce wasteful meetings, eliminate misleading information.
Introduce Value Stream Costing	All Value Stream team-members, particularly Accounting, Information Systems, and Management	Eliminate transactions, simplify processes, provide accurate cost information, free up accountants' time.
Increase scope of technical support to support the new ZX12 products and the configuration software. Increase working hours and depth of technical support processes to increase customer value.	Technical support	Provide additional value to the customer in ways that are unique to BMA, Inc.
Introduce marketing campaign based around the flexibility and ease-of-use of the ZX12 product family. Emphasize the company's technical support and product innovation.	Sales and marketing. Customer service. Technical support.	Increase sales, develop market share, enhance the company's reputation, increase customer value.

	New ZX12 Home Automation Product			
	Current product design	With design changes	Purchasing improvements	With process changes
Product value	$400.00	$400.00	$400.00	$400.00
Required profit	57.0%	57.0%	57.0%	57.0%
Allowable cost	$172.00	$172.00	$172.00	$172.00
Conversion cost	$50.84	$49.12	$49.12	$43.75
Material cost	$155.00	$135.00	$128.25	$128.25
Total cost	$205.85	$184.12	$177.37	$172.00
Cost gap	$33.84	$12.12	$5.37	$–
Expected sales quantity	500	500	500	500
Total current costs	$102,921	$92,060	$88,685	$86,000
Total target cost	$86,000	$86,000	$86,000	$86,000
Total cost gap	$16,921	$6,060	$2,685	$–
Current return on sales	48.5%	54.0%	55.7%	57.0%

Figure 16.16: Financial Effect of the Improvement Initiatives on the ZX12 Products.

and the process will be more dependable and of higher quality. The purchasing improvements further reduce the material costs leaving a cost gap of $5.37. This cost gap is fully bridged by the remaining process improvements.

These financial savings are quite conservative and contain only hard and verifiable numbers. No account has been taken for additional sales coming from the improved design and the enhanced sales campaign.

The overall effect of these changes on the value stream is shown in Figure 16.17. As a result of these improvements, the value stream will be brought very close to the required hurdle rate of 50 percent. Many of the improvements provided benefits within the whole value stream, not just the ZX12 products.

Figure 16.18 shows the box score developed from the team's analysis. The first column shows the current state value stream information. The second shows the effect on the box score of introducing the new products. The far right column shows the box score as it will be when all the improvement projects are successfully implemented. The operational and financial results are monitored every week by the value stream team-members.

At ECI target costing is a primary driver of the ongoing continuous improvement process. The improvements within the value stream are based upon the need to increase customer value and increase the company's profitability.

	Total value stream cost including the ZX12 products	
	Current design & processes	With design, purchasing, & process changes
Product value	$562.03	$562.03
Required profit	50.0%	50.0%
Allowable cost	$281.02	$281.02
Conversion cost	$81.73	$70.33
Material cost	$223.86	$212.67
Total cost	$305.60	$283.00
Cost gap	$24.58	$1.99
Expected sales quantity	2,634	2,634
Total current cost	$804,947	$745,431
Total target cost	$740,200	$740,200
Total cost gap	$64,747	$5,231
Current return on sales	45.6%	49.6%

Figure 16.17: Financial Impact of the Overall Value Stream

SUMMARY

Target costing is a powerful tool for lean improvement. The target costing process integrates the entire value stream and focuses the team's attention on the need to drive the business from customer value. While target costing is a set of formal tools designed to bring the team-members from an understanding of customer value through to the development of a practical action plan, the primary purpose of target costing is to instigate cross-functional improvement within the value stream.

Target costing closes the loop of value stream management. It starts with customer value. It addresses the entire value stream. It recognizes the need to grow the business and make exceptional profits. It leads to practical, cross-functional improvement. It is a never-ending process of pursuing perfection. Lean companies move beyond random improvement and use target costing to instigate radical and ongoing change, aimed at increasing customer value and making tons of money.

	Current state 4-Apr-03	With new products 2-May-03				Future state goals 26-Sep-03
Units per person	34	41				45
Order to invoice days	12.50	12.5				4.5
On time shipment	92%	92%				98%
First time through	67%	67%				82%
Average cost	$329	$306				$283
Accounts receivable days	52	52				40
Productive	37%	44%				43%
Non-productive	47%	55%				39%
Available capacity	16%	1%				18%
Revenue	$1,280,400	$1,480,400				$1,480,400
Material costs	$512,160	$589,660				$560,177
Conversion cost	$189,866	$215,287				$185,254
Value stream profit	$578,374	$675,453				$734,969
Value stream ROS	45.2%	45.6%				49.6%

Figure 16.18: Box Score for the Target Costing Action Plan

CHAPTER 17

Expanding Value Streams Outside Our Four Walls

Up to now we have spoken of value streams as though they consist of those activities within the four walls of our plant. But, in the broadest sense, our value stream includes all the activities from the mining of the ore in the ground, extracting the elemental raw materials from which product will be fabricated, right the way through to the delivery of the product to the end-user consumer in his local store; and possibly to the recycling of the product or its materials. Our company lies somewhere within this larger value stream. In this chapter, we will broaden our definition to include the upstream supplier and the downstream customer of our company. The purpose will be the same as in earlier chapters: how to add shape and definition to the measurement, management, and control of lean value creation. Our suppliers, our customers, and our own organization all provide value for the benefit of the ultimate customer.

THE LEAN VALUE STREAM REVISITED

As described earlier in this book, lean thinking has five basic principles as shown in Figure 17.1.

Value: Lean is all about creating value for customers. This involves understanding what the customer wants, which may be very different from the product we deliver. A critical examination of value from the customer's point of view provides the basis for more effective product and process design.

Value Stream: Value is delivered through a value stream, which, up to now, we have defined as all the activities performed by a lean company to create and deliver its product or service, from receipt of an order, to delivery into the arms of the immediate customer. Some of the activities that appear to create

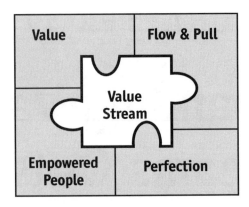

Figure 17.1: Lean Principles

value from the point of view of the individual, may not create value from the point of view of the broader value stream. For example, our efforts to improve flow and eliminate inventories in our companies, may result in an increase in the inventories of our customers and suppliers — a net reduction in value for the broader value stream. Looking at the broader value stream and the entire flow will lead to more savings, better flow, and increased value.

Flow and Pull: Lean thinking demands that work should flow smoothly and be initiated by the pull of the customer demand. Production upstream should not commence until it is requested by a downstream operation. This contradicts traditional mass production thinking, which seeks to produce in large batches, so as to create the lowest per unit part cost. This principle applies as well to the broader value stream: to the interface between our suppliers and customers, where the flow within the company is often interrupted by large distribution and receiving warehouses.

Perfection: Waste can be defined as anything that interrupts the smooth flow of value through the value stream. That should include the way the customer uses the product in his value stream—how well the product works in his value stream, and whether there is a smooth flow of the delivered product into his production. It also includes how smoothly the supplier can respond to the demand. The goal of lean is to create perfect continuous flow throughout the value stream at the pull of the customer. We now broaden this to include the supplier and customer of the lean company.

Empowerment: Lean demands that there be continuous attention to maintaining flow and eliminating waste by all employees in the value stream. To achieve this goal, employees must be given the right information concerning flow and waste in a timely manner. They must know how to fix the problems that impede flow and create waste. They must be given the authority to fix the problems, and work continuously to improve the flow and eliminate waste. The ability of lean to free up capacity in the form of key manufacturing, engineering, accounting systems, and other resources, creates an opportunity to deploy these resources to create more and more customer value. This pursuit of perfect cannot be achieved solely through the work of managers; all employees must be engaged and empowered to serve the customers, create more value, eliminate waste, and increase profitability. There is powerful new potential for radical improvement when these empowered employees work cooperatively with their peers throughout the larger value stream. The role of lean outside the four walls of the plant involves blurring the roles that normally mark the boundaries between corporate entities.

A VISION OF THE EXPANDED VALUE STREAM

The traditional value stream flow consists of a sequence of functional processes:

- Marketing to determine customer needs
- Sales to work with customer purchasing to generate an order
- Engineering to design the product and process based upon requirements received from sales
- Purchasing to procure the materials required to produce the product to engineering specifications
- Manufacturing to produce the product based upon specifications received from engineering
- Logistics to receive raw materials from suppliers and store and ship the product
- Support services such as Human Resources, Accounting, and Information Systems to provide the management and information flows to run the value stream

The prime point of contact with customers and suppliers traditionally is between the sales department of the supplier company and the purchasing department of the customer company, as shown in Figure 17.2—depicted for our case study company, ECI. This single point of contact creates problems for the flow of information between customer and supplier companies. The problem is particularly acute in flows of information about customer needs that are filtered through the sales point of contact before getting to the engineers, who need to know specifically what these needs are. Even more convoluted is the case in which the key technology resides in a supplier that is upstream of the direct point of contact.

For ECI to overcome these information flow problems, it must view its role in the overall value stream differently. Rather than filtering information through a sales department, there needs to be a network of relationships among suppliers and customers, to enable fast and free exchange of information, regardless of where the people are in the value stream hierarchy. Thus, an engineer working on the circuit supplier of BMA might play a key role in the

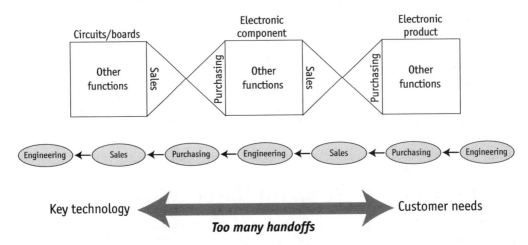

Figure 17.2: Traditional Customer-Supplier Interfaces at ECI

design of a customer's new product. Another possibility is that customer and supplier companies might integrate their information systems across the companies to eliminate existing obstacles to the free flow of information.

A vision of this changing role is set out in the book, *Beyond Partnership: Strategies for Innovation and Lean Supply*,[1] by Dr. Richard Lamming, Professor of Purchasing and Supply Management at the School of Management, Bath University, England. The change in role envisaged by Professor Lamming entails a shift from arms-length relationships with suppliers and customers to one of collaboration among customers and suppliers, in order to maximize the value delivered to the end customer. The role of any one company, as such, is less important to that end than the capabilities it can provide to the end product. The resulting network of trans-company capabilities becomes a virtual organization formed for the delivery of a particular product or service. From the point of view of any company along the value stream, its role is one of providing capabilities that add value to the end product. This is a major shift from just delivering a product to the next customer-supplier in the extended value stream. This change in roles simplifies the extended value stream by eliminating duplicate functions among companies, and adding to its overall capability by assigning key functions to partners that have the greatest capability to perform them. The diagram in Figure 17.3 depicts this new relationship for ECI, its suppliers and customers.

There must be collaboration among ECI, its suppliers, and its customers in eliminating duplicate functions, improving the flow of information, and

---

1. Richard Lamming, *Beyond Partnership—Strategies for Innovation and Lean Supply* (Prentice Hall International Limited, 1993 (Hertfordshire, UK)). The vision is most clearly articulated in Chapter 9 (pp. 238–259), in which Dr. Lamming provides examples of ways to rationalize the supply chain. This is an excellent reference for those who would like to explore this topic in more depth.

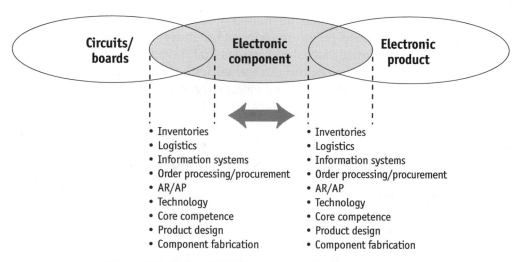

Figure 17.3: The Extended Value Stream—a Blending of Functions

allocating key functions to those entities having the greatest capability to add value. Examples of this collaboration are:

- Eliminating duplications
  - Finished goods and raw materials inventories at supplier and customer
  - Accounts payable and receivable at supplier and customer in favor of electronic payment scheme
  - Duplicate product design capability
  - Duplicate information systems in favor of integration across companies
  - Duplicate sales and purchasing staffs dedicated to processing orders in favor of a relationship management role for these functions
  - Simplifying logistics by housing more key supplier assembly in customer facilities
- Improving the flow of information through aligning functions, from customer our company to supplier
  - Customer design engineering alignment with our engineering and our supplier's engineering
  - Customer procurement with our procurement
  - Customer manufacturing with our manufacturing and with our supplier's manufacturing
  - Networked information and accounting systems, such as accounts payable and receivable
  - Process engineering
- Allocating key functions to the entities having the most competence
  - Identifying value added within our company, our customer, our supplier
  - Identifying competencies and technologies needed
  - Selecting core competence providers across the value stream

Achieving this vision entails formation of alliances among value stream participants that transcend the boundaries of the individual companies. Such alliances, in essence, create virtual companies that have their own networked information flows and cultures and are staffed with dedicated people who can move comfortably across the extended value stream.

However, the first step for our company is to determine where we add value and cost.

EXAMINING VALUE AND COST WITHIN OUR OWN COMPANY

To get at value and cost, we pick up the ECI example where we left off in the preceding chapter. You recall that as part of its target costing exercise, the company had defined the cost and value of each of the business processes in its value stream. Table 17.1 ranks each process on these two dimensions.

Table 17.1: ECI—Business Process Cost-Value Ranking

Business Process	Percentage of Conversion Cost	Cost Ranking (Highest=13)	Percentage of Total Value	Value Ranking (Highest=13)
Customer Service	6.0%	5	2.7%	4
Purchasing	8.9%	10	8.2%	8
SMT Cell	18.2%	13	10.3%	10
Hand Load and Wave Post	14.0%	12	6.8%	7
Test and Rework	11.5%	11	2.5%	2
Assemble and Burn-in	6.6%	8	9.8%	9
Shipping	1.5%	1	0.4%	3
Quality Assurance	5.7%	4	4.4%	5
Manufacturing Engineering	6.0%	7	16.0%	12
Accounting	6.0%	6	Not rated	1
Information Systems	4.0%	3	4.9%	6
Design Engineering	4.0%	2	21.4%	13
Technical Support	7.6%	9	12.6%	11

Having recorded these rankings, we can now see what they mean and begin to direct the allocation of functions within the extended value stream. A useful way to look at this is shown in Figure 17.4

As we saw in the last chapter, the cost-value diagram (Figure 17.5) compares the value a business process contributes versus its cost. The analysis of

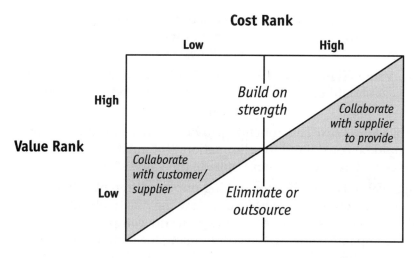

Figure 17.4: The Cost-Value Strategy Framework

cost and value is performed by each of the companies making up the extended value stream alliance, as the basis for determining where the value stream processes should be performed. For each of the companies, then, the value stream processes are positioned on the cost-value framework. For each of the dimensions, a rank of 1–7 is low, and a rank of 7–13 is high. The diagonal is the cost/value relationship at which the relative cost and value are equal; that is, the ratio of the cost rank to the value rank is 1. Above this line, the process adds more value than cost; below the line the process adds more

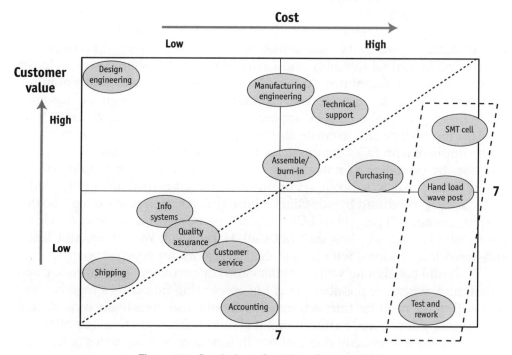

Figure 17.5: Developing a Cost-Value Strategy at ECI

cost than value. For each company in the extended value stream, the cost/ value position of each process provides general guidance as to the role of its processing in the extended value stream, as follows:

- **Cost Low, Value High.** A core competence of the company possessing it, the process should be capitalized on by the extended value stream to create even more value for the customer.

- **Cost High, Value Low.** This function provides low value and is expensive. It should be considered for elimination. If it must be provided, it should be considered for purchase outside the value stream.

- **Cost High, Value High.** This positioning implies different actions depending on whether it lies above or below the diagonal. Above the diagonal, the process should be considered a core competence of the evaluating company. Below it, the cost of using the evaluating company to provide the high-value process is too high. Potentially, a member of the value stream alliance that has this as a core competence could provide this process.

- **Cost Low, Value Low.** This positioning also implies differing actions above and below the diagonal. Above it, a member of the value stream that has the core competence should provide the process. Below it, the process should be eliminated or purchased from a supplier outside the value stream.

Having described the method, we are ready to see how it can be used in one of the value stream companies. We will use the BMA, Inc. example to demonstrate its use.

For ECI, the strategy is clear. It should focus its energies on its alliance with customers towards its value-added strengths, its product and process design, and in its final assembly and technical support. It should seek to foster opportunities for collaborated design of value-added products, incorporating its superior technical competence in electronic component design and assembly. In this regard, it should seek opportunities to perform the key design functions for the alliance and to create assemblies that combine components from other suppliers with ECI's components, to eliminate customer assembly processes by capitalizing on its strength in electronic component assembly.

It should seek to subcontract or purchase circuit boards already loaded with circuitry, produced by suppliers whose core competence is circuit board loading, because 40 percent of ECI's total conversion cost is dedicated to loading circuit boards (including the SMT Cell, Hand Load, Wave Post, and Test and Rework operations) with a great deal of rework for off-spec boards.

It should collaborate with suppliers and/or customers to eliminate duplications and, wherever possible, get rid of accounting functions altogether by eliminating the need for transactions. ECI should also investigate outsourcing its accounting functions. Furthermore, it should collaborate with suppliers and customers to eliminate duplications in functions and obstacles to information flow in Shipping/Receiving, Information Systems, Quality Assurance,

Purchasing and Customer Service.

There are enormous savings and benefits when each of the parties to the supplier-customer value stream alliance perform a similar analysis and work together to create the highest value for end customers of the extended value stream.

EXAMPLE OF EFFECTIVE VALUE STREAM EXPANSION

The Superior Meter Company is a supplier of speedometers to a supplier of automobile interiors. Superior found itself with free capacity after having successfully completed an initial lean program in its manufacturing facility. It decided to explore how it could increase the value delivered to its customer by expanding the definition of how it created value to include the complete interior dashboard assembly, and thereby employ the free capacity.

At the time there were several suppliers to the customer, each requiring the expenditure of resources in logistics and storage, planning, scheduling, transportation, fabrication, and accounting and administration. Figure 17.6 shows the current-state map of the customer's manufacturing process.

To execute its strategy, Superior Meters created a joint project with its customer to maximize the value that the extended value stream created, including the two companies. They formed a joint project team comprised of representatives from the customer's purchasing, quality, manufacturing, scheduling, materials, shipping, receiving, and manufacturing engineering departments and from Superior's manufacturing, finance, process engineering, sales and marketing departments. Their charter was to research the following questions related to the extended value stream:

- Where do the core competencies lie?
- Where are the duplicate activities?
- Where is the inventory?
- Where are the fixed assets?
- Where are the duplicate information systems?
- Where are the obstacles to the information flows?

The objective of the team was to identify potential improvements to the value stream efficiency. Examples of improvements sought were:

- reduced packaging materials
- reduced number of inventory items
- reduced supplier lead times
- reduced transaction costs
- reduced scrap and rework
- increased flow of the interiors production process
- improved financial returns on assets employed

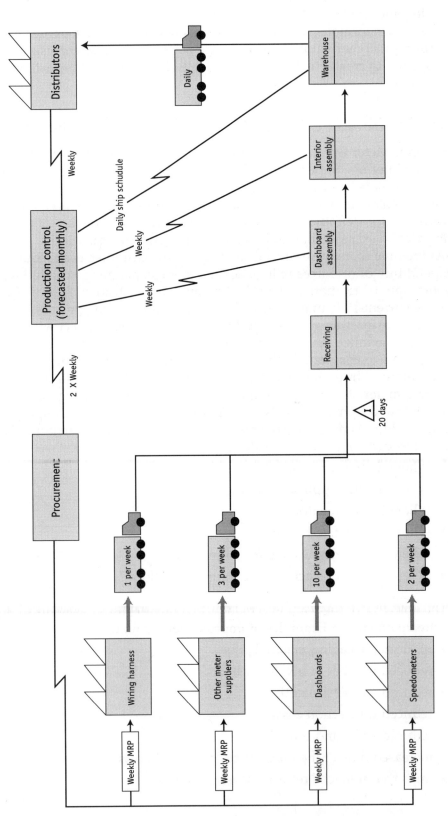

Figure 17.6: Automobile Interiors Manufacturer—Current-State Map

The team concluded that significant savings could be achieved by reducing the number of suppliers from seven to four, using Superior to assemble the purchased dashboard housing, tachometer, miscellaneous gauges, wiring harnesses, and speedometer assemble the entire dashboard. This assembly would proceed directly into the automobile interior assembly process. This solution is shown in Figure 17.7.

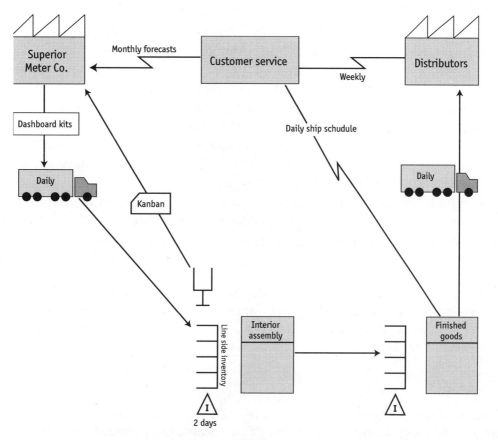

Figure 17.7: Automobile Interiors Company—Future State Map

These improvements would have the effect of eliminating Dashboard Assembly from the customer's production operation. This would eliminate the frequent rework and scrap problems that the customer was experiencing in this operation and would thereby improve the flow through the process. Superior now delivers the fully assembled dashboards directly to the Interior Assembly cell of the Auto Interiors Company. The dashboards kits are pulled every day from Superior using kanban cards to replenish the line-side supermarket adjacent to the cell.

The study showed that there were indeed significant savings to be achieved:

- Reduced inventory costs
- Reduced purchase order costs

- Reduced scrap
- Reduced tooling expense
- Reduced supplies
- Reduced people cost
- Reduced production equipment.
- Reduced transportation costs
- Eliminated shortages
- Increased on-time delivery to the customer
- Significantly reduced customer returns and complaints

Superior and the customer agreed to divide the annual savings on an equitable basis. They planned to explore future value improvements:

- Superior delivers the dashboard assemblies in production sequence each day to fill the end customer's orders. This will largely eliminate the cell supermarket of dashboard kits.

- Superior not only can deliver the dashboard assembly directly to the customer's assembly cell, but can also install it on site.

- Extend the value improvements further upstream into the supply chain.

The experience of Superior demonstrates the possibilities for even a minor supplier to contribute significant value, even in slow economic conditions, by identifying its unique competence and deploying its free capacity to the benefit of its customer.

Summary

This chapter has explored the process of creating value outside the lean company by extending the definition of the value stream. As organizations mature into lean enterprises, their view of the value stream extends beyond their own four walls. They create close, cooperative relationships with their suppliers, their customers, and other third-party partners. These relationships lead to closer peer-to-peer communication throughout the value stream, leading to the elimination of waste, improved flow, and increased customer value.

We have shown that by drawing macro value stream maps we can identify where cost and value are created in a company, supplier, and customer. By working together, significant improvements and savings can be made in total value stream and product flow, which eliminates duplications of inventories and functions, obstacles to information flow between companies, and employs value stream resources to their highest value in the production, design, logistics, and administrative processes.

CHAPTER 18

The Lean Accounting Diagnostic

In Chapter 2, we introduced the concept of the maturity path to lean accounting. The remaining chapters of this book have presented the methods of lean accounting that were introduced in the earlier chapter. What remains to be discussed is how to get started on the lean accounting journey. This entails assessing where on the maturity path the company's accounting and control processes currently lie, and developing the steps for proceeding forward from that point. What is needed is a diagnostic tool. This chapter deals with just such a tool, which has been tailored to the needs of companies that want to know where they currently are on the lean accounting maturity path.

THE MATURITY PATH REVISITED

The path to lean accounting parallels the path to lean manufacturing. Figure 18.1 shows this progression proceeding in step with lean manufacturing.

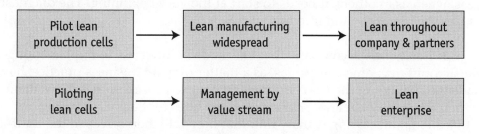

Figure 18.1: The Maturity Path to Lean Accounting

This progression was discussed in some detail in Chapter 2, and the details of each of these three stages have been the subject of the earlier chapters of this book. The important questions are:

1. For each of the areas of finance and accounting, where do we stand now?

2. Given where we are now, where do we want to go?

3. What are the steps that need to be taken to progress from where we are now to where we want to be?

This format provides a structured diagnostic approach to addressing these questions, gauging where each aspect of finance and accounting currently is along the spectrum from traditional to lean business management.

Overview of the Diagnostic Tool

The first thing to do in starting your lean accounting journey is to create a plan. You will want to chart an overall course that will enable a progression along the maturity path to Lean Business Management.

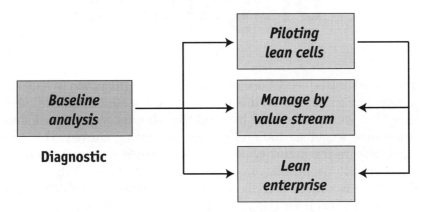

Figure 18.2: Creating the Lean Accounting Action Plan

As shown in Figure 18.2, the first step in creating this plan is to baseline where you currently are. The best way to work out this information is to employ a diagnostic tool that covers all these areas. Based on the results of the diagnosis, you may find that the company is ready to jump ahead in some areas, whereas in others, it needs to start at the very beginning. The diagnostic divides the maturity path into four stages:

Stage 1: Traditional—A company that has made no progress in implementing lean accounting. Some companies, as a matter of good business practice, have made the changes in their accounting and control processes that move them beyond the traditional level. However, companies that are just starting out with lean manufacturing usually find that they rate themselves in the traditional stage in most categories.

Stage 2: Piloting Lean Cells—A company that is just getting started with lean manufacturing can begin to implement the changes that are summarized in Table 18.1 This is possible when the company has successful pilot lean cells in place and has conducted extensive training in lean manufacturing principles.

Stage 3: Managing by Value Stream—A company that has implemented pull systems in the factory and has created value streams to link the individual cells of Stage 2, above, can begin to think about managing the company by value stream. This is characterized by the changes listed in Table 18.2.

Table 18.1: Piloting Lean Cells

- New cell level performance measurements and targets
- Calculate financial benefits of lean improvements
- Eliminate cell operational transactions through backflushing (labor and materials)
- Eliminate variance reports
- Identify value streams

  Provide clear goals and objectives
- Drivers of performance and cost

  Root causes
- Eliminate waste from financial accounting processes

The value stream management step is a major leap for many companies and enables them to eliminate many of the transactions required by traditional companies to manage their production process.

Table 18.2: Managing by Value Stream

- Integrated performance measurements at value streams and strategic or corporate levels
- Direct costing with features and characteristics replaces standard costing
- Performance measurements and value stream cost analysis drive continuous improvement
- Expand value stream cost analysis
- Assess and track performance and cost improvements of lean projects
- Value stream cost analysis linked to sales and operations planning

Stage 4: Lean Enterprise—Companies have lean value streams in place and they function as the core of the strategic business system. The next step entails extending these value streams beyond the corporate limits and into suppliers and customers. Target costing is an important tool for companies in this stage.

Table 18.3: Lean Enterprise

- Target costing driven from the voice of the customer linked to features and characteristics

- Target costing drives product and process design and improvement

- Profound cooperation with suppliers and customers

- Extend value stream analysis outside the company to suppliers, customers, and partners

- Automate routine bookkeeping activities

- Many part numbers expensed and not tracked

These four stages of the lean accounting maturity path mark milestones along the path to maturity in each of the major areas of accounting control encompassed by lean accounting. These milestones are characterized by narrative descriptions in the diagnostic (two descriptions for each stage) that make up eight discrete gradients for each diagnostic area.

Table 18.4: The Diagnostic Areas of Lean Accounting

Financial Accounting	Accounts payable and procurement
	Accounts receivable
	Authorizations and sign-offs
	Month end
Operational Accounting	Material costs
	Labor and overhead costs
	Inventory tracking
	Product costing
Management Accounting	Alignment of company strategy and lean goals
	Performance measures
	Budgeting and planning
	Managing product profitability
Support for Lean Transformation	Role of finance people
	Continuous improvement
	Empowerment and learning
	Financial benefits of lean changes
Business Management	Value stream organization
	Customer value and target costing
	Rewards and recognition

Each of these areas trace the progression from complexity to simplicity in accounting and control, relying increasingly on the visual control and simplicity of the production and information flow afforded by lean manufacturing, in place of the transactions-intensive control processes of the traditional manufacturer. The goals in each of these areas demonstrates this:

- **Financial Accounting**—shifting from highly transaction-oriented processes with considerable auditing control, to processes with minimal transactions and control built into the structure of the process itself.

- **Operational Accounting**—shifting from multiple postings of labor and materials tracked through the production process to reliance on visual controls, low and level inventories, and short lead times afforded by lean manufacturing to provide the control.

- **Management Accounting**—shifting from a historical/results-based orientation, to performance measurement and control to one based on predictive and causal-based measures, from departmental to value stream, and from cost-based to value-based orientations.

- **Support for the Lean Transformation**—shifting the financial professionals and financial reports from a results orientation to integral supporters of the lean effort in guiding improvement initiatives, disclosing waste and benefits of lean, and in providing real-time information that is actionable by the operations team.

- **Lean Business Management**—shifting from a functional organization to a value stream organization, and an approach to decision making that measures the contribution to customer value as the primary criteria.

Thus, the diagnostic assessment provides a comprehensive view of the alignment of the control processes with lean at each stage of the lean journey.

WORKING WITH THE DIAGNOSTIC TOOL

A copy of the tool is provided on the accompanying CD with this book. The format of each assessment area is as shown in Table 18.5.

For each area there are four statements—one for each of the stages of the maturity path. Place an X in the space provided for the statement that most closely describes where the company currently is, with respect to that lean accounting area. You place an O for the statement that most clearly describes where the company would like to be in the foreseeable future.

The overall questionnaire results can be summarized visually in a radar chart depiction, shown in Figure 18.3. Such a depiction provides a lean team with a basis for developing an action plan that will help them reach the desired future state of lean accounting.

Table 18.5: Filling Out the Diagnostic Questionnaire

Accounting, control, and measurement questionnaire

INSTRUCTIONS

1. Read all four statements carefully—the left hand statement defines 1–2 on the scale; the second statement covers the 3–4 range on the scale, the third covers 5-6 and the right hand statement 7–8 on the scale. Please note: the statements and the numerical ratings do not precisely align. Some judgment is needed.

2. Honestly evaluate the present position of your organization in terms of the four statements by marking an **X** (one of 1, 2, 3, 4, 5, 6, 7, 8) over the number which best represents your *present* position.

   If you are using a computer, change the number you choose to **X** in the "current" row.

   If you are doing this analysis manually, write the number that corresponds to your choice under "current" at the right.

3. Decide where you would like your organization realistically to be *in the foreseeable future* by marking an **0** on the scale (one of 1, 2, 3, 4, 5, 6, 7, 8). This goal should be challenging yet realistic.

   If you are using a computer, change the number you choose to **0** in the "future" row.

   If you are doing this analysis manually, write the number that corresponds to your choice under "future" at the right.

To illustrate this and the previous point, the following diagram shows a typical and valid response:

Current	1	2	X	4	5	6	7	8
Future	1	2	3	4	0	6	7	8

SUMMARY

This chapter has provided an overview in the use of the lean accounting diagnostic tool, a copy of which is provided on the accompanying CD. It is recommended that the tool be employed at the beginning of the lean accounting journey, and that it be updated to reflect changes as improvements are made. In this way, this tool will become a living document in the management of the transformation to a lean accounting control world.

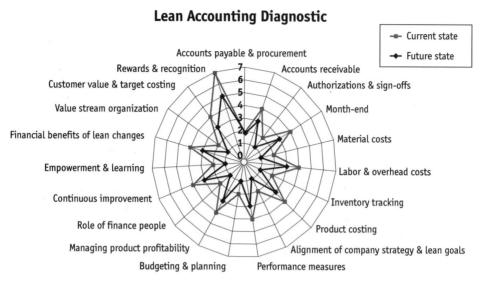

Figure 18.3: Depiction of Overall Diagnostic Results

CHAPTER 19

Performance Measurement Linkage Chart

In Chapters 3 and 8, we described a set of measurements for a starter set for lean manufacturers. These were presented at the cell, value stream, and plant levels as examples of the type of measures that support lean goals, and that many lean companies have found helpful in sustaining their lean programs. We do not claim that these are the best or only measurements. The term "starter set" implies that the company will modify the measurements to suit the unique circumstances. In this chapter, we develop a method and rationale for tailoring these measures.

The chapter focuses on the following general topics:

- The performance measurement framework
- Creating the performance measurement starter set
- Steps for developing performance measurements in your company

THE PERFORMANCE MEASUREMENT FRAMEWORK

As we have stated repeatedly, existing measurements and control processes do not work in a lean environment. To discover what should be measured requires thought about the process of measurement and control, defining the characteristic of a good measure, and developing a set of principles that can be translated into a framework. This framework can then be applied to any situation in which measurements need to be defined. This section lays out that framework.

Key Questions About Measurement and Control

To be useful, our framework must assist in answering the following questions, listed in Figure 19.1.

The questions themselves are:

- What to measure
- How often to measure
- How to control

Key Questions

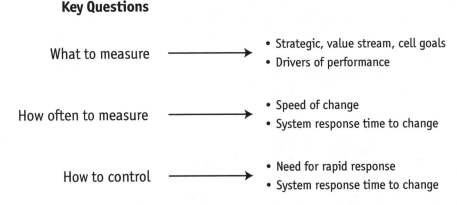

Figure 19.1: Key Questions About Measures and Controls

What to Measure

Measures are needed to monitor the performance of a system related to expectations. Therefore, we can state as a general rule of thumb that the purpose of a measure is to monitor performance compared to some specific goal set for the system. A goal should state the specific result and time frame desired. An example of such a goal would be "I plan to lose 10 pounds in two months." This is a good goal because it states specifically what must be done and when. We could also posit secondary goals, "to lose five pounds in one month," "to lose 1.25 pounds by the end of the week," and so on. A measurement shows the extent to which a goal has been achieved. If you tell me what I am to do, and by when, then I can establish a measure to determine whether I have achieved that goal.

Lean organizations operate in teams. They do not operate as individuals. Our measurements should focus on the success of the team at attaining its goals. The relevant teams making up a lean organization are value streams and cells. However, we have not fully defined what should be measured because we have not defined what the organization is trying to achieve. This is set forth in the strategy of the enterprise within which the lean structure operates. The strategy dictates the direction of the organization. It defines all subordinate goals and measures. For example, a strategy might define an overall growth in sales and market share during the coming year by sales of new products to existing customers. This strategy would then define the goals of each value stream and cell within that company.

However, for a goal to be achieved, it is not sufficient to simply monitor the extent to which it has been attained. Every team must be successful in its goal, if the overall strategy is to be attained, just as in the army, every unit must reach its objective if the overall mission is to be successful. To follow our example of the weight-loss scenario, if I want to be assured of losing the ten pounds in two months, I must then define what has to happen to enable me to lose the weight. The resultant factors are what we call the drivers of performance. In this case the driver of weight loss is caloric intake minus calories burned. The resulting difference determines the amount and rapidity of the weight loss, and the factors critical to success are diet and exercise. If I am to lose the ten pounds, I must institute these disciplines in my daily schedule sufficient to achieve my weight-loss goal. It might be that I decide that such a program would constitute, for example, running three miles a day on the treadmill and limiting my intake to 1500 calories per day. These are called critical success factors. They are the drivers of the achievement of my weight loss goal, and they must be measured regularly, in this case, daily, to ensure achievement of the overall goal. So we need to measure both the results (the weight loss) and the drivers, or causes, of that weight loss if we want to ensure attainment of our goals. In this case, we can check our weight weekly to answer the question, how are we doing? We measure exercise and caloric intake every day: Did we run three miles this day? Did we consume less than 1500 calories? Then, if we see we are not on track to our goal, we change our program: perhaps more exercise; perhaps fewer calories; perhaps both.

Figure 19.2 illustrates exactly what we have described above: a causal-based measurement process that defines both the measures of desired results and the causes or determinants of those results.

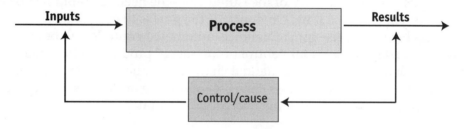

Figure 19.2: Causal–based Measurement and Control

Now we will turn to the second important question, how often to measure?

How Often to Measure

To deal with this issue we need to refer to Figure 19.2. The frequency of measurement is determined by the characteristics of the process that we want to control and goals for those characteristics. If, for example, the desire is to control the quality of units produced by a production process within very tight tolerances, we will need to monitor conformance of produced units to specifications very frequently, perhaps every second, and then modify production controls to maintain the quality within tolerance limits. If, on the other hand, our goal is to identify the effectiveness of the system as the basis for identifying root causes of problems and introducing structural change, a longer period, perhaps a week, will be better, in order to have a long enough period to identify systemic, as opposed to random, variation. If the variation is due to random causes, then we do not need to pay attention to it, but if it is caused by a problem in the process (a systemic error), then we should initiate a project to get at the root causes of the problem and fix them.

So, the determinants of measurement frequency will be:

- The speed of system change: how rapidly the system needs to change to adapt to changing conditions. The more rapid the change, the more frequent the measurement.

- The system response time to change: how long it takes for a change in process to be reflected in process performance. For example, a system design change takes longer to be reflected in performance than a programmed change in production tolerances.

The third important question in designing performance measures is deciding how to control the process.

How to Control

As we have alluded above, there is a great difference between process measurement and process control. Ineffective measurement processes are often due to a misunderstanding of this difference and the belief that measurement in itself is control. The control methods used will be determined by the same factors that govern the frequency of measurement—the need for rapid response and the system response time. Obviously if the goal is to control an automated process within six sigma tolerance, automated controls will be required. The day-by-the-hour control of the rate of production for a manufacturing cell can be tracked using manual charts and policies, giving the cell team the latitude to make process changes to increase or decrease the rate of production as required to meet the takt production rate.

The Shift in Focus

The parameters of the measurement system defined above represent a shift in focus from traditional measurement, employed by traditional accounting-based measurement.

The nature of this shift is shown in Figure 19.3.

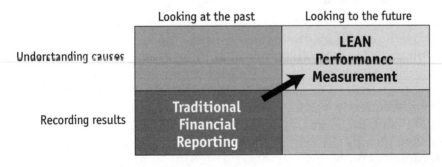

Figure 19.3: The Shift in Measurement Focus Required

To be effective, measurement must shift from the traditional historical orientation, which looks only looking at results, then analyses the causes of those results, to identifying the causes of desired performance beforehand and designing the measurement and control processes that maintain these causes, within prescribed limits. This new focus, then, identifies goals, and links those goals to the critical factors required to achieve them. It does this at each level of the organization. For a lean company, this means at the plant, the value stream, and the cell level. This, of course, applies equally to the company as a whole and to both the production and the non-production processes.

The Linkage Analysis Framework

The shift from historical-results approach to a future-oriented causal-measurement focus alters the orientation of measurement in some quite profound ways:

- Measurement now focuses on the goals of the organization and the direction that the organization intends for the future.

- Measurement now focuses on the few factors that are critical for attaining those objectives. These few factors are referred to as "critical success factors," or CSFs, and they represent what the organization must do extremely well if the goals are to be achieved.

By defining this linkage between goals and critical success factors, senior management can embed its policies into every level of the organization, so that every person will be motivated towards behavior that is congruent with these policies.

The resulting framework is a set of linked strategies, goals and measures at the plant, value stream, and cell/process levels that set the direction and motivate the performance of the entire organization toward the attainment of the aims of the company. The diagram in Figure 19.4 portrays the way such a linkage is worked out in a lean organization.

Strategic Objectives	Strategic Measure	Value Stream Goal/Target	Value Stream Measure	Cell CSF	Cell Goal/Target	Cell Measure
Set the direction for the value stream Determine the product/market goals Determine financial goals Determine resource goals	Measures the attainment of strategic objectives	Specific value stream results that need to be attained to achieve strategic objectives Specific target Specific time for achievement	Measures the attainment of value stream goals/targets	The specific lean cell initiatives that need to be accomplished to achieve the value stream goals/targets	Specific cell results that need to be attained to achieve value stream goals/targets Specific target Specific time for achievement	Measures the attainment of cell goals/targets

Figure 19.4: Future-Oriented Measures Link Measurements to Strategic Objectives

This linkage framework will be employed to define performance measures for the lean organization. The remainder of the chapter describes how this framework was used in defining the Starter Set of Lean Measurements described in Chapters 3 and 8. Next, it will provide step-by-step guidance for creating a set of performance measures for your own firm.

CREATING THE PERFORMANCE MEASUREMENT STARTER SET

To summarize:

- Performance measurements start with the company's strategy, objectives, and goals.
- The success of the measurements is determined by how well they motivate people throughout the organization towards its strategic objectives and goals.
- Strategic issues—those things that must be done very well to achieve the overall strategy of the organization—are related to value stream goals.
- Value stream goals are related to cells and processes within the value streams by critical success factors.

As we are dealing with a lean organization, it is important to reiterate the principles of lean because they define what must be done very well in order to achieve the company's lean strategy.

Lean Principles[1]

Whether or not it has explicitly done so, a company undertaking the lean journey has adopted the set of lean principles depicted in Figure 19.5 as its operating strategy.

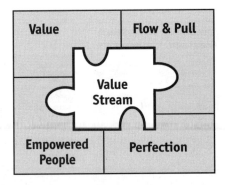

Figure 19.5: The Principles of Lean

These are the principles of lean thinking that must be reflected in the performance measurements:

---

1. The principles of lean were derived from Womack, James P. and Daniel T., *Lean Thinking*, Simon & Schuster, New York, 1996.

- **Value:** lean starts with a precise definition of what constitutes value from the customer's point of view in terms of the product features and characteristics that are values by the customer.

- **Value Stream:** the sequence of processes through which a product is transformed from raw material to delivery at the customer's site. Normally a value stream is defined by a group of related products that employ the same production processes.

- **Flow and Pull:** the production process is designed to maximize the flow of the product through the value stream, initiated by the pull of customer demand.

- **Perfection:** defined as 100 percent quality flowing in unbroken flow at the pull of the customer. Stated another way, anything that interrupts the flow to the customer results in less than perfection.

- **Empowerment:** the system of measurements and controls that provides each employee with the information and authority to take the necessary action at the time it is required.

The measurement framework for a lean company, therefore, will measure and control the extent to which a value stream achieves the critical success factors of value, flow and pull and perfection. The measurements and controls themselves must empower the employees to achieve these factors.

The Linkage Chart Developed

Figure 19.6 depicts how the framework elements are linked from Strategic Objectives to Cell Measures for a typical manufacturing value stream.

In fact, this chart was developed at a real company. Note that it is common for measures and critical success factors to be linked to more than one goal/measure. The linkage chart you develop for your company is likely to look like Figure 19.6 in this respect.

The Resulting Measurement Set

The linkage chart resulted in the starter set shown in Figure 19.7. For the purpose of this explanation, only the Primary Measures are shown in Figure 19.7. The complete list of primary and secondary measures is described fully in Chapters 3 and 8.

STEPS FOR DEVELOPING PERFORMANCE MEASURES IN YOUR COMPANY

This section lays out the steps for creating your own starter set for your company. This methodology applies equally well for all companies in all industries. The eleven steps are listed in Table 19.1.

Each of these steps will be described in the remainder of this chapter.

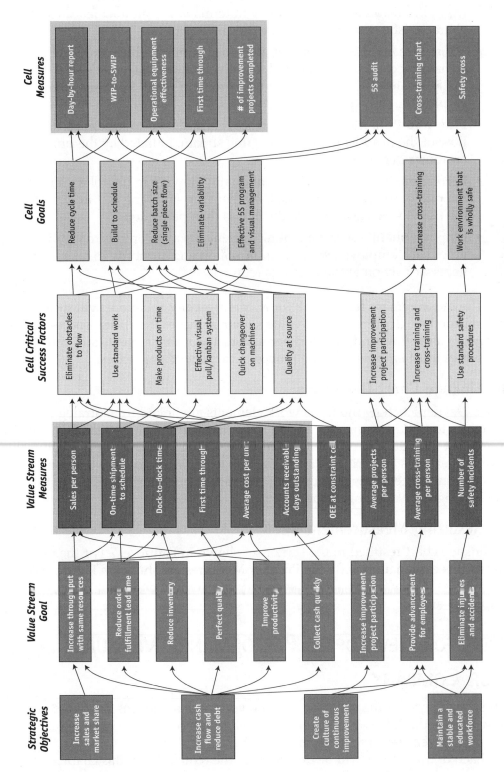

Figure 19.6: Developing the Performance Measurements Starter Set for a Typical Manufacturing Value Stream

Strategic Issues	Strategic Measures	Value Stream Measures	Cell/Process Measures
Increase cash flow Increase sales and market share Continuous improvement culture	Sales growth EBITDA Inventory days On-time delivery Customer satisfaction Sales per employee	Sales per person On-time delivery Dock-to-dock time First time through Average cost per unit AR days outstanding	Day-by-the-hour production WIP-to-SWIP First time through Operation equipment effectiveness

Figure 19.7: Starter Set of Performance Measures for Lean Manufacturing

Table 19.1: Steps for Developing Performance Measurement Sets for Your Company

1. Define business strategy.

2. Define company strategic goals and objectives.

3. Define the value stream.

4. Define strategic goals related to the value stream.

5. What must we be very good at to achieve these value stream goals?

6. Define value stream goals.

7. Define value stream performance measurements.

8. Review these performance measurements with those currently in use.

9. Cell and process level critical success factors (CSFs).

10. Cell and process goals and targets.

11. Cell and process measurements.

12. Review these performance measurements with those currently in use.

The template, shown in Table 19.2, works very well with lean companies. You can blow it up into a laminated wall chart and it will serve as a great working document for the team.

Let us look at the steps. We have divided them into three sections, dealing with strategy, value stream, and cell.

Articulating Strategy

The first step is to get the company's strategy straight. Some companies have a clearly defined and coherent business strategy. Other companies do a poor job of articulating their goals, answering questions such as:

- How do they plan to grow—which products, which markets?
- What are the specific financial targets for sales, cash flow, and earnings?
- When do they want to achieve these targets?

Table 19.2: Linkage Chart Template

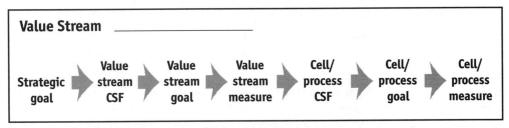

If your company's strategy is clearly defined, use it for the Performance Measurement Linkage Chart. If not, have the team document the strategy that is revealed by the company's actions. It is not our role to define the strategy, but merely to document the strategy inherent within the daily actions and decisions of the company's executives. It is best to verify these strategies with the company's leadership team.

Table 19.3 provides some things that you will want to think about as you define your **corporate strategy**.

Table 19.3: Step 1—Get the Strategy Straight

- Write down the company's (or the group's) business strategy.

- List the important strategic issues relating to lean manufacturing in your division.

- List (or define) the relevant strategic objectives for your division.

- List (or define) the relevant strategic goals for your division.

Linking to Value Stream

Next, define the value stream you want to measure. Another name for a value stream is a product group. So, Step 2 is to define the value stream. Table 19.4 provides some of the things you should pay attention to, including defining the flow in terms of a value stream map.

Now that you have defined the value stream, it is time to pull your team together to define the value stream measurements. This will entail, as Table 19.5 states, listing the strategic goals that relate to your value stream, creating CSFs for the value stream to achieve those goals, and linking the CSFs to goals for the value stream.

Finally, you should create a set of performance measures related to those goals and then link the strategic goals, CSFs, value stream goals and measures

Table 19.4: Step 2—Decide Which Value Streams

- List the value streams within your business unit.

  Grouping products families together by similarity of flow.

- Select a primary value stream to work on.

- Define the steps in the flow for the value stream.

  Remember the value stream extends outside the manufacturing process.

- Draw a map of the value stream.

- Discuss where the value streams overlap with each other.

  How can we overcome this confusion?

Table 19.5: Step 3—Creating Value Stream Measures

- List the strategic objectives & goals that relate to the value stream you have chosen.

- Define the critical success factors within the value stream related to these strategy goals/objectives.

  What must we be very good at to achieve these goals?

- Define the goals of the value stream.

- Draw the linkage diagram.

- Create a list of the performance measurements that support these goals.

  Try to "think outside the box."

  Ignore your current measurements at this time.

  Remember these measurements are primarily focused on continuous improvement of the value stream.

- Prune your list down to the vital few.

- Add to the linkage diagram.

on the linkage chart template. Here is where the laminated template will come in handy, as you, through trial and error, create the linkage chart that says what you want it to say. Remember the goal of the value stream measurements is to measure the effectiveness of the value stream in fulfilling its CSFs, and these CSFs are driven by the principles of lean.

Before you go on to develop the Cell-level measures, take a few minutes to compare your value stream measures with your existing measures. It is likely these new measures will be more focused and relevant to achieving the strategy of the company than the existing (plant-level) measures.

In most cases, fewer measurements are required. Most companies measure too many things and create confusion rather than insight. The primary value stream measurements should be restricted to between five and seven measurements. If you have less than five, you probably have not included all the relevant issues. If you have more than seven, you are (almost certainly) losing focus, and therefore confusing the team members with conflicting objectives.

Now that you have evaluated the new measurements, it is time to create the cell- or process-level measures.

Production Cell or Process Measures

We will look at this from the perspectives of both cell- and process-level measures.

For cell-level measures, the procedure followed is exactly the same as for the value stream measures. These are listed in Table 19.6.

Table 19.6: Step 4—Creating Production Cell Measures

- Define the cells and processes within the value stream.

- List the value stream measurements that are relevant to each production cell.

- List the critical success factors for that cell.

  What must we be very good at to achieve these goals?

- List the goals of the cell.

- Draw the linkage diagram.

- Create a list of measurements for the production cells.

  Remember these measurements are used to enable the cell team to achieve today what is expected of them.

- Prune your list down to the vital few.

- Complete the linkage diagram.

- If necessary, split the list into primary and support measurements.

Create the linkages for these critical success factors, goals and measures. If there are non-production processes, perform the same analysis for these, as described in Table 19.7, and update the linkage chart. In cases where production and non-production processes in a value stream have different CSFs and goals, you may find it helpful to use the forms provided on the CD accompanying this book in place of a single template. One template will not handle the complexity imposed by the multiple goals. Once again, compare the new measurements with the existing ones for the operations units.

Table 19.7: Step 5—Develop Non-Production Process Measures

- List the value stream measurements that are relevant to each process.
- List the critical success factors for that process.

  What must we be very good at to achieve these goals?

- List the goals of the process.
- Draw the linkage diagram.
- Create a list of measurements for the process.
- Prune your list down to the vital few.
- Complete the linkage diagram.
- If necessary, split the list into primary and support measurements.

Implementation Considerations

Review all the measurements and linkages to test the logic. Redraw the linkages as appropriate. Eliminate measures that duplicate linkages to goals and CSFs. The goal is to reduce the number of measures to a minimum.

Then define each of the measures:

- How will they be calculated?
- Where will the data come from?
- Can the data be easily obtained? (If it is difficult to obtain, it is not a good measure.)
- How often do we need to measure?
- How will the measure be presented?
- Who is accountable for the measured results?
- Who is responsible for collecting the data and reporting the results?

Finally, you should review and update the linkage chart periodically particularly when the business strategy changes.

SUMMARY

This chapter has presented a performance measurement framework that represents a shift in focus from traditional measurement, from historical results to future-oriented causal orientation. This framework was then demonstrated by showing how it was used to develop the starter set of measures described in Chapters 3 and 8 of this book. Finally, a step-by-step process was presented for developing a set of measures tailored to your company.

CHAPTER 20

Transaction Elimination Maturity Path Table

In Chapters 5, 6, 11, and 13, we discussed how to eliminate transactions from a lean company's business processes. All transactions are wasteful and time-consuming, and eliminating them relentlessly is very important in lean accounting, especially in the beginning. Transactions, however, are useful used in lean accounting. Transaction based tracking systems are used to maintain operational and financial control of the organization when those processes are unstable and likely to go out of control.

We are not advocating the cavalier elimination of transactions merely because they are wasteful. Transactions should be eliminated only when the need for those transactions has been eliminated. The changes and improvements made as lean manufacturing is introduced bring a company's processes under control. Such methods as short cycle times, kanban pull, cell performance measurements, value stream performance measurements, and visual management work together to bring processes under control. As the processes come under control, the need for the transactions is eliminated. At this point the transactions can be eliminated.

In Chapter 5, we discussed the circumstances under which transactions can be eliminated by introducing the approach in which we ask what must be in place in lean manufacturing that will ensure good, or better, control of these processes? In order to eliminate transactions, we need to decide what must be present in our current processes to show that those transactions are no longer necessary. The Transaction Elimination Maturity Path Table is designed to answer these questions in advance of the changes being made.

If we can describe in advance the lean manufacturing changes that will bring the processes under control, then we can create a planned and orderly move away from the complex, wasteful transaction-based control systems to lean methods.

How to Use the Maturity Path Table

The first two pages of a typical maturity path table are shown in Figures 20.1 and 20.2.

These pages describe the progress the company has made, or expects to make in the foreseeable future, with lean manufacturing. Each page of the table contains five rows that describe different aspects of lean manufacturing, including such issues are inventory levels, kanban pull, standardized work, visual systems, and so on. The columns of the pages show the company's progress with lean manufacturing. The first column shows the company "Making a Start with Lean," then proceeds through the columns, ending with the fifth column, which describes the Lean Enterprise.

There are four steps to the development of a Transaction Elimination Maturity Path Table:

1. Develop a lean manufacturing maturity path (Pages 1 and 2 of the Transaction Elimination Table).

2. Assess the company's current level of maturity with lean manufacturing.

3. Establish which transactions can be eliminated at each level on the lean manufacturing maturity path. This is Page 3 of the Transaction Elimination Maturity Path Table (Figure 20.3).

4. Develop a detailed action plan to move from the current state to the future state by eliminating the transactions and systems shown on Page 3 of the Maturity Path Table (Figure 20.3).

Step 1: Describing the Lean Manufacturing Maturity Path

The first step in using the Maturity Path Table is to describe what aspects of lean manufacturing are introduced as the company progresses from "Making a Start with Lean" through to "Lean Enterprise." There are no right answers with this process. The Lean Accounting Implementation Team must review each aspect of the lean maturity path and define what they expect to see at each of the five steps, for each of the ten aspects of lean manufacturing.

In reality, most companies do have other tables showing these kinds of maturity path progressions. These tables are used to establish the implementation plan for lean manufacturing throughout the organization. Lean assessment tools seek to give a picture of what lean manufacturing will look like at each stage of the implementation process. These tools can be used to develop a Transaction Elimination Maturity Path Table that is in line with the company's approach to lean manufacturing.

Step 2: Assessing Lean Manufacturing Progress

In Step 2, you assess where your company currently stands on the Maturity Path to lean manufacturing. In the Maturity Path Table shown in Figures 20.1 and 20.2 above, the current status of the company is shown through the shading of the boxes on the table. This assessment can be worked out for the entire

Category	Making a Start with Lean	Lean Pilots in Place	Lean Production	Lean Value Stream Management	Lean Enterprise
Cycle time	• 6–12 months • Just beginning to understand lean concepts • Batches are smaller	• 4–6 months • Value streams have been mapped • Start creating flow in pilot cells • Bottlenecks are reduced	• 2–3 months • All production is linked for a balanced flow • Pull system in place • Producing to customer takt time.	• 1–2 months • Cells continue to shorten cycle time • All production is linked to customer takt time.	• 2 weeks • Supplier is linked to customer takt time • 100% customer service level.
Inventory levels	• 5 turns–48 days • High raw, WIP, and finished goods inventories • While inventories are high it's not the right stuff	• 15 turns–16 days • Using kanbans • Using supermarkets and FIFO lanes	• Kanban is used to pull from all internal areas • Visual systems • No supermarkets • Consistent level of inventory at point of use	• 24 turns–10 days • Kanban pull from customer	• 48 turns–5 days • Supplier making mild runs and monitoring inventory levels • All inventory at point of use
Kanban & pull	• MRP • Push System • No or very little kanban pull • Introducing kanban in cells	• Introducing kanban in cells • Kanban with some suppliers • Pull system used in pilot cells • Pull bottlenecks minimized	• Pull system in all areas of organization • Pull system with all suppliers • No more batch jobs	• 1 piece flow or equivalent • Kanban pulled from customer • Kanban throughout • Level production • Supplier kanban • Customer pull from us	• 1 piece flow or equivalent. • Delivery directly to customer's cell • Kanban from customers to suppliers
Standard work	• Using work instructions and routings that are used for standard costing	• Standard work is used • Started 5S • Lines are balanced • Started eliminating sub-assemblies	• Visual work instructions • Standard work for all cells • Workers are cross trained	• Paperless • Standard work across value stream including non-production areas • Lean team monitors performance	• Visual systems • Continuous improvement • Line balancing based on customer takt time.
Supplier quality	• Many suppliers but few certified • No measurement system • Frequent supplier delivery problems • Receiving inspects most incoming material • Inspection shows erratic supplier quality	• Identified core suppliers • Decreased the number of suppliers • Developed a supplier certification program • Have some certified suppliers • No longer inspect receipts from certified suppliers	• Core suppliers are all certified • Certified suppliers delivering 99.5% direct to point of use • Frequent deliveries using kanbans • Measuring suppliers as responsible for quality • All certified suppliers address quality issues • Value stream manages the inventory	• Moving to six sigma • Material is delivered directly to point of use • Certified suppliers are lean too • Most, if not all, other suppliers are certified	• Six sigma • Customer is involved with supplier quality • All suppliers are lean • All suppliers are certified

Figure 20.1: Transaction Elimination Maturity Path Table, Page One

Category	Making a Start with Lean	Lean Pilots in Place	Lean Production	Lean Value Stream Management	Lean Enterprise
Cell quality	• Large batches • Scrap rework issues • Only 75% on-time delivery to next operation	• Formed cells • Using pull system • Smaller batches • Cross-trained and certified the operators • There is better quality and less rework	• Single-piece flow • Proactive on quality issues • Operators inspect • Time to stop and fix	• Moving to six sigma • Quality is part of the process • Mistake proofing processes ("Poke yoke")	• Six sigma quality
Cell performance measures	• Using detailed labor reports for efficiency • Using machine utilization measures • Measures are primarily accounting	• Start using lean performance measures, e.g., scrap, day-by-hour, 1st time through and other lean performance measures	• Running to takt day-by-hour report • Add more lean performance measures that are tracked by cell • Have a uniform measurement system for all cells	• Have value stream measures • Have cell measurements that are linked to the value stream measures	• Cell measures and value stream measures are integrated with strategic goals • Continuous process of using measures to refine and improve
Visual systems	• No visual systems. It is basically, paper, paper, and more paper. • MRP work orders, and ad hoc reports are used.	• Measures are vital and visible • Measure boards in cells • Measures posted real time • Display is simple to understand	• Line of sight • Measure boards are by value stream. • Kanban pull signals	• Manage the customer order • Pull system triggered by customer orders (kanban)	• Customer tied in to supplier • Visual systems used throughout value stream
Engineering data	• Have multiple level bills of material • Routings and bill of materials are inaccurate	• Bills of material and routings are simple and accurate • Engineering responsible to keep BOM and routings accurate	• Cell personnel participate in concurrent engineering and process reviews • Cell takes appropriate actions to update the requirements	• Bill of material and routings are maintained by value stream	• Paperless. • Information flows from customer to us to supplier • Improvements by continuous improvement teams
Organization and control	• Organized by department • Use department continuous improvement teams and only limited results	• Identified the value streams • Started educating on value streams • Formed some value streams • Moving towards value stream • Buyer planner in cell	• Value streams clearly identified with some allocations and some direct costing. • Measurs by value stream	• All functions are in the value stream • Organized and managed by value stream • Support functions within value stream • Cross functional training • Addressing compensation structure for alignment • Matrix management	• Suppliers and customers are included in the value streams

Figure 20.2: Transaction Elimination Maturity Path Table, Page Two

company, for one segment or division of the company, or for an individual value stream. It is not necessary for the entire company to be on the same level of lean manufacturing before transactions can be eliminated for the more advanced sections of the business. In fact, the more advanced sections can be used as pilots for the elimination of transactions. The successful methods can be proven in the advanced value streams, and then rolled out to other parts of the company as they reach additional levels of maturity within lean manufacturing.

Step 3: What Transactions and Systems Can Be Eliminated?

The most creative part of the Transaction Elimination Maturity Path Table comes in Step 3. The team decides which transactions and systems can be eliminated at each stage in the maturity path. The maturity path table describes what must be in place to enable us to eliminate the transactions and still maintain good, or better, control of the business.

The team starts with a review of the primary, transaction-driven processes within the organization. These usually include such processes as:

- Labor reporting
- Shopfloor tracking and control
- Procurement, purchasing, receiving, and payables
- Inventory planning and control
- Physical inventory and cycle counting

The team-members then describe, on page 3 of the Maturity Path Table, the changes and eliminations that can be made to the selected processes as a result of achieving each of the maturity path levels of lean manufacturing. The team determines which transactions and systems can be eliminated as each stage of lean manufacturing is achieved. The Transaction Elimination Maturity Path Table provides a roadmap for the elimination of wasteful transactions throughout the lean manufacturing process. An example of page 3 of the Transaction Elimination Maturity Path Table is given in Figure 20.3

The financial controller is a key member of the team at this stage, and is responsible for the accuracy of the information reported in the company's financial accounts. These financial accounts are (usually) reported every three months to external bodies like the Internal Revenue Service and the Securities and Exchange Commission, as well as to stockholders and owners of the organization. In the past, the financial controller has ensured the accuracy of the financial information, through the use of detailed transaction-based systems. These systems are about to be eliminated as a result of lean manufacturing and lean accounting. The financial controller must be thoroughly satisfied that the changes introduced through the lean implementation are creating the right level of control for the transactional systems to be eliminated.

Category	Making a Start with Lean	Lean Pilots in Place	Lean Production	Lean Value Stream Management	Lean Enterprise
Eliminate labor reporting	• Since labor is small % of total product costs, there is some backflushing and/or elimination of labor reporting • Many units will still use detailed labor reporting	• Some backflushing of labor • Detailed labor records are starting to go away	• For pay purposes, either salaried workforce or exception based reporting for hours • For cost purpose, all labor (direct and indirect) is charged to the cell	• Exception based reporting minimized to labor law requirements	• Non exempt salary workforce
Eliminate production tracking & inventory	• Backflushing some material • Still running MRP • Still cycle counting for inventory problems	• Eliminate receiving stock withdrawal tickets and associated moves by scanning parts in at receiving (supplier will barcode) • Developing plans for Kanban process	• Full pull system • Scrap-exceptions • Supplier managed inventories • Low value multiple use stock to be expensed when purchased	• Inventories are minimized • Eliminate cycle counting • No stockroom transactions • Stock is delivered to point of use	• Complete pull system from customer through supplier • Everything is period cost
Eliminate requisitions, purchase orders, receiving, & AP	• Have blanket POs with release schedule • Implementing ERS to eliminate invoices and 3 way match • Implementing P Cards for low dollar non-inventory purchases • Implementing EDI purchasing • Set up long term agreements	• Eliminate some PO's with pull system • Autopay; no more invoicing and/or 3 way match • Eliminate some PO releases by having kanban system • No longer receive invoices • Web based purchasing • More auto-vouchering as supplier and have fewer monthly releases • Expanding Web based purchasing	• Backflush inventory and pay by backflush • Eliminate receiving function • No POs since full pull system • Increase P card usage to inventory items (low value) • Supplier managed inventories • Initial blanket PO with no updates. Suppliers will [ ] shipments	• Initial blanket PO for each Part no. with annual review of pricing • Purchasing group engineering group and accounting group are all part of the value stream • Pay on receipt (no invoice)	• Eliminate accounts payable function because of limited amount of checks to cut • Eliminate receiving with suppliers delivering to point of use • Consigned inventory at point of use • No backflushing

Move to Lean Value Stream Management

Figure 20.3: Transaction Elimination Maturity Path Table, Page 3

Step 4: Develop an Action Plan

Nothing is achieved until a plan is put into action. The purpose of the Transaction Elimination Maturity Path Table is to create an orderly introduction to low-waste, low-transaction processes. Having decided the method for eliminating transactions as lean manufacturing matures within the organization, the Lean Accounting Team in Step 4 creates a practical action plan for making these changes occur. This action plan needs to be thought out, through and through. It will include a list of all the tasks required to move transaction elimination from one level on the maturity path to the next. This will include defining the changes to the accounting systems, the chart of accounts, the transaction posting tables, and so on; defining the changes to the reports produced throughout the company; and defining the changes to the accounting and control procedures. Also, the plan includes providing the necessary training for the finance people, the operational people, and the company managers.

There may be a parallel run of these changes when they are first introduced. This requires additional work to run the old and the new methods, and to verify the two approaches. This requires additional work and it must be planned out carefully. It is very important that the parallel runs be short and purposeful. If the parallel runs continue for any length of time, many people within the company will continue to rely on the old familiar information, and no benefit will be gained from the parallel run.

TRANSACTION ELIMINATION PROCESS MAPS

Figure 20.4 shows a typical process map that can be used to understand the transactions used in a process. It is not always apparent how many transactions are required and which transactions are needed within a process. It is useful to draw a detailed process map of the flow and show where the transactions are required and how many transactions are needed. This exercise is useful for understanding the process, but will often be quite shocking to the people involved in the process. Most people do not understand the number of transactions required to complete their processes and are shocked when this waste is made plain to them.

These process maps can also be used to show, graphically, how the transactions will be eliminated. Figure 20.5 shows the first step of the transaction elimination for the Pro-Bo product.

SUMMARY

The Transaction Elimination Maturity Path Table enables the Lean Accounting team to develop an action plan for the elimination of transactions. The team draws a table that shows the steps in the lean manufacturing maturity path. They then add to this table the major transaction elimination methods that can be applied at each stage of the maturity path. The team can then develop a detailed action plan showing how the changes are made and the transactions eliminated.

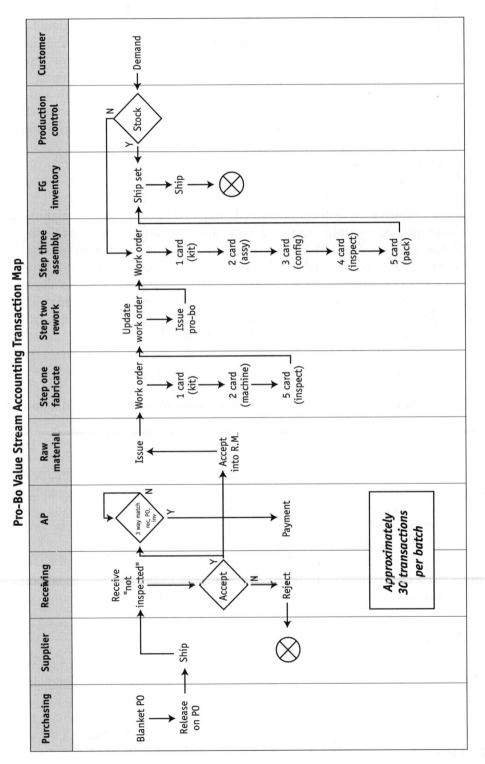

Figure 20.4: Process Map to Show Transactions

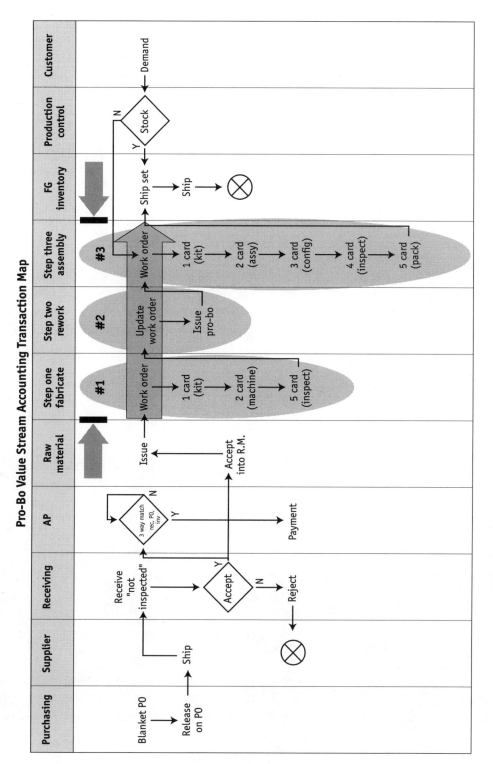

Figure 20.5: Process Map Showing How Transactions Can Be Eliminated in the Process

CHAPTER 21

Value Stream Cost Analysis

Value stream cost analysis (VSCA) is an important tool of lean accounting. VSCA shows how the resources within the value stream are being used. For each step within the value stream, how much capacity is being used productively? How much is being used non-productively? And how much available capacity is there at this value stream step?

Lean thinking emphasizes the flow of materials, information, and cash through the value stream. This flow is determined by amount of available capacity within the value stream and how that capacity is used. VSCA provides a simple and practical method for assessing these capacity issues and using this information to maximize the benefits of lean manufacturing and other lean initiatives. The value stream manager always needs to have a good understanding of how the capacity is used, where the bottlenecks are in the flow, and how the capacity can be used to provide maximum financial benefit to the organization. The VSCA provides this vital information.

Table 21.1 lists some of the ways VSCA is used.

Lean manufacturing frees up large amounts of resources that can then be used for value-creating activity. The challenge for management in lean companies is to be able to predict the volumes of resources that will become available sufficiently in advance, so plans can be put in place for their productive use. Too often, management's only recourse is to eliminate the resources freed up, with the consequence that the company loses the significant benefits that would result from their use in more creative and profitable ways. VSCA is an important planning tool.

The purpose of this chapter is to show in detail how value stream cost Analysis is calculated. We will use the example of ECI from Chapter 4, Financial Benefits of Lean Manufacturing, to describe the steps in the process. The example in Chapter 4 was given to show how VSCA is used to assess the financial benefits of lean improvements by comparing the capacity usage depicted on the current state value stream map with the capacity usage of the future state value stream map. By working through this detailed example and playing with the spreadsheet workbook provided on the CD accompanying this book, the reader will gain a clear understanding of how VSCA is calculated.

Table 21.1: The Many Uses of VSCA

Box Score for weekly reporting	Shows the summary capacity usage for the value stream as a whole
Box Score for the financial impact of lean improvements	Shows how the capacity usage changes from the current state to the future state. From this a strategy is put in place to maximize the financial benefit of these changes.
Box Score for strategic changes and investment	When planning (for example) new capital investment the Box Score shows how the capacity, operations, and financial results of the value stream will change.
Features and Characteristics Costing	VSCA used to determine the bottleneck in the value stream. The bottleneck determined the flow through the value stream and therefore the product costs.
Target Costing	VSCA used to identify places within the value stream where potential changes will impact the overall value stream cost.
Value Stream Manager	The VSM needs to understand the flow of materials, information, and cash through the value stream. For example, VSCA is used to assess the financial and capacity impact of a make/buy decision.
Continuous Improvement Team	Capacity usage information is required when selecting improvement projects. To increase the flow, the team must work to provide more capacity at the bottleneck cells.
Financial Controller	To show the financial capacity usage on the Income Statement
Lean Champions	Use VSCA to select lean events and to determine the financial benefit of the changes proposed.
Marketing	Use the capacity analysis to do "what-if" and optimization analyses. For example, to determine the product mix that will maximize the value stream profitability leading to changes in marketing plans.
Sales, Operations, and Financial Planning	The capacity information is required to match the production output to the sales needs from the customers.

WHAT IS VALUE STREAM COST ANALYSIS?

Value stream cost analysis (VSCA) is the tool used for calculating the resource utilization implied by value stream maps, drawn by the lean manufacturing implementation team. A value stream map depicts the flow of production through the studied value stream and the factors that determine the rate of flow. Such factors as cycle time, changeover time, scrap and rework percentages, overproduction, and downtime,[1] etc., determine how long it

---

1. Some of these terms may not be familiar to those who are not manufacturing experts. Brief definitions are provided below:
   - **Cycle time**—the time in seconds to perform an operation on one product at a work center. For any work center, some products may be easy to make and others may be more difficult. If a product is more difficult, then its cycle time to complete is longer.

takes a manufacturing process to complete its operation on a given product. These factors, combined with monthly demand, determine the amount of total time spent by the people and machines in the process and, by extension, the time required to process the monthly production of the value stream. One of the important functions of lean manufacturing is to free up people and machines by eliminating the waste that restricts the flow of the product, the information, and the cash. The purpose of VSCA is to provide a simple tool for converting the information in the value stream map into resource utilization data. Basing VSCA around the value stream map provides a way for the operations members of the lean team to communicate how their planned lean initiatives affect the profitability of the company to the finance department and others in the company. It also provides a way for the sales and marketing and the engineering departments to understand how the lean initiative impacts their planned activities, and how they fit into a successful lean program.

PERFORMING THE VSCA CALCULATIONS[2]

This chapter is primarily a how to discussion and we assume the reader has already read Chapter 4. We also assume that the reader has assembled the data about the value stream costs, value stream maps, and box score data concerning the current and future states for the value stream. So, now the reader is eager to get on with the task of determining how lean affects the employment of resources. So let us get on with describing how to do it.

This chapter provides step-by-step instructions for completing the box score for the Resource Capacity captions in the Current State, Future State, and Long Term Future State. Table 21. 2 is a copy of the box score from Chapter 4, with operational and financial data filled in for the current and future states.

There are three steps on the VSCA journey. These are depicted in Figure 21.1.

- **Changeover time**—the time it takes to get ready to produce a different product at a work center. Often the changeover time determines the economic batch size. If the changeover time is long, generally, larger batch sizes are called for. Therefore, most lean companies strive to make changeover times as short as possible.

- **Scrap and rework percentages**—scrap percentage equals the proportion of total parts made at a work center that are so defective that they must be discarded. Rework percentage equals the proportion of total parts made at a work center that are defective but can be repaired so that they meet quality specifications.

- **Overproduction**—the number of items produced at a work center during a shift that exceeds the amount scheduled for that shift. In a lean company the amount scheduled for a work center is equal to the amount demanded by the customer.

- **Downtime**—the amount of time that a work center cannot produce because of machine malfunction requiring repair or personnel absence.

 2. A simple VSCA spreadsheet workbook is provided on the CD accompanying this book.

Table 21.2: Box Score for the Current and Future States, without Resource Capacity Data

Lean Value Stream Box Score

Value stream: Electronics controllers

		Current state	Future state	Change	Long term future state	Change from current state
Operational	Dock-to-dock days	20.5 days	4.5 days	16 days		
	First time through	48%FTT	96%FTT	48%		
	On-time shipment	90%	99%	9%		
	Floor space	34000 sq. feet	17,000 sq. feet	(17,000) sq. feet		
	Sales per person	$25,230	$26,380	$1,150		
	Average cost per unit	$328.27	$308.61	($19.66)		
Resource capacity	Productive					
	Non-productive					
	Available					
Financial	Inventory value	$58,502	$13,997	$44,505		
	Revenue	$1,292,640	$1,292,640	$0		
	Material costs	$512,160	$477,160	($35,000)		
	Conversion costs	$189,866	$181,416	($8,450)		
	Value stream profit	$590,614	$634,064	$43,450		

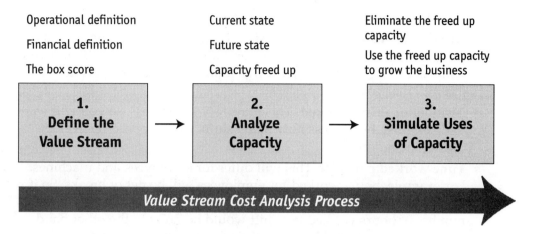

Figure 21.1: Value Stream Cost Analysis Steps

These steps are as follows:

- Step 1: Define the Value Stream
- Step 2: Analyze Capacity
- Step 3: Simulate Uses of Capacity

STEP 1: DEFINE THE VALUE STREAM

To begin you will need to complete the box score for the current and future state for the operational data and financial data tabs, as was described in Chapter 4. In addition to that, you will need to collect some basic data about the value stream and you will also want to define an analytical framework for calculating the capacity information. We show you how to do these things in the paragraphs that follow.

Collect Basic Value Stream Data

As part of this step, review the current and future state maps for completeness.

Do they have data boxes? Data boxes appear on the value stream maps beneath each of the process boxes and define what is going on in the processes. This should include information about cycle time, changeover time, scrap rate, down time, etc.

Are the data boxes complete? Complete data boxes should include all the relevant data about the value stream, such as the items identified in the previous paragraph.

If the data boxes are incomplete, you will need to ask the lean implementation team to help you find the data needed to update them.

You will need other information about the value stream:

- **Number of workdays in the period.** Normally this is 20 because most companies work five days a week and four weeks per month, but you will want to identify whether it was more or less for the period (month) that you have selected

- **Number of shifts worked.** This may vary by process, so you will want to distinguish by process how many shifts were worked on average during the month.

- **Time worked per shift.** This will differ for employees and machines. For example, hours worked for employees will be net of breaks. So if employees took one 20-minute break per eight-hour shift, then the number of hours worked per shift would be 7.67. On the other hand, machines are not eligible for breaks and are considered to work the full eight hours per eight-hour shift.

- **Customer order quantity.** This is measured by number of units of the product that was shipped to the customer that month.

Create an Analytical Framework for Your Calculations

There is no one best way to collect the information you will need so you can calculate how the capacity was used. The format depends somewhat on how automated you want to make the process. The framework that we have found to be useful as a starter set is quite straightforward and can be applied manually or by using a PC spreadsheet to make the calculations for you. Table 21.3 provides an example of such a framework. We have also provided a copy of the framework in Appendix A, on the CD provided with this book.

Let us run through the sample in Table 21.3 so that you get an idea of the kinds of information that you will need:

- In the top row, list the name of the value stream, your name, the date, and the sequential page number of the current study.

- You will note that the next row contains column headings:
  - The name of the process step being studied. This should coincide with the name of the process on the value stream map. Other information to be included under this heading are the number of employees (or machines, if it is a machine study), the number of shifts being worked, and whether the time will be denominated in hours, minutes, or seconds.
  - A listing of activities performed by the process during the period. For the most part, information about these activities will be found on the data box beneath the process box on the value stream map.
  - The amount of non-productive and productive time spent on each activity during the period, derived from the information in the data boxes. This information is collected for the current state first, and is then collected for the future state.

Table 21.3: Sample Framework for Analyzing Resource Capacity Usage

Value Stream Study	Value Stream:	Observer:				Date			Page		
			Current State				Future State				
Process Steps	Activity		Non-productive	Productive			Non-productive	Productive			
	Total time by value creating category										
	Total time used current/future state										
	Total time not used per month										
	Total time available for use per month										

- – The change in the time expected to be spent on the activity at the time the future state has been implemented.
- At the bottom of the form there are several summary totals:
  - – The total time spent in each of the non-productive and productive categories for both the current and future states, as well as the changes in the times from current to future states.
  - – The total time used in each of the current and future states, calculated by adding the non-productive and productive summary totals for both current and future states.
  - – The total time not used during the month, derived by subtracting the total time used (found in the row above) from the total time available for use (found in the last row).
  - – Total time available for use, calculated by multiplying the hours (minutes or seconds, if that is your unit of measure) available per shift per person, times the number of shifts worked per day times the number of days worked. For example, if it is the normal practice to work eight hours per shift, but during each shift the workers take two ten-minute breaks, then the total time available per shift is 7 hours and 40 minutes (8 hours minus (2 times 10 minutes)). In minutes per shift this would be equivalent to 460 (7 hours times 60 minutes per hour plus 40 minutes). In seconds this would be equivalent to 27,600. The time worked per day is equal to the time per shift times the number of shifts per day worked at that workstation. The total time per month, then, is equal to the time worked per day times the number of days worked at that workstation. Thus the formula for total time worked per month is as follows:

Total time per month (Minutes) = [(hours per shift * 60) – (minutes of breaks per shift) * number of shifts per day] * [days worked per month]

You should have one form per process-resource type. By resource type, we mean employees and machines. So if the process uses both machines and people, there should be one form for each of these two resource types within that process.

If you are creating these forms manually, it is a good idea to place all the forms you will need in a binder, heading up each form for the process and resource type being studied. Alternatively, you can create a spreadsheet "Workbook" identifying each worksheet tab with the name of the process and resource type included in the worksheet. You should label one tab for each of the processes defined in Table 21.4, which defines the value costs by process that we worked with in Chapter 4.

So now that you have defined the value stream and pulled together the information and framework for gathering the data, you are ready to go ahead with the analysis.

Table 21.4: Controllers Value Stream Costs by Process

Company	Location	Value Stream	Type	Date			
Electronic Components	Nirvana, CA	Controllers	Current				
	Material costs	Outside process cost	Employee costs	Machine costs	Other costs	TOTAL COST
Customer service			$11,921			$11,921
Purchasing			$14,902			$14,902
SMT cells	$358,512		$16,704	$16,956	$20,000	$412,172
Hand load & wave cell	$25,608		$22,968	$2,016		$50,592
Test & rework cell			$16,704	$3,528		$20,232
Assemble & burn-in cell	$128,040		$10,440			$138,480
Shipping			$2,088			$2,088
Quality assurance			$7,978			$7,978
Manufacturing engineering			$7,978			$7,978
Accounting			$7,978			$7,978
Information systems			$3,989			$3,989
Design engineering		$7,760	$3,989			$11,749
Maintenance and other support			$11,967			$11,967
TOTAL	$512,160	$7,760	$139,606	$22,500	$20,000	$702,026

STEP 2: ANALYZE CAPACITY

Use the value stream map to analyze capacity in the current state first, and then to perform the job again, for the future state. To guide our discussion we will use the Electronics Company case that was used in Chapter 4. So you may want to go back to Chapter 4 to refresh your memory about case, because we will not go into detail about ECI or its products again here.

Current State

We are concerned with two tasks:

- Gathering the data
- Posting the data to our analytical framework for both employee and machine capacity

Gathering the Data

The first step is to get hold of the current state map for the value stream we studied in Chapter 4. We have reproduced the map in Figure 21.2.

Review the current state map. Note that there are process boxes for this map for each of the four production processes (SMT, hand load/wave post, test and rework, and assemble and burn-in). There are also process boxes for some, but not all, of the support processes (shipping, customer service, purchasing). That leaves the other support processes of quality assurance, manufacturing engineering, accounting, information systems, design engineering, and technical support as being in the value stream, but not defined in the value stream map. This is a fairly typical situation and is appropriate, given the purpose of value stream mapping to capture those processes that are in the flow; and this map has done a good job of that. However, from the point of view of finding out how the lean implementation will impact the use of resource capacity, it is important to include all processes that support the value stream, not only those that are directly in the flow. We will discuss this further later in the chapter.

Take a look at the process entitled "Hand Load/Wave Post." Note that the process box has the information about the resources. It says that there are 11 people working in the process and there is one machine. So you know right away that you will need one VSCM form for the employees and one for the machine.

Now, let us take a look at the data box for that process shown in Figure 21.3. It provides quite a bit of information about the operation of the process during the month. It says that the process has a cycle time (C/T) of 12 minutes, meaning that it takes a circuit on average of 12 minutes to move through the process. The data box shows that it took 10 minutes to change over (C/O) from one type of component to another. This time was consumed by employees getting ready to make the different component. In addition, there were two minutes of preparation time for 3735 of the components made during the period (on average there were approximately 1.8 circuit boards per component).

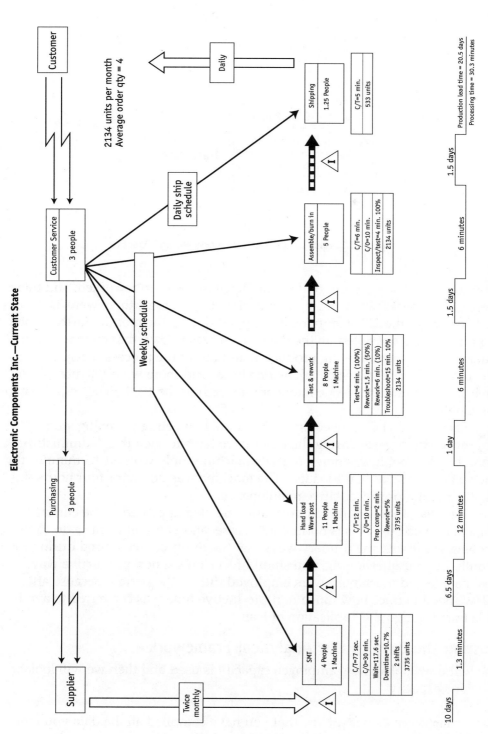

Electronic Components Inc.—Current State

2134 units per month
Average order qty = 4

Figure 21.2: Current State Map for the Controllers Value Stream

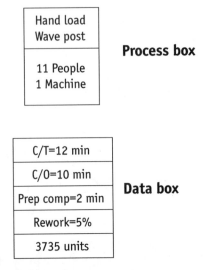

Figure 21.3: Hand Load/Wave Post Process Box and Data Box

Approximately five percent of the total items made were reworked, and there were 4435 boards loaded during that period. On average, there were 2.07 circuit boards for the 2134 components shipped during the month. Furthermore, although it was not noted on the data box, it was known that there was considerable time spent moving product in and out of the process. There were 60 moves into the process, each taking one hour; and there were 100 moves out, each taking 20 minutes—one move out for each of the 100 batches run during the month.

Each of the 11 employees spent 53 hours in meetings, training, and improvement projects during the month; we have termed this "administration." In addition, it was noted that the machines only worked 1.5 minutes for each board that was hand-loaded. The machine was down for four hours during the month for preventative maintenance.

It is clear that not all the information needed appeared in the current state map data box. This is normally the case, and you will want to do some probing to identify the primary ways that the resources were used during the month. In your questioning, you should focus on the non-productive ways that people and machinery were employed during the period, because after all, we need to trace how much non-productive time was converted to available time through the application of lean.

Posting the Data to Our Analytical Framework

We will now look at how employee capacity is used and then we will look at machine capacity.

Uses of Employee Capacity. Now that you have compiled all the data you will need, let us assemble it using the Hand Load/Wave Post process and the employee resource type as an example.

Table 21.5: Using the Data Box to Understand Capacity Usage

Value Stream Study	Value Stream: Electronics	Observer:		Date		Page	
		Current State		Future State			
Process Steps	Activity	Non-productive	Productive	Non-productive	Productive		
Hand load/	Make for Demand (3735 x 12 minutes)		853.6				
Wave post							
11 persons							
1 shift							
hours							
	Total time by value creating category						
	Total time used current/future state						
	Total time not used per month						
	Total time available for use per month						
	Productive Percent						
	Non-Productive Percent						
	Available Percent						

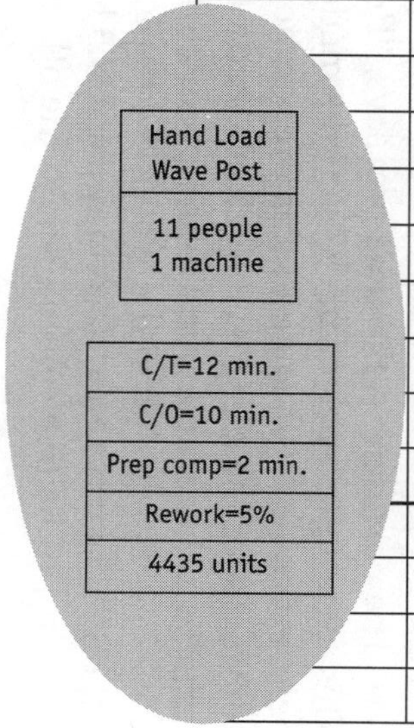

Hand Load
Wave Post

11 people
1 machine

C/T=12 min.
C/O=10 min.
Prep comp=2 min.
Rework=5%
4435 units

Note on Table 21.5 that we have written, under the "Process Steps" information, the name of the process ("Hand Load/Wave Post"), the number of people (11) and shifts per day, and that we are going to account for the time in hours. We are now going to use the data box information to determine how the hours were spent. We have included a thumbnail diagram of the process data box to aid in understanding the discussion that follows.

The first activity, "Make for Demand," is listed in the "Activity" column. The number of items made during the period, 3,735 boards hand loaded/wave posted, was obtained from the production records for the month. Each time the item was made, it took one person 12 minutes to make it. This information was obtained from the first line of the data box, where cycle time was listed as 12 minutes. These two items are noted in the "Activity" column within the parentheses where the formula for the amount of time spent in making for demand appears (3735 items times 12 minutes per item). The time in hours is then calculated by dividing this product by 60 minutes per hour. The result is shown as 853.6 hours spent during the month hand loading boards and wave posting them. In this process, the circuit boards are loaded by hand rather than by machine, as they are in the SMT process. This is written in the current state—Productive column, to signify the productive nature of the activity.

We now come to the next set of activities listed on the data box shown in Table 21.6.

The next three items of information on the data box, seen in Table 21.6, tell us that Changeovers took an average of 10 minutes per changeover. Preparing Components for hand loading took an average of two minutes per board; and approximately five percent of the items made contained errors that caused the item to be reworked. We will discuss how each of these items was treated.

In the "Activity" column, note that the first new item is titled, "Get Ready." We term all activities such as changeovers, preparation, set-ups, etc., as "getting ready to do work," because in fact that is what is going on. The real work is to make the items on customer demand. Time spent on changeovers, etc., is simply getting ready to do the real work. As can be seen, there were 100 times that the team got ready to Make for Demand, and each time they did this it took one person 10 minutes. We know that they did this 100 times because there were 100 batches run during the month, according to production records. The product of 10 minutes times 100 is 16.7 hours. Note that this number appears in the "Non-Productive" current state column, because getting ready to do work is a non-productive activity.

The next item in the data box says, "Prepare Components=2 minutes." This means that each of the 3735 units made had to be prepared in some way before it could be made and this preparation took 2 minutes. Once again, this comes under the category of getting ready to do work, because the preparation did not add any value to the product from the customer's point of view. It was necessary due to the way the company performs its work. So the product of 3735 units times two minutes, 124.5 hours, is calculated and placed in the non-productive column under the other "Get Ready" items.

Table 21.6: Adding More Information from The Data Box

Value Stream Study	Value Stream: Electronics	Observer:		Date		Page
		Current State		Future State		
Process Steps	Activity	Non-productive	Productive	Non-productive	Productive	
Hand load/	Make for Demand (3735 x 12 minutes)		853.6			
Wave post	Get ready (100 batches x 10 min.)	16.7				
11 persons	Get ready—prep components (3735 units x 2 min.)	124.5				
1 shift	Rework/remake (227 errors x 6 min.)	22.7				
hours						
	Total time by value creating category					
	Total time used current/future state					
	Total time not used per month					
	Total time available for use per month					
	Productive Percent					
	Non-Productive Percent					
	Available Percent					

Data Box:

Hand Load
Wave Post

11 people
1 machine

C/T=12 min.
C/O=10 min.
Prep comp=2 min.
Rework=5%
4435 units

You should begin to see how the information in the data box on the value stream map has been used to derive the amount of time spent by the process in making the product demanded by the customer. It is also clear that there is a good deal more things going on than simply making the product, and these additional things take up a great deal of the peoples' time in the process.

Let us proceed to the other activities performed by the process team.

We know from experience that there are other activities, normally performed by a process team, than those shown in the data box. Our inquiries revealed that the team spends some time moving materials in and out of the work center. In this case, the record of issues from inventories informed us that there were 60 issues during the month to the Hand Load/Wave Post operation, and, on average, it took one hour to perform this task. Moves from the operation back into work-in-process inventory took 20 minutes and there was one move after each of the 100 batches run during the month.

In addition, we found by inquiry that each process team spent 53 hours during the month attending meetings, attending training, and performing improvement projects, all of which were accounted for in order to get a rough idea of the time worked during the month.

So looking at the summary of how time was spent (Table 21.7), at the last item in the column, there were 1650 hours available for use during the month. That is, each of the 11 people had 150 hours available for work during the month. Of the 1650 hours, 1693.8 hours were employed in productive and non-productive work. That implies that 43.8 hours were provided by working overtime or by part-time workers, since there were more hours worked than were available. So there was no time unused in the Hand Load/Wave Post operation. In fact, the additional hours were provided by cross-trained workers in the SMT operation.

What we are aiming to do, if you remember, is to define the number of hours that will be freed up when the lean program is completed. So what we are very concerned about is how the available capacity changes; the number of hours that shift from "Used" to "Not Used" as a consequence of the lean initiative.

Now we will take a look at how the machine in the Hand Load/Wave Post operation was used during our current state test month.

Uses of Machine Capacity. From the process box on the current state map, we know that there was one machine in the operation. Our examination of the machine records shows that the machine was available for use 160 hours during the month (8 hours a day) times 20 days during the month, working one shift. This is shown in the last row of the current state column in Table 21.8.

The machine was used by all 11 employees for making demand, and it took 1.5 minutes for each of the 3735 boards loaded. In addition, from the machine records there were four scheduled maintenance procedures performed and each of these took one hour. There were no other uses of the machine, as it was not involved in changing over, moving materials, and administration, and the reworked items were done by hand.

Table 21.7: Other Work Performed by the Process Team

Value Stream Study		Observer:			Date		Page
	Value Stream: Electronics						
			Current State		Future State		
Process Steps	Activity		Non-productive	Productive	Non-productive	Productive	
Hand load/	Make for Demand (3735 x 12 minutes)			853.6			
Wave post	Get ready (100 batches x 10 min.)		16.7				
11 persons	Get ready—prep components (3735 units x 2 min.)		124.5				
1 shift	Rework/remake (227 errors x 6 min.)		22.7				
hours	Move in material (60 moves x 1 hour)		60				
	Move material (100 batches x 20 min.)		33.3				
	Administration (11 employees x 53 hours)		583				
	Total time by value creating category		840.2	853.6			
	Total time used current/future state		1693.8				
	Total time not used per month		-43.8				
	Total time available for use per month		1650				
	Productive Percent		0.517333333				
	Non-Productive Percent		0.509212121				
	Available Percent		-0.026545455				

Hand Load Wave Post

11 people
1 machine

C/T=12 min.
C/O=10 min.
Prep comp=2 min.
Rework=5%
4435 units

Table 21.8: Current State Use of Machine

Value Stream Study	Value Stream: Electronics	Observer:			Date		Page
			Current State		Future State		
Process Steps	Activity	Non-productive	Productive	Non-productive	Productive		
Hand load/	Make for demand (3735 units x 1.5 min.)		93.375				
Wave post	Scheduled maintenance (4 procedures x 1 hour)	4					
1 machine							
1 shift							
hours							
	Total time by value creating category	4	93.375				
	Total time used current/future state	97.375					0
	Total time not used per month	62.625					
	Total time available for use per month	160					
	Productive Percent	0.58359375					
	Non-Productive Percent	0.025					
	Available Percent	0.39140625					

So now we have taken into account the resources of one process used during the month. This analysis should be done for each of the processes defined in the value stream map, as supplemented by the analysis of value stream cost. We have included the completed VSCAs for all the processes on the CD, and you should take some time to review these to see how various conditions were handled in practice. In particular, you should pay attention to the non-production processes, such as Customer Service, Shipping, Purchasing, Quality Assurance, etc. A summary is provided in Table 21.9.

We now need to look at the future state.

FUTURE STATE

Let us look at the Future State Map prepared by the lean implementation team for the Controllers Value Stream. This is depicted in Figure 21.4.

There were significant changes that were made and performed by the lean team. These are discussed in Chapter 4 in the section entitled ECI Future State, and will not be discussed further here, as this is a technical/tools chapter. We do need to trace through the effects of these changes into the VSCA. To do this we need to access the data boxes, and once again we will trace through these effects in the data box for the Hand Load/Wave Post process. This is shown in the comparative data boxes for that process in Figure 21.5.

Note that the changeover time has been reduced to zero in the future state. Also, through changes to the prior process, the need for preparation of each component was eliminated. Finally, the number of items reworked was reduced from 5 percent to 1 percent.

These changes were reflected in the VSCA showing both the current and future states. It can be seen that, in addition to the changes mentioned, moves were eliminated through the placement of inventory at the cells and administration was cut in half, as shown in Table 21.10.

Note that the changes planned for the future state will eliminate 543.9 hours of non-productive work. This will increase the amount of employee resource capacity available for use by an equivalent amount. As there were no improvements to the future state for the machine in that cell, we have not shown the completed VSCA for the machines.

As in the current state, the next step is to complete the VSCA exercise for each of the processes, calculating the numbers of hours freed up for both employees and machines for the planned future state. The results of that exercise are shown in Table 21.11.

The final step in the calculation of available capacity is to prepare a summary of the number of hours freed up from the individual VSCAs by process. Table 21.12 shows this summary, concluding that there will be approximately 19 equivalent people freed up as a result of the lean exercise.

If you have been following the analysis carefully, you are now prepared to try this out in your own company, using one of your own value streams that you want to lean-out. You should expect that it will take you and your team a couple of days to complete the exercise, as the methodology will be

Table 21.9: Summary of Current State Capacity Usage for the Controllers Value Stream by Process

Current State Value Stream Cost Analysis by Capacity Category

EMPLOYEES	Totals	SMT	Hand load / wave post	Test and rework	Assemble and burn-in	Shipping	Customer service	Purchasing	Quality assurance	Accounting	Design engineering	Information systems	Manufacturing engineering	Technical support
Cost	$139,624	$16,704	$22,968	$16,704	$10,440	$2,088	$11,928	$14,902	$7,978	$7,978	$3,989	$3,989	$7,989	$11,967
Productive		0%	52%	0%	28%	71%	0%	0%	0%	0%	0%	0%	0%	0%
Non-productive		62%	51%	70%	67%	0%	90%	25%	99%	71%	80%	91%	64%	83%
Other		0%	0%	0%	0%	0%	0%	0%	0%	0%	0%	0%	0%	0%
Available capacity		38%	-3%	30%	5%	29%	10%	27%	1%	29%	20%	10%	36%	17%
MACHINES														
Cost	$22,500	$16,956	$2,016	$3,528	$-	$-	$-	$-	$-	$-	$-	$-	$-	$-
Productive		25%	58%	0%	0%	0%	0%	0%	0%	0%	0%	0%	0%	0%
Non-productive		67%	3%	80%	0%	0%	0%	0%	0%	0%	0%	0%	0%	0%
Other		0%	0%	0%	0%	0%	0%	0%	0%	0%	0%	0%	0%	0%
Available capacity	0%	8%	39%	20%	0%	0%	0%	0%	0%	0%	0%	0%	0%	0%

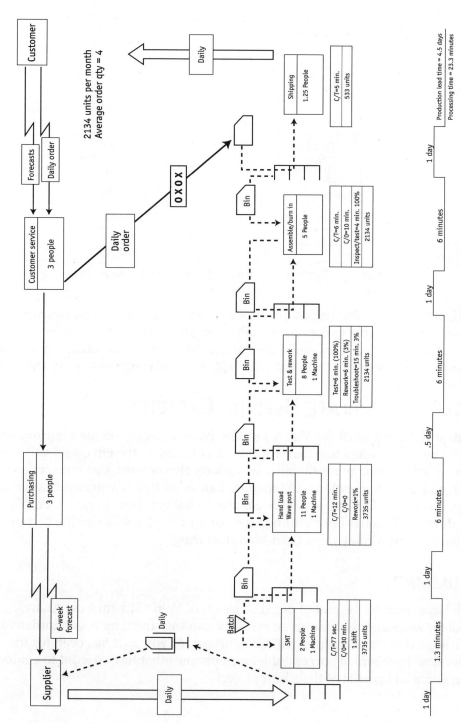

Figure 21.4: Future State Map for the Controllers Value Stream

Current State	Future State

Hand load	Hand load
Wave post	Wave post
11 People	11 People
1 Machine	1 Machine

Current State	Future State
C/T=12 min	C/T=12 min
C/O=10 min	C/O=0 min
Prep comp=2 min	Rework=1%
Rework=5%	3735 units
3735 units	

Figure 21.5: Comparative Data Boxes for the Controllers Value Stream

unfamiliar to you, but as you practice and gain experience, you and your team should be able to complete analysis in an afternoon.

After you have completed the current and future state analyses, you will be ready to proceed to Step 3 of your VSCA, simulating uses of capacity.

STEP 3: SIMULATE USES OF CAPACITY

This is the fun part of the VSCA process. Now you can use the information that you have pulled together in Table 21.11 to assess the effects on value stream and company profitability of various alternatives. Use your imagination and involve people in all functional areas, as this is a strategic undertaking. It is beyond the scope of this chapter to tell you how to go about this evaluation. This has been outlined for you in Chapter 4, under the section titled Making Money from Lean Manufacturing.

SUMMARY

We have come to the end of our discussion of Value Stream Cost Analysis, the tool for assessing the amount of resource capacity freed by a lean initiative. We hope that the technique will be as useful for you as it has been for the countless numbers of successful lean companies that have used it to evaluate the financial benefits of their lean projects.

Table 21.10: Completed Value Stream Cost Analysis for the Hand Load/Wave Post Process

Value Stream Study	Value Stream: Electronics	Observer:		Date		Page
		Current State		Future State		
Process Steps	Activity	Non-productive	Productive	Non-productive	Productive	
Hand load/	Make for Demand (3735 x 12 minutes)		853.6		853.6	
Wave post	Get ready (100 batches x 10 min.)	16.7		0		Eliminated
11 persons	Get ready—prep components (3735 units x 2 min.)	124.5		0		Eliminated—components okay from SMT
1 shift	Rework/remake (227 errors x 6 min.)	22.7		4.3		Cut to 1% from 5.3 %
hours	Move in material (60 moves x 1 hour)	60		0		Eliminated
	Move material (100 batches x 20 min.)	33.3		0		Eliminated
	Administration (11 employees x 53 hours)	583		292		Cut in half
	Total time by value creating category	840.2	853.6	296.3	853.6	
	Total time used current/future state		1693.8		1149.9	543.9
	Total time not used per month		−43.8		500.1	
	Total time available for use per month		1650		1650	
	Productive Percent	0.517333333		0.517333333		
	Non-Productive Percent	0.509212121		0.179575758		
	Available Percent	−0.026545455		0.303090909		

Hand Load Wave Post
11 people 1 machine

| C/T=12 min. |
| C/O=10 min. |
| Prep comp=2 min. |
| Rework=5% |
| 4435 units |

Table 21.11: Summary of Planned Future State Capacity Usage for the Controllers Value Stream by Process

Future State Value Stream Cost Analysis by Capacity Category

		Totals	SMT	Hand load / wave post	Test and rework	Assemble and burn-in	Shipping	Customer service	Purchasing	Quality assurance	Accounting	Design engineering	Information systems	Manufacturing engineering	Technical support
EMPLOYEES	Cost	$139,624	$16,704	$22,968	$16,704	$10,440	$2,088	$11,928	$14,902	$7,978	$7,978	$3,989	$3,989	$7,989	$11,967
	Productive		0%	52%	0%	28%	0%	0%	0%	0%	0%	0%	0%	0%	0%
	Non-productive		28%	18%	38%	67%	71%	90%	1%	99%	71%	80%	91%	64%	83%
	Other		0%	0%	0%	0%	0%	0%	0%	0%	0%	0%	0%	0%	0%
	Available capacity	0%	72%	30%	62%	5%	29%	10%	80%	1%	29%	20%	10%	36%	17%
MACHINES	Cost	$22,500	$16,956	$2,016	$3,528		$–	$–							
	Productive		25%	58%	80%	0%	0%	0%	0%	0%	0%	0%	0%	0%	0%
	Non-productive		16%	3%	0%	0%	0%	0%	0%	0%	0%	0%	0%	0%	0%
	Other		0%	0%	0%	0%	0%	0%	0%	0%	0%	0%	0%	0%	0%
	Available capacity	0%	59%	39%	20%	0%	0%	0%	0%	0%	0%	0%	0%	0%	0%

Table 21.12: Summary of Freed-Up Resources in the Planned Future State

Summary of Freed Up Resources

Value stream: Controllers

	Available hours in the current state	Available hours in the future state	Freed up hours	Equivalent resources	Comment
SMT					
People	481.4	867.5	386.1	2.5 people	Reduced changeover time. Eliminated downtime and material moves.
				4 people	In addition there is potential to eliminate one shift; people no longer need to tend the machine.
Machines	25.3	190.1	164.8	1 machine-shift	Reduced changeover time and eliminated downtime. Reduced to one shift from two.
Hand load/wave post	-43.8	500.1	543.9	3.6 people	Eliminated changeover time. Eliminated material moves.
Test and rework	360.9	747.4	386.5	2.5 people	Cut defects by two-thirds.
Shipping	54.2	98.7	44.5	.3 person	Reduced shipping time from 15 to 10 minutes.
Customer service			487.7	3.2 people	Eliminated expedites. Reduced customer complain calls due to better service.
Purchasing			395.8	2.6 people	Implemented kanbans—eliminated production schedules. Reduced POs due to master POs. Eliminated suppliers and certified remaining.
Accounting			58.3	.4 people	Eliminated invoices due to purchasing initiatives.
				19.1 people	

CHAPTER 22

Value Stream Mapping

Value stream mapping is a fundamental tool of lean manufacturing and lean enterprises. The purpose of a value stream map is to enable us to see the flow of materials, information, and sometimes cash, through the value stream. Traditional companies often have little understanding of the flow of materials or information through their processes because the routes taken by products and processes are convoluted and difficult to recognize. Value stream mapping is the starting point for lean manufacturing and is also the starting point for Lean Accounting.

It is not the purpose of this chapter to explain how value stream maps are created; a number of very good books already do this.[1] The purpose is to show the use of value stream maps within lean accounting, and what additional information is required from the maps to complete the lean accounting picture.

Almost every aspect of lean accounting starts from a value stream map. Performance measurements are established around value streams and their production cells and non-production steps. The financial impact of lean improvement is calculated from the current state and future state value stream maps. Value stream costing is driven from the value streams defined by their maps. Value stream cost and capacity analysis uses the information available from the value stream map data boxes. Sales, operations, and financial planning (SOFP) is achieved through value streams and their associated maps. Lean organizations use value stream maps as living documents, enabling continuous improvement, including lean accounting.

A simple example of a value stream map is shown in Figure 4.1. This map shows the production flow for ECI. The map shows the flow of the product, the inventory, and any other waste that impedes the flow. The map also gives a harvest of detailed information about each step in the value stream. This information includes such things as the production cycle time, the changeover (or set-up) time, scrap rates, downtime, etc. This information is essential when designing improved flow across the value stream. Figure 4.2

---

1. Shook, John and Rother, Mike, *Learning to See*, Publisher, LEI, MA, 1999; Duggan, Kevin, *Creating Mixed Model Value Streams*, Productivity Press, NY, 2002; Tapping, Don, *Value Stream Management*, Productivity Press, NY, 2002.

showed an improved value stream design for ECI's value stream. This is not the perfect lean flow, but it does show considerable improvement on the previous (current state) approach. The production flow has fallen from 20 days to only 4 days. This improvement can be seen from the time line shown across the bottom of the current state and future state maps. The right hand summary box on the current state map shows that it takes 20 days for the material to flow through the value stream. The future state map shows that the flow has been reduced to 4 days.

Value Stream Maps and Lean Accounting

Three primary needs are met by value stream mapping within lean accounting:

- Recognizing the value streams
- Including more value stream steps
- Data box information required for lean accounting.

Many companies are unable to recognize value streams. Their production processes are so ingrained in the people working in the company, they find it difficult to see anything different. A value stream map lets people see and understand the flow of production and see how their products and processes flow. A clear understanding of the company's value streams is essential for a lean enterprise, and a successful lean business is managed by value stream.

When contemplating lean accounting, the place to start is with the company's value stream maps. They show what level of financial and operational information is required. They indicate where the major wasteful processes are located. They describe the size and complexity of the organization, and how the information flows from one entity to another. In lean accounting, all costs are gathered and reported by value stream. It is essential to have well defined value stream maps.

The current state value stream map shows the value stream information as the process is currently designed. The future state value stream map shows process flows as they will be in the future, when more lean improvement has been implemented. The future state value stream map is the company's vision for the future. A primary purpose of lean accounting is to engender relentless continuous improvement. The future state map is the immediate goal of that continuous improvement. We use the current state and the future state maps to identify how the available capacity changes when lean improvements are made, and to develop strategies to use the newly available capacity for the financial benefit of the organization.

More Value Stream Steps on the Value Stream Map

Most company's value streams restrict themselves to the production processes only, as do the books on value stream mapping. In reality, there are many

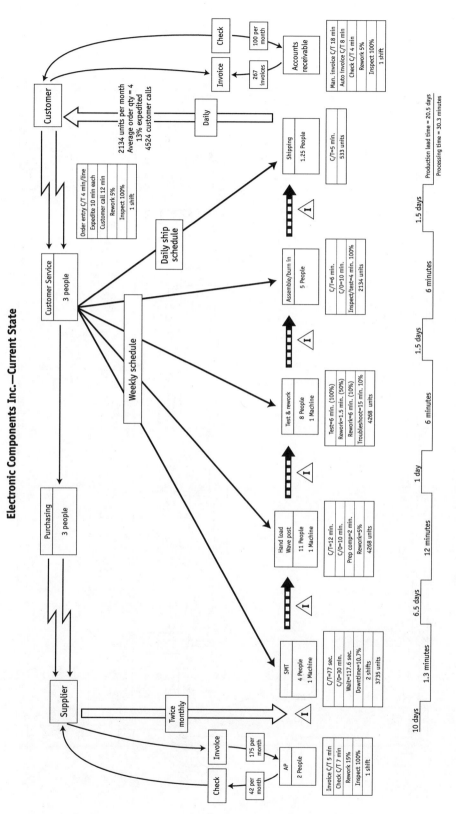

Figure 22.1: Value stream map showing additional non-production steps

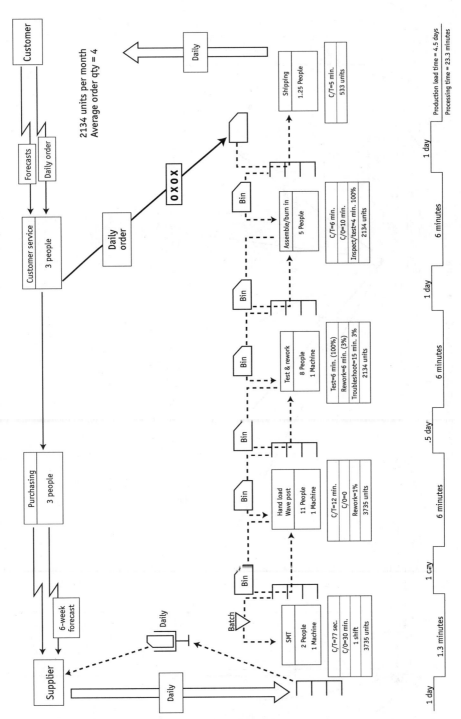

Figure 22.2: Future State Map for the Controllers Value Stream

other tasks are performed through the flow of a value stream. These include such processes as customer service, quoting, invoicing, purchasing, production planning, etc. They also include support operations like maintenance, materials handling, engineering, accounts payable, accounts receivable, and cost accounting.

It is helpful to add many of these tasks to the value stream maps. These tasks have just as much effect on the flow through the value stream as the manufacturing steps. Lean accounting methods, such as value stream costing, take account of all the steps and activities within the value stream, not just the production steps. From a financial perspective there is little difference between costs required on the shop floor and costs required in support activities. They are all costs directly associated with the manufacturing of the product, the production of the service, and the generation of value for the customer.

Figure 22.1 shows the ECI value stream map, with some of these additional tasks included in the map. An invoicing and accounts receivable process is shown, as is the accounts payable process for incoming materials. These processes have their data boxes giving the information required to assess their capacity and cost information. While it is not necessary to show every detailed process, which can make the value stream map difficult to read and use, it is helpful to include major support processes and their associated data.

DATA BOX INFORMATION

There is no definitive list of information that must be included in a value stream map data box. Some of the books about value stream mapping provide a suggested list, but are at pains to explain that the specific information changes according to each company's needs. The data box information is used to change the processes and improve the flow of the value stream.

A data box will generally include such information as the production cycle time, the machine changeover time, scrap rates, downtime, the number of shifts or available time per day. This information is also the information required for Lean Accounting, but we often need additional information. To complete a value stream cost analysis (VSCA), the following production information is usually required:

Number of employees	Number of machines	Number of shifts
Employee shift time	Production demand quantity	Number of parallel cells
Unit of measure	Average batch size	Machine downtime
Cycle time	Set-up time	Scrap rate

It is helpful when this information is always made available on the value stream map. This information is essential for the design of the flow within a cell or production process.

A more thorough and detailed VSCA would also take account of the following additional information:

Cycle time (employee)	Cycle time (machine)	Set-up time (employee)
Set-up time (machine)	Inspection %	Inspection time
Rework rate	Overproduction quantity	

While it is not usual for this additional detail to be shown on the value stream map, it is helpful for this information to be readily available for the production steps of the value stream. When this information is available, the cost and capacity analysis of the value stream production steps can be largely automated and the capacity usage divided into productive, non-productive, and available capacity.

The non-production value stream data boxes require different kinds of information. With few exceptions, the non-production steps of the value stream perform repetitive tasks, having cycle times, set-up times, rework, and inspection. An order entry process, for example, is performed exactly the same way, many times every day. There is a cycle time for the process, there may be a set-up time required, and there may be frequent rework. This process requires similar information to that of a production step.

The non-production steps, however, often have additional tasks that need to be included. The order entry process (in our previous example) may also schedule production, expedite orders, answer customer inquiries, etc. A sharp-eyed lean facilitator will notice that these tasks will be eliminated as the process flow is improved. In fact, the entire order entry process may be eliminated as the relationship with the customer is improved and the wasteful activities removed. However, when these tasks are in place, Lean Accounting will need to include them, highlighting them as waste that is taking up valuable capacity that could be used to increase value, grow the business, and increase profits.

It is helpful for as much of this kind of information to be included in the value stream maps, together with their cycle times, rework rates, and other relevant data. We do not want to make the maps too busy and complex, but we do want to show as much relevant information shown as possible.

SUMMARY

Value stream maps are the starting point of Lean Accounting, just as they are the starting point for other aspects of lean. They enable us to see the flow of the process. We use value stream maps to identify the value streams that will be used in value stream costing. We use the information on the value stream maps to calculate the value stream analysis that is so vital to understanding the process costs, the process flow, and the use of our assets.

For these value stream maps to be useful for lean accounting, they must be complete, must contain the non-production steps, as well as the production steps usually shown on the maps, and must have the appropriate process information shown in the data boxes.

Index